The 1992 Study of the American School Superintendency

America's Education Leaders in a Time of Reform

by Thomas E. Glass

 AMERICAN ASSOCIATION OF SCHOOL ADMINISTRATORS

The 1992 Study of the American School Superintendency
is available from the American Association of School Administrators.
1801 North Moore Street, Arlington, VA 22209-9988; (703) 875-0748.

© American Association of School Administrators, 1992

Library of Congress Catalog Card Number: 92-073480

ISBN: 0-87652-177-4

AASA Stock Number: 21-00189

This report was reviewed by AASA and approved for publication.
Approval does not signify that the contents reflect the views or policies of AASA.

AASA is an equal opportunity employer.

Table of Contents ᵢ

FOREWORD vii

EXECUTIVE SUMMARY ix

AUTHOR'S OBSERVATIONS xiv

1. THE SUPERINTENDENCY 1

Historical Perspective 1

From Schoolmaster to Manager 1

    Establishing Professionalism 1

The Era of Scientific Management 2

    Toward a Corporate Model...2

    Superintendents as "Experts" 2

Practice Into Theory: A Revolution in Training 2

Challenges in the 1960s and 1970s 3

    Superintendents Under Fire 3

Reform in the 1980s and 1990s 3

The Growth of Mandates 4

The Untold Story 4

The Future of the Superintendency 4

2. DESIGN OF THE STUDY 5

Survey Objectives 5

Content Areas 5

Instrument Development 6

Sample Selection 6

Survey Implementation and Return 6

Data Analysis 7

3. PERSONAL CHARACTERISTICS 9

Gender 9

Race 10

Age 10

    Early Retirement 11

    Attrition 11

Marital Status 12

Political Party Preference 13

Community Background 13
    Exodus...14
    Small-Town Roots 14
Family Characteristics 15
    Parents' Education Level 15
    Parental Activities 16

4. PROFESSIONAL EXPERIENCES **19**
Entry Into Administration 19
    The Dominance of Former Teachers 19
What's in a Name? 20
    Where Were They Then? 20
Extracurricular Activities 22
Career Patterns 22
Gaining the First Superintendency 23
    When the Decision Is Made 24
Number of Superintendencies 24
Tenure in the Superintendency 24
    Big City Turnover 25
    Size of District..26
Mentoring, Discrimination, Hiring 27
    Old Boy/Old Girl Network 27
    Gender Discrimination 27
    Discrimination Against Minorities 27
    Recruitment of Women and Minorities 28
Selection to the Superintendency 29
    Search Committees 29
        School Board Searches 29
    Reasons Why a Superintendent Is Selected 29
    Movers, Shakers, and Peacemakers 30
        Change Agent...30
        Developer 30
        Maintaining the Status Quo 30
Salaries and Contracts of Superintendents 31
Participation in Professional Organizations 32
Mentoring and Being a Mentor 33
Future Plans of Superintendents 33

5. SCHOOL BOARDS AND SUPERINTENDENTS **35**
Evolution 35
Power Struggles 35
    Overlapping Roles..35

Who Initiates Policy? 35
   Shared Responsibility 35
How Are Board Members Oriented? 36
School Board Meetings 36
   Who Sets the Agenda? 37
Community Participation 37
   Heightened Need...37
   Increased Willingness 38
   When Is Participation Sought? 38
   Do Boards Seek Community Involvement? 38
Community Pressure Groups 39
Board Abilities 40
Elected or Appointed? 40
Evaluations and Job Descriptions...40
   Taking it Personally...41
   The Why and How of Evaluation 41
   What Counts With the Board? 42
Board Expectations..42
Problems Board Members Face 43
Problems Superintendents Face 46
   Self-Perception 46
   Factors That Inhibit Effectiveness...47
   Reasons To Leave a District 47
   Troubling Issues...47
   Reasons To Leave the Field 50
Fulfillment 50
Prestige 51
Stress 51
Communication Sources 53
If They Could Do It All Over Again 54

6. MINORITY AND WOMEN SUPERINTENDENTS 55
Demographics 55
   Age 55
   Political Affiliation...55
   Political Posture 56
   Education Level of Parents...56
   Type of Community Lived in Before College 57
Career Paths—The Road More Traveled 57
   First Administrative Position 57
   Length of Classroom Service Before Entering Administration 58
   Age When Appointed to First Administrative Postion 58

Nature of Superintendents' First Administrative Position 58
Career Pattern Prior to the Superintendency 59
Place-Bound Succession 59
Duration of Career in the Same District 60
Length of Time Spent Seeking First Superintendency 60
Populations of Communities 61
A Leg Up: Mentoring, Hiring Practices 61
Are Superintendents Mentors? 61
Do Minority and Women Superintendents Have Mentors? 61
Who Manages the Search? 61
Influence of the Old Boy/Old Girl Network 62
Discrimination 62
Discriminatory Hiring Practices Faced by Women...62
Discriminatory Hiring Practices Faced by Minorities 62
Prestige, Satisfaction, Fulfillment 63
Prestige and Influence of the Superintendency 63
Who Would "Do It All Over Again"? 63
Degree of Fulfillment 63
Power, Influence, and Decision Making 63
Who Takes the Lead in Developing Policy? 63
Who Prepares the Agenda for Board Meetings? 64
Parent/Community Participation in Decision Making 64
Community Group Pressure on the Board 65
The Most Difficult Problems Facing School Boards 65
Highest Academic Degree Held 65
Usefulness of Research 65
Essential Responsibilities in School Administration 65
Area 1: District Climate 66
Area 2: Obtaining Support for Education...66
Area 3: Providing an Effective Curriculum Program..66
Area 4: Effective Instructional Programs..66
Area 5: Continuous Improvement and Evaluation...66
Area 6: Financial and Budget Management 67
Area 7: Operations Management..67
Area 8: Using Research 67
Stress 67

7. PROFESSIONAL PREPARATION AND TRAINING 71
Past History 71
Meeting Needs 71
How the 1992 Study Differs 71
Formal Academic Training and Degrees 71

Schooling Prior to the Superintendency 72
    Degrees Held 72
    Full-Time Vs. Part-Time 75
    Financial Support 75
    Age and Experience 75
    Specialist Level 75
    Sabbatical Leave 75
    Method of Payment 76
Quality of Educational Administration Programs 77
    Different Strokes 77
    Quality of Programs 77
    Quality of Instructors 79
    What Counts in Preparation Programs? 79
Educational Research 80
Rating Performance Areas 80
Summary 84

8. DISTRICT CHARACTERISTICS 85
Types of School Districts 85
Age of Superintendents 85
School Reforms 86
    Early Childhood Education 86
    School-Business Partnerships 87
    School Volunteers 87
Changing Demographics 88
    Decreasing Enrollments 88
Central Office Administrators 89
    Number of Central Office Personnel 89
    Women and Minorities 90
Chain of Command 91
    Collective Bargaining 91
District School Board Characteristics 93
    Women and Minorities on School Boards 93

CONCLUSIONS 97

REFERENCES 99

ACKNOWLEDGMENTS 103

v

Foreword

School superintendents hold some of the most challenging, yet satisfying, positions in American society. These chief executive officers of what are often the largest employers in town have become the lightning rod for every social and economic problem facing our nation.

What makes the job difficult? What are the backgrounds and career paths of superintendents? What is the average tenure of a superintendent? These are just a few of the questions you'll find answered in *The 1992 Study of the American School Superintendency.*

This study is based on the opinions of about 12 percent of the nation's superintendents. More than half of the nation's school children are served by the survey sample group.

Since the 1920s, the American Association of School Administrators has conducted a study of the superintendency each decade. The only lapse came in the 1940s during the height of World War II.

These studies have helped us, as school leaders, track the progress of our profession, explore a panoply of issues that affect education, and see ourselves, up close and personal.

As this benchmark study has gone to press, our nation has been facing a stubborn recession. Teacher and administrator layoffs have become commonplace. Social and economic conditions affecting children and youth are getting worse.

Yet, expectations are on the rise. President Bush and the nation's governors helped set the stage by establishing a series of goals for education, and the Bush administration has announced an "America 2000" strategy for achieving those goals.

AASA's 1990-91 Status and Opinion Survey has revealed that more than 50 percent of superintendents plan to retire during the '90s. That fact alone will mean a loss of talent and years of experience. At the same time, it will bring opportunities for those who have

been waiting in the wings, especially women and minorities.

We are grateful to Tom Glass, professor of educational administration at Northern Illinois University, for conducting this study. He spent endless hours meeting with key groups, developing the survey instrument, drawing an appropriate sample, tabulating and interpreting results, and writing this report.

This *1992 Study of the American School Superintendency,* like those decennary studies of the past, will find many uses. Aspiring superintendents will use it to explore career paths. Those who hold superintendencies will compare their experiences and concerns with those of colleagues nationwide. Colleges and universities will probe this publication for significant changes in the profession to project what the superintendency will be like in the future. For others who care very much about education, this book will provide an in-depth look at the dedicated professionals we expect to lead us.

The 1990s promise even greater challenges for school superintendents. Their vision and inclusive leadership will be center stage. Their leadership skills, no matter how finely honed, will be stretched to the limits.

Despite these challenges, superintendents will continue to find great satisfaction in what they do best...helping others to learn and grow. Because of their dedicated efforts, millions of young people in our nation will be prepared to take on the responsibilities of citizenship, to perform well in their chosen careers, and to gain a deep sense of personal fulfillment.

Richard D. Miller
Executive Director
American Association of School Administrators

viii

Executive Summary

The American school superintendency is a multifaceted and complex role. Enrollment size, ethnic composition, and community expectations of the nation's school districts differ drastically. In most cases, school districts reflect the communities in which they are situated. As expected, districts with a sizable supply of fiscal resources have more and better financed programs than districts without ample amounts of tax dollars.

Just as communities and districts differ, so do the backgrounds, roles, and expectations for superintendents. Superintendents are former teachers, principals, and sometimes central office administrators. Therefore, they have served many years in the schools and demonstrate and exhibit many opinions, attitudes, and behaviors consistent with having spent their professional lives in one social institution.

HIGH VISIBILITY

The contemporary jurisdiction of the superintendent is not solely situated in a district office or in the schools. It extends into the community, where the superintendent is expected to participate and represent the school district. This increased visibility may pose the most serious challenge in the 1990s, as many citizens are demanding increased accountability for learning and use of their tax dollars.

Current literature on the superintendency calls for superintendents to cease being bureaucratic managers and become "executive leaders" akin to chief executives of private sector corporations, whose success or failure is predicated on the quality of their products.

The survey finds that superintendents of larger and more complex districts appear to somewhat fit the mold of the "executive leader" or CEO. By the nature of their districts they must form administrative teams, be conciliatory with various special interest groups, find consensus among employee groups, and shed strictly managerial duties to have sufficient time to be reflective and visionary. The purpose of the survey was not to ascertain if superintendents were or were not

"executive leaders," but hints to that effect do occur in many of the 110 questions.

A CHANGING LANDSCAPE

In an era when the school curriculum is expanding (what is taught today in junior high science was often taught 10 years ago in high school) and computers are becoming tools used by students daily, the enrollment of thousands of school districts is declining. During the 1980s small districts generally became smaller. Many large districts became larger due to shifts of population to urban centers. And in some cases there were significant shifts of population from urban centers to the suburbs. In the case of large districts, such as Chicago, much of the population loss was replenished by minority groups in migration.

The number of small districts with enrollments of under 300 (some 4,000 districts) often employ a combination principal/superintendent. The responses of superintendents (principals) of these small districts were significantly different from superintendents of larger districts. Small district superintendents indicated they were subject to demands to perform a wide array of administrative tasks and saw themselves primarily as managers.

The survey data also indicate that perhaps 50 percent (15,000) of American school districts have a superintendent and one other administrator in the district office. This probably accounts for the historical image of the superintendent being a "manager." Survey data also indicate small district school boards expect the superintendent to be a general manager.

Rural Districts Persevere

For the most part, the organization of America's school districts has not changed to reflect current national demographics. America is no longer a rural nation, but the majority of its school districts are located in very small towns and rural areas.

The Census Bureau recently released data showing

X

that only 24 percent of Americans now live in rural areas. However, of some 15,000 school districts in the country, more than 12,000 have fewer than 3,000 students. Nearly 6,000 have fewer than 600 students. Even though substantial school district consolidation has occurred in most states in the past 40 years, a significant number of school districts still are located in rural areas. As Americans have migrated to the city, small districts have hung on tenaciously.

The observable effect of the "small and rural" nature of America's school districts is that the superintendency in the small and large districts has become more dissimilar than ever before. However, superintendents are certified by state departments of education to serve any district, regardless of enrollment, problems, program, or community composition.

WHO ARE THE NATION'S SUPERINTENDENTS?

Many studies show that a large majority of superintendents are white males. The 1992 10-year study confirms this is still true; only a small percentage of the nation's superintendents are women or members of a racial or ethnic minority group. However, women and minority superintendents are more often found in larger, more urban school districts. This is especially true of minority superintendents, many of whom serve on the "hot seat" of a large urban superintendency. Only a couple of the nation's 20 largest school districts have enrollments reflecting a white majority; most have student populations whose majority is composed of minorities, with a minority or female superintendent.

Although women are represented to a greater extent in the 1992 study sample than in 1982, their numbers do not reflect their majority status among professional educators in the nation's schools. The need for more preparation and placement of women and minorities in the superintendency is reflected in the study data and is one of the major challenges facing the profession in the 1990s.

Superintendents generally come from small-town and rural backgrounds representing the demography of the 1930s, 1940s, and 1950s. Their mean age is close to 50, meaning that more than half of them were born in the 1930s and 1940s, when the country was much more rural. Politically, they represent the traditional moderate-conservatism of their small-town and rural backgrounds. They are split nearly evenly between the two major political parties and Independents. However, in spite of their expressed political party preference, they see themselves over-

whelmingly as political moderates.

Back to the future. It will be interesting in the 1990s to see whether more new superintendents will be younger and from the suburbs and large population centers. This would seem logical because of shifts in American demographics towards more urban and suburban living. However, once again, the majority of superintendencies currently are not located in the suburbs and large urban centers, but rather in small towns and rural areas. It does not appear now that large-scale district consolidation efforts are under way nationwide that would reduce the number of superintendencies and likely increase the number of central office positions.

For the most part, superintendents rarely move from larger districts to smaller ones to assume their first superintendency. Superintendents of smaller districts seem to have grown up in, taught in, and been a principal in a small district.

Average "Joes." To characterize superintendents as "mainstream" would be fairly accurate. They are of the average age to lead a public organization, come from traditionally blue-collar families, have a college education, are political moderates, and are white males. This profile has not changed greatly over the 70-year period of the 10-year studies, but it likely will change in the future, as the nation's workforce composition changes. Meanwhile the American school superintendent remains a white male who comes from and fits comfortably into traditional "Main Street America."

In future studies, more women and minority superintendents, many of them having been reared and trained in urban areas, likely will be represented more fully in these ranks. In addition, the forces of urbanization undoubtedly will continue to exert pressure on small school districts to consolidate as states and local communities find costs unacceptable.

In future decades the public school superintendency likely will become better aligned with the population distribution of the nation, and this may well mean fewer positions for those aspiring to the superintendency in the 21st century.

CHANGES IN THE SUPERINTENDENCY

The 1992 10-year study found that superintendents have more formal education than their counterparts in previous decades. The complexity of the position also has increased, and the states as well as the superintendents themselves have thought that increased training and preparation is necessary to lead districts of all sizes effectively.

The traditional career route of superintendents—of classroom teacher, principal, and then superintendent—is changing. Today, more superintendents begin their administrative career as assistant principal and spend some years in a central office position before becoming superintendent. This new pattern is not as widespread among superintendents of very small districts, who tend to begin their teaching career in a small school, become a principal, and then superintendent in a small district.

Career Ladders

Superintendents spend about five years as classroom teachers before gaining their first administrative position. Many superintendents are former secondary teachers of social studies, science, or math. About one-fourth of superintendents are former elementary teachers. A large number of superintendents were engaged in coaching some type of sport, but very few were certificated physical education teachers.

HIRING, FIRING, AND PAY

The superintendency is often portrayed by the press as a position with a high turnover rate. However, the 1992 study shows that most superintendents spend about 15 years as superintendents in no more than three districts. Approximately three-quarters of the nation's superintendents have been in their current position for five or six years.

The average tenure in the 1982 study actually was briefer than in 1971 or 1992. During the 1970s and early 1980s, many districts were undergoing declining enrollments, which often resulted in budget cuts and staff dismissals, both prime factors in changing superintendents. The superintendency is not a highly transitory position, except in the larger urban school districts. Because the firing of a superintendent attracts a great deal of attention in the media, relatively few firings can create an impression that many superintendents are fired each year, which is not true. In fact, reasons most superintendents leave one position to move to another are better pay and greater responsibility in a larger district.

School boards hire superintendents for various reasons. The most common one, according to superintendents, is their personal characteristics. The relationship between a superintendent and board is highly personal, and good interpersonal relationships are critical. Superintendents who are fired or encouraged to leave usually do so when their personal relationships with school boards break down. At the same time, however, superintendents in the 1992 study say that school boards are much more interested in the superintendent as an instructional leader than in past years.

Most superintendents have multiple-year contracts with annual salaries in excess of $70,000. Those selected to work in the larger districts usually are recommended by professional search firms or by professional organizations. Most believe there is an "old boy/old girl" network that influences these decisions, and that it is important to have a mentor. Most indicate they are willing to or are serving as a mentor to someone preparing for the superintendency.

SCHOOL BOARDS AND SUPERINTENDENTS

Superintendents say that they most often initiate policy decisions in their school districts. This is especially true in the smaller districts. They also say they lead the orientation of new board members, and they think most board members are "qualified" but not "well qualified" for their responsibilities. Most superintendents believe they are firmly in charge of their districts and work well with their school boards.

The increase in pressure from special interest groups in the community is a particular concern for superintendents in the 1992 study. They say they and their boards are under greater pressure from such groups than ever before. Most welcome community participation in district activities, especially in planning activities that attract the interest of parents. Superintendents say their board members would like more parent/community participation in the school district.

A large majority of superintendents are evaluated annually by their school boards in a formal and informal process. Most superintendents have written job descriptions, but say they often are not evaluated according to the formal criteria. Most evaluations are conducted in a closed session. Superintendents believe the most important evaluation criterion is overall effectiveness (in contrast to the primary reason why they believe they were hired—personal characteristics).

Superintendents say the most serious problems facing school board members are those related to school finance and interest group pressure—the same problems they believe present the greatest challenge to their districts. However, the most serious challenges they face as superintendents are finance, student assessment/testing, general district accountability, changing demographics, and developing selected new programs. This is somewhat different from responses in 1982 and 1971, when collective bargaining issues ranked behind finance problems as key concerns.

JOB SATISFACTION

When asked what would cause them to leave the superintendency, superintendents in nearly all cases say lack of district fiscal resources. The lack of adequate funds for programs is a never-ending source of frustration for superintendents. One of the reasons they give for lack of effectiveness is not enough time to "get things done," a situation which could be alleviated by additional funding to hire more administrators, especially in districts where the superintendent is the sole administrator.

A majority of superintendents experience a moderate degree of job stress. The current levels of stress are slightly greater than in previous studies. But superintendents also indicate they feel very fulfilled in their jobs, which suggests that stress is an occupational hazard they are willing to tolerate as long as they believe the job is worthwhile. Considering the increased levels of pressure on superintendents from interest groups, state mandates, staff, the community, legal issues, and lack of adequate funding, a certain amount of stress is to be expected. However, the high levels of stress felt by some superintendents call for a greater awareness in professional training programs and especially institutions of higher education that superintendents should be better prepared to cope with stress.

Despite the serious problems facing their districts, superintendents believe they are doing a "good" to "excellent" job. Considering the modest turnover in the position, their school boards must agree. This is less true in small districts.

WOMEN AND MINORITIES IN THE SUPERINTENDENCY

Though the numbers of women and minority superintendents in the 1992 study have increased from previous surveys, they still are very few. In the study sample of 1,734 superintendents, only 115 are women, and only 67 are minority.

The credentials and backgrounds of women and minority superintendents are different from their white male colleagues. Both women and minority superintendents tend to have more academic degrees and to have spent more years as a principal and teacher.

Compared to men and nonminorities, women and minority superintendents were more frequently hired through professional search firms. However, local school boards still managed the search for a majority of superintendents, regardless of race or gender. Politically, women and minorities tend to be Democrats and lean more to the political left, perhaps reflecting their more urban background.

Their career patterns also differ. Women are more likely to have moved from classroom teaching into a central office position or some "non-line" position in the school, such as coordinator of a special program. Both women and minority superintendents more often begin their teaching and administrative careers at the elementary school level.

Women superintendents do not appear to be place bound; most obtained their first superintendency in a district other than the one in which they were working. And most women superintendents found their first superintendency within their first year of searching.

Both women and minority superintendents perceive some hiring discrimination. However, both groups indicated they had taken advantage of the "old boy/old girl" network to gain their positions.

Women and minority superintendents indicate they place a higher priority than do their white male counterparts on curriculum and instruction activities in their preparation for the superintendency and once they become a superintendent. In most other respects, the differences between women and minority superintendents compared to their white male counterparts are not great. They also are frustrated by lack of adequate school financing and pressure from special interest groups, and they feel similar amounts of stress in their jobs.

TRAINING AND PREPARATION OF SUPERINTENDENTS

The preparation of superintendents is controlled in part by state departments of education through certification requirements. In most states, a master's degree is the minimum degree required for certification as a superintendent. In a majority of states, about 30 additional semester hours of preparation in educational administration are required. Most preparation programs are located in institutions of higher education. More than 300 higher education programs cooperate with their respective states in granting the superintendency certificate.

Superintendents think that preparation and training programs could be improved substantially. However, they indicate a higher level of support for the higher education program in which they participated.

About one-third of superintendents have earned a doctoral degree, nearly all of them in educational administration, and only a handful in a field outside of education. The larger the district, the more likely the superintendent has a doctoral degree.

Most superintendents begin a master's program in educational administration after about three years of classroom teaching, and the majority attended both their master's and doctoral programs on a part-time basis after regular work hours. Very few ever were full-time graduate students, and even fewer had graduate assistantships. Nearly all of the superintendents obtained their master's degrees in their late twenties or early thirties and their doctorates by their late thirties or early forties. The older the superintendent, the more likely he or she earned advanced degrees later in life.

Superintendents indicate that preparation programs should be better coordinated, contain more practical experiences, and extend to later professional development. Superintendents say the kinds of preparation and training most essential to their effectiveness are in establishing a productive learning climate, developing effective instructional and curriculum programs and managing district finances. The emphasis on instruction is greater than in previous decades, reflecting the growing importance of instructional leadership to superintendents.

SELECTED CHARACTERISTICS OF DISTRICTS

A sizable majority of the districts sampled provide schooling in grades K-12. A majority offer pre-kindergarten programs, and about one-fourth have day-care programs. Some 80 percent of the districts have some kind of school-business partnership, as well as community volunteer programs, both of which factor in the school reform movement.

About half the superintendents say the community in which their district is located has fewer than 10,000 people, which reinforces the finding that many American school districts are located in small and rural areas. Superintendents in smaller districts also indicate

that during the past 10 years their enrollment generally has declined. Enrollments in the very large districts vary. Some have increased significantly, and some have decreased.

The overall picture of the American public school superintendency indicates it is a challenging and fulfilling position with varying levels of stress and frustration. The 1992 study data show the superintendency is in a state of flux as the composition of the profession changes—however slowly—to more closely represent the total group of professional educators, especially minorities and women.

Younger superintendents are leading many changes, especially in the areas of emphasizing instruction, academic preparation and meaningful community involvement in district activities. Superintendents' responses indicate that many aspects of the profession must change if schools are to meet the challenges of the 21st century. Also superintendents in the 1990s may find fewer positions because of consolidation of smaller districts, pressure for accountability, and increasing enrollments without significantly increased funding. Children have not been considered a high priority in the political realm of our society, but other surveys indicate this may be changing. Superintendents, in sum, must be prepared to be executive leaders in the 1990s to help schools and society meet the challenges in the decades ahead.

CONCLUSION

After examination of thousands of pieces of data self-reported by the nation's superintendents, it can be seen that they are a well-educated and experienced group of fairly "typical" American middle class citizens. They find a great deal of self-fulfillment in their moderately stressful positions, but are willing to soldier on despite perceived lack of fiscal resources, special interest group demands, and sometimes less than qualified school board members. They are an important link between the children they serve, the community they wish to involve, and the school programs they strive to have supported in the community. In brief, the superintendency is a position that many times must serve many masters; parents, board, state office, community, and employee groups.

Author's Observations

THE SUPERINTENDENCY AND REFORM

As the title of this study implies, superintendents are indeed a part of this era of national, state, and local school reform. Along with their school boards, superintendents have been characterized as part of the problem, rather than as part of the solution. Some accuse superintendents and board members of desiring to retain the "conservatism" of keeping things the way they are.

Many superintendents and school boards are besieged by hints, suggestions, and threats that schools must get better or "else." What the "else" might be generally is not very well defined, but one can assume it means no support at the polls the next time the district must ask for additional local taxes. Frequently, private sector groups are seen complaining in the media that schools are not turning out graduates capable of filling their needs. For many, a general panacea for education reform is that schools should operate more like a business, turning out products, making profits, and keeping overheads low.

Unfortunately, schools are not institutions that have ever operated on a profit motive. In fact, the school institution is one that must, and should, always be motivated to reach out, seek, and obtain consensus among its many constituents (parents, students, teachers, citizens, agencies, religious and political groups, and the private sector).

Not surprisingly, the future of the American public school superintendency is linked integrally to the future of the school institution. Whether superintendents and schools are going to emerge stronger in the 1990s is currently questionable, as the nation's priorities seem to be far away from the interests of children. Hopefully, the nation's school superintendents will be leaders in awakening the American public to realize that schools are not an expense, but a vital national resource. The overall findings of this study indicate that school superintendents are also a national resource, and much more attention should be paid to their views and strengths.

Thomas E. Glass
Northern Illinois University

The Superintendency

American public education is now entering its second decade of "reform." Beginning in 1983 with the publication of "A Nation at Risk," schools and educators came under greater scrutiny than ever from the public, media, and politicians. Previous reform movements, such as the Sputnik "scare" in the 1950s and progressive education in the 1930s, were less far-reaching compared to the many measures that have been proposed and implemented since the 1980s. The kinds of reforms the 1990s will bring are subject to debate, but whatever significant changes are made in school organizations and schooling, they surely will involve the position of superintendent. The men and women who hold these approximately 15,000 key leadership positions so important to the future of the nation will be at the center of the movement toward creating more effective schools.

HISTORICAL PERSPECTIVE

The position of superintendent of schools has existed in American public education since the mid-1800s, when many school districts located in larger cities appointed an individual to be responsible for the day-to-day operations of a number of schoolhouses. By 1860, 27 cities with school districts had created superintendencies. During the next century, the growth of the superintendency paralleled the growth of the public schools (Callahan, 1966), and was inextricably linked to the evolution of school boards .

Many early superintendents faced serious challenges, including the survival of the common school movement itself. Those men (mostly men—then as now) taking up the call of the superintendency and the common school were true school reformers. They traveled from large cities to villages preaching the gospel of a free public education. In some respects, many early superintendents were like secular clergy. They served as moral role models, spreaders of the democratic ethic, and, most important, builders of the American dream.

FROM SCHOOLMASTER TO MANAGER

The American public school superintendency has changed a great deal since its inception in the first half of the 19th century. The original role was that of a schoolmaster, with a board of education making almost all decisions of any importance. By the end of the 19th century, most superintendents in the cities had shed this role of supervisor of students and teachers to become managing administrators. Superintendents became responsible for operations in the district, and their day-to-day decisions usually were not subject to examination by the board of education (Callahan, 1966). Schools reflected the transition in the late 19th and early 20th centuries from an American economy and culture dominated by rural farm concerns to one where heavy industry would play an increasing role.

Establishing Professionalism

Gaining operational authority separate from the board did not occur overnight. Ellwood Cubberley, a former superintendent who wrote books and articles on school administration in the early 1900s, called this transition the struggle to become true professionals (Cubberley, 1922).

Historically, the partnership between superintendents and school boards has been a subject of discussion and substantial research. The function of the board and its relationship with the superintendent has been important in the development of the superintendency.

The position of superintendent as we know it today evolved from superintendents struggling to become professionals during the first part of the 20th century. The "grand old men" of the superintendency —Cubberley, George Strayer, and Frank Spaulding— championed the cause of the common school, and advocated an executive type of leadership. They wrestled with boards of education in large cities such as

Chicago, where political spoils systems determined which teachers would be hired, what textbooks would be purchased, and which vendors would be patronized (Callahan, 1966).

In addition to their efforts to reform schools and school boards, the early educational leaders also worked to prepare future school executives who would be able to provide civic leadership, scientific management, and established business values in the schools.

Early superintendents also were aware of the need for those in their field to be current in their knowledge of curriculum and instruction, teacher preparation, and staff training.

THE ERA OF SCIENTIFIC MANAGEMENT

In his 1966 book, *The School Superintendent,* Daniel Griffiths discusses a second phase in development of the role of the superintendency. He describes the "quasi-businessman" attempting to form school districts into industrial models, through principles of scientific management. During this period, a significant degree of control over decision making was moved from boards of education into the hands of the superintendent. The tenets of scientific management, and the resulting bureaucracy, still guide the practices of some local schools today, despite the fact that many researchers and reformers believe highly centralized, hierarchical structures are a chief obstacle to school restructuring.

School organizations based on bureaucracy and scientific management first were found in cities, where school districts, hard-pressed to keep up with escalating enrollments, were won over by the promise of management efficiency and increased "production" levels. Scientific management principles were tempting to big city superintendents struggling to "Americanize" immigrants from abroad and migrants from the rural countryside in this pre-World War I society.

In this second phase of the American superintendency, the majority of school districts were still in rural areas, but the majority of schoolchildren were beginning to attend city schools.

Toward a Corporate Model

During the first half of this century, larger school boards slowly moved toward a more corporate model. Then, the board was a policy-making body that met periodically, while day-to-day decisions were made by management. By the 1920s, most states had spelled out the legal responsibilities of both parties in statute. In most cases the superintendent still was responsible to the school board, and lines of authority were more clearly drawn.

Superintendents As 'Experts'

As superintendents became more secure in their role with the school board, they became more assertive. Meanwhile, as the country became more urban and school districts grew, more efforts were made to centralize control of all management activity. This move was consistent with scientific management principles, but was seen by many nonsuperintendent educators as not in the best interest of schools and schoolchildren. Nonetheless, the drive for hierarchical bureaucracy and scientific management continued mostly unabated until the late 1980s, when the role of the superintendent as "expert manager" came under questioning of school reformers.

In fact, during the 1980s and, to some extent earlier in the 1960s and 1970s, the unhappiness with American public schools voiced by minority groups and school reformers often focused on the authority and control principals and superintendents held. Minority parents and school critics often claimed that school administrators (educational experts) who would not or could not change the educational system (bureaucracy) obstructed equal educational opportunity and reform. Likely, most citizens still perceive the superintendent as the "chief expert on schools in the community." Certainly, school boards look to the superintendents for "expert" knowledge and leadership that will result in peace and harmony in the district. However, as Arthur Blumberg points out, the modern superintendency, as opposed to earlier in the century, must be more politically driven; meaning that traditional views and expectations of the superintendent for the 1990s many times directly conflict with desires and demands for substantial institutional restructuring (Blumberg, 1985).

PRACTICE INTO THEORY: A REVOLUTION IN TRAINING

A third phase in the development of the superintendency essentially began in the 1950s, and is just now coming to a conclusion. Daniel Griffiths and Jacob W. Getzels describe this period of "professionalism" as one of great debate about what superintendents should do and how they should be trained.

Most of the early professors of educational administration such as Strayer, Cubberley, and Spaulding were former superintendents of large city school districts who later turned to the college classroom to train and place students in key superintendencies across the nation. These teacher-educators focused on solving what they saw as educational problems. In contrast, more recent training has been based on theory development and its application to practice.

In the first half of the century, textbooks written by the "founding fathers" of the superintendency were compendia of "best practices" gained from their experiences. But as social science theory began to influence preparation programs, growing numbers of professors of educational administration who had never been practicing superintendents began to dominate the preparation of administrators (Sass, 1989).

Today, "superintendent scientists" now develop or alter theoretical models, test them, and through training pass them on to practitioners. This is a subtle but very critical change (Sclafani, 1987).

CHALLENGES IN THE 1960S AND 1970S

The 1960s were a time of immense social tension that brought significant changes to American public schools. Issues such as equal educational opportunity for minority groups, community control, compensatory programs, and desegregation resulted in a greater performance focus by policymakers on the training, and selection of superintendents.

One of the most dynamic changes during the 1960s and 1970s was the dramatic transformation in the role and composition of school boards. In the 1950s, authors such as Charles Reeves held that the role of the board was that of a legal interest group elected by the public. The professional backgrounds of board members often reflected the composition of the local Chamber of Commerce or Rotary Club. In the late 1960s and 1970s, board members became more representative of the total community, as many blue-collar workers, homemakers, and others were elected who were intent on changing the system to make it more responsive to their needs (Getzels et.al., 1968, pp. 352-358).

There are few first-person accounts by school leaders on how the role of the superintendent and board changed during the 1960s and 1970s. However, Larry Cuban, in *The Managerial Imperative and the Practice of Leadership in Schools*, furnishes a portrait of the nature of changes in school boards and the superintendency during the 1970s and 1980s. The tension that existed in society during this tumultuous time spilled over to the schools and led to a superintendency much

different from the one that existed during the quiet years of the 1950s. Relationships between boards and superintendents began changing, and in many districts, boards assumed greater leadership in formulation of policy (Campbell, et. al., 1990).

Superintendents Under Fire

Perhaps the greatest challenge to the superintendency during the Civil Rights era was the encroachment into the authority of the superintendency by a more involved citizenry and school board. At the same time, a wide array of legislative mandates also were lessening school system autonomy. The superintendent's traditional role of "expert" was challenged by many parents and board members, because the schools were not meeting community expectations (Tucker and Ziegler, 1980). As the person in charge, the superintendent was the most visible school figure and the target of criticism, which was easier to project onto one individual than hundreds of school staff. The displeasure of parents and citizens during the 1960s and 1970s, combined with growth in the number of unionized teachers, created a superintendency where leaders often found themselves in continuous defensive postures, both personally and on behalf of their districts. The disenchantment with American schools was especially pronounced in large urban systems, where increasing numbers of disadvantaged students dropped out or were chronic underachievers. In such school systems, superintendent firings often were front-page news (Cuban, 1988).

REFORM IN THE 1980S AND 1990S

During the 1980s and early 1990s, the policymaking pendulum has swung back and forth between the superintendent and school board, reflecting the fact that education leaders and theoreticians disagree about what constitutes policymaking and what constitutes management. This fuzzy division between policy and management is a continuing area of concern. Most researchers on the superintendency favor a model of the superintendent as chief executive officer, partially borrowed from corporate America. In many cases, what has been viewed as policy development in the world of public education is seen as management prerogative in the private sector (Konnert and Augenstein, 1990).

The 1980s likely will be remembered as the time in American public education when the private sector and citizens of all races and socioeconomic levels became sufficiently displeased to trigger a nationwide reform movement. With the publication of "A Nation at Risk" in 1983, a diverse group of civil rights and corporate interests led a national movement inspired by concern over equity issues and the inability of industry to compete successfully in world markets because of low education and skill levels of graduates.

THE GROWTH OF MANDATES

4

Top-down reform programs were initiated in many states in the '80s. Many of these so-called reforms focused on testing of students and teachers. Legislation created more extensive systems of teacher evaluation and, in some cases, curriculum review.

The effect of these actions often was more bureaucracy but few changes, as mandates—but not always funding—increased. In states such as Illinois, superintendents concluded that the state reform programs initially had no impact or a negative impact on their school districts (Glass, 1989). In response, many superintendents and their districts resisted demands made by state legislatures.

The 1980s era of school reform, dominated by state and federal initiatives, created a backseat role for superintendents and school boards, thus putting a damper on successful results. The emergence in 1990 of "choice" movements across the country, as well as advocacy for more control at the local level by principals, parents, teachers, and students themselves, have brought additional challenges to superintendents' authority and policymaking leadership.

THE UNTOLD STORY

The contemporary role of the superintendent has not been thoroughly researched, compared to earlier generations of superintendents. Theories are few about why the superintendency and superintendents have not been studied in depth. Many early professors of educational administration conducted massive surveys both of school district practices and the behavior of school leaders.

While recent research on the superintendency has been scarce, James March speculated in his 1987 study that experienced superintendents might provide practical services that make school bureaucracies work. March also stated that superintendents, as a group, often appear to have similar personalities and behaviors (Crowson, 1987). In a 1988 study, Emily Feistritzer found that school administrators, including superintendents, were similar not only in their demographic characteristics, but in their opinions about issues facing American public education. Her study sampled principals and superintendents and claimed to have found the existence of an "old boys club" environment in public school management. In general, the study agreed with many of the findings of the 1982 AASA study of the superintendency authored by Luvern L. Cunningham and Joseph Hentges.

THE FUTURE OF THE SUPERINTENDENCY

What will be the role of the superintendent in the 1990s and beyond? Will it be as a facilitator of a number of school buildings located in a certain geographical locale, as "choice" and site-based management would indicate? Or will it be as a professional educational executive with a vision for the direction and means by which the district will improve the quality of public education?

In 1982, AASA endorsed a series of essential skills for school administrators, known as "Guidelines for the Preparation of School Administrators," and a subsequent book, titled *Skills for Successful School Leaders* by John Hoyle, Fenwick English, and Betty Steffy (1990). These two documents now serve as signposts for the establishment of professional standards for the practice and preparation of future superintendents.

For the superintendency to survive and flourish into the 21st century, superintendents will have to serve as role models, demonstrating a high degree of professionalism in order to increase their influence in policymaking at the local and state levels.

No definite answers have emerged as to who will develop educational policy and who will control schools in the 1990s. If school boards and superintendents are to retain their leadership, they must be open to significant change in areas such as board training and superintendent preparation—and they must examine whether their current roles and behaviors are consistent with the needs of school systems of the 21st century.

Design of the Study

The 1992 Study of the American School Superintendency follows similar reports issued each decade, beginning in 1923 under the auspices of the Department of Superintendence of the National Education Association. In 1952, the American Association of School Administrators took over the responsibility of the 10-year studies, and has since produced a major survey project each decade. Reports of the previous studies have appeared in various formats, including yearbooks, and most recently in formal survey project reports. The formal names of each of these studies are, "The Status of the Superintendent in 1923"; "Educational Leadership, 1933"; "The American School Superintendent, 1952"; "Profile of the School Superintendent, 1960"; "The American School Superintendent, 1971"; and "The American School Superintendency in 1982." No survey was conducted during the 1940-41 period due to World War II.

The content and the direction of the studies have been varied. So have the sampling techniques, titles, and issues covered. However, all of the studies have defined the superintendency, who superintendents are and what they do in their school districts. The 1933 study, conducted during the height of the Depression, looked ahead to the future of the nation, as well as to the role schools would play in the economic and social growth of a rapidly changing world. Special attention has been devoted in some of the studies, such as the one in 1952, to the similarities and differences between urban and rural superintendents. The 1960 study, in a yearbook format, discussed the preparation of individuals who wanted to become superintendents. During this period, the nation's schools were expanding rapidly, and the preparation of new leaders was of great concern.

The 1971 study took a different direction. Profiles of urban and rural superintendents were discontinued, and a new format was adopted that subsequently was used for the 1982 and 1992 studies. Some comparisons between the 1971, 1982, and 1992 survey studies are possible because of similarities in format and survey instrument content.

Research for the 1992 study was conducted through a survey mailed in 1990 to practicing superintendents across the nation.

Additional data used in this report were obtained from other studies conducted in recent years under the sponsorship of AASA.

SURVEY OBJECTIVES
The study has four objectives:
- To provide current information on the superintendency to national, state, and local education policymakers; the media; and superintendents themselves.
- To provide trend data that could be compared to studies conducted in 1971 and 1982.
- To provide an overview of public education from the perspective of its professional leaders.
- To provide researchers data and analysis about public education and educational leaders in the 1990s and projections into the 21st century.

CONTENT AREAS
The content of the 1992 survey relies partially on previous surveys, especially those conducted in 1971 and 1982, with particular attention paid to maintaining trend data.

The 1992 study includes data on the following:
- Personal profiles of superintendents including gender, age, family status, education, and area of residence.
- Relationships with board members, including evaluation and terms of employment.
- Characteristics of school districts, including staffing, hiring practices, programming, and size.
- Selected community characteristics, including their involvement and influence in district decision making.
- Superintendents' opinions on key problems and issues in education.

- Issues surrounding the preparation of superintendents and professional development of practicing superintendents.
- Career patterns of superintendents.

INSTRUMENT DEVELOPMENT

The 1992 survey instrument was developed in cooperation with AASA executive staff and the AASA Committee for the Advancement of School Administration.

The 1982 instrument was used as a prime reference document. The 1971 and 1960 instruments were substantially different and did not blend as well with the objectives of the 1992 study.

Some items from the 1982 survey were accepted without change, while others were updated or reworded. Additional items were written by the principal researcher, based on the objectives of the study and its selected topical areas. The final instrument for the 1992 study contained 110 items, mostly multiple choice.

The trial instrument was reviewed by AASA executive staff and members of the CASA committee. In addition, copies of the trial instrument were shared with selected educational administration professors for their comments and suggestions.

At a January 1990 meeting, held at the AASA offices, members of the CASA committee, the AASA executive staff, and the principal researcher discussed objectives for the study. Participants were asked to study trial items and be prepared to make suggestions.

The final 110 items were selected, and AASA staff and the principal researcher refined the items and arranged them in the final survey instrument, which went to press in June 1990. The instrument contained a short set of instructions and a cover letter from Dr. Richard Miller, executive director of AASA at the time of the study. It was 12 double-sided pages in length.

SAMPLE SELECTION

The stratified random sample was obtained from the 1988 Common Core of Data Public Education Agency Universe maintained by the U.S. Department of Education, which generates summary information for 15,449 school districts by type and total enrollment. There are many types of districts, even some without students. The 15,499 districts identified by the U.S. Department of Education must be said to "approximate descriptions."

Samples by types of districts and enrollment categories selected were the following:
- **GROUP A:** Districts with enrollments greater than or equal to 25,000 pupils: 172 sampled.
- **GROUP B:** Districts with enrollments greater than or equal to 3,000 but fewer than 25,000 pupils: 676 sampled.
- **GROUP C:** Districts with enrollments greater than or equal to 300 but fewer than 3,000 pupils: 825 sampled.
- **GROUP D:** Districts with enrollments of fewer than 300 pupils: 863 sampled (see **Table 2.1**).

An examination of the sample drawn (2,536) of a population of 15,449 was thought to be of an adequate size and proportion to reflect the immense diversity of public school districts and superintendents in the nation.

In addition, special attention was paid to ensure that gender and racial diversity in previous studies be brought forward to meet the objectives of continuing trend data. The sample reflects the fact that a significant number of American public school districts are still rural, even though about one-third of U.S. students attend school in one of the 10 largest school districts.

In the smallest districts, those with 300 or fewer students, where no one person holds the title of superintendent, it was assumed that someone was a de facto superintendent. It also was assumed that individuals receiving instruments addressed to the superintendent would not fill them out if they did not feel they were performing in that or an equivalent role.

Large-city superintendents serve many of the minority students in the entire country. Also, the 10 largest districts in the nation are majority-minority, as are most of the other 25 largest. A majority of these superintendencies are held by minority superintendents (Rist, 1991).

SURVEY IMPLEMENTATION AND RETURN RATE

The 2,536 survey instruments were mailed to superintendents in August 1990. A second mailing was made in October. There were few requests for additional information or assistance in filling out the instrument. A trial test showed that a superintendent would need about 20 to 25 minutes to complete the instrument. All information needed to complete the instrument normally is available in the office of a superintendent.

By January 1991, all completed surveys were forwarded by AASA to the principal researcher for tabulation and analysis. The number of usable surveys returned was 1,724, for a return rate of 68 percent, or 11 percent of all U.S. superintendents. **Table 2.2** describes the sample and return rate in more detail.

DATA ANALYSIS

Data contained in the 1,724 usable surveys were coded and processed at Northern Illinois University by February 1991. The statistical analysis was performed using Social Science Statistical Package software. Data were analyzed for the total response group, as well as the four enrollment strata, on an item-by-item basis. In general, simple, straightforward percentiles were used to illustrate similarities and differences among various response groups.

While the return rate was low for superintendents of districts enrolling fewer than 300 students, this should not be a concern to policymakers who seek to influ-

ence schooling of large numbers of students, because the smallest districts, even when counted as a whole, serve a comparatively small number of students.

The very high return rates for the other three groups, especially superintendents from districts with more than 25,000 students, further strengthens the validity of the data.

In **Table 2.3** the decline of enrollment in many small districts can be seen between 1982 and 1992. The shifts in the national population, as well as number of children in families, illustrated in this table suggest district demographics be considered in policies addressing reform or restructuring. Some large districts are getting much larger and small rural districts are declining.

The composition of the sample groups in terms of demography and personal characteristics is discussed elsewhere in the report.

TABLE 2.1 1992 SURVEY SAMPLE GROUPS

PUPIL ENROLLMENT CLASSIFICATION	INCLUDED IN EACH ENROLLMENT GROUP		PUBLIC SCHOOL SUPTS RECEIVING QUESTIONNAIRES		RETURNED QUESTIONNAIRES	
	NUMBER	PERCENT OF TOTAL SUPTS	NUMBER SAMPLED	PERCENT SAMPLED OF EACH GROUP	NUMBER	PERCENT OF THOSE SAMPLED
GROUP A: 25,000 OR MORE	172	1.1	172	100.0	145	84.3
GROUP B: 3,000 TO 24,999	2,706	17.6	676	25.0	610	90.2
GROUP C: 300 TO 2,999	8,255	53.4	825	10.0	716	86.8
GROUP D: FEWER THAN 300	4,316	27.9	863	20.0	253	27.3
TOTALS	15,499	100.0	2,536	16.4	1,724	68.4

TABLE 2.2 SIZE OF DISTRICT PARTICIPATING IN SAMPLE

PUPILS SERVED	NO. OF DISTRICTS	TOTAL %
MORE THAN 100,000	19	1.1
50,000-99,999	40	2.3
25,000-49,999	86	5.0
10,000-24,999	146	8.5
5,000-9,999	212	12.3
3,000-4,999	252	14.6
1,000-2,999	426	24.7
300-999	290	16.8
LESS THAN 300	253	14.7
TOTAL	1,724	100.0

TABLE 2.3 CHANGE IN ENROLLMENT SINCE JANUARY 1980

RESPONSE CLASSIFICATIONS	GROUP A: 25,000 OR MORE	%	GROUP B: 3,000-24,999	%	GROUP C: 300-2,999	%	GROUP D: FEWER THAN 300	%	TOTALS	%
INCREASED 25% OR MORE	20	13.8	83	13.6	56	7.8	19	7.5	178	10.3
INCREASED 20-24%	9	6.2	26	4.3	25	3.5	10	4.0	70	4.1
INCREASED 15-19%	6	4.1	18	3.0	28	3.9	8	3.2	60	3.5
INCREASED 10-14%	15	10.3	40	6.6	57	8.0	8	3.2	120	7.0
INCREASED 5-9%	12	8.3	58	9.5	60	8.4	15	5.9	145	8.4
INCREASED LESS THAN 5%	19	13.1	101	16.6	98	13.7	38	15.0	256	14.8
DECREASED 25% OR MORE	6	4.1	36	5.9	61	8.5	42	16.6	145	8.4
DECREASED 20-24%	11	7.6	40	6.6	45	6.3	12	4.7	108	6.3
DECREASED 15-19%	8	5.5	40	6.6	67	9.4	16	6.3	131	7.6
DECREASED 10-14%	10	6.9	66	10.8	87	12.2	31	12.3	194	11.3
DECREASED 5-9%	24	16.6	91	14.9	121	16.9	46	18.2	181	16.4

DISTRICT SIZE CLASSIFICATIONS

Personal Characteristics

3

What are the personal characteristics of superintendents in America's public schools? Who are they? Where do they come from? Are they married? Do they have children? How old are they? These are just a few of the questions posed to the sample of superintendents that provided a framework for developing a composite picture of the typical superintendent based on district enrollment size.

Married white male. The American school superintendent has been characterized in recent research studies as a white male, of middle age, coming from a small town, having advanced degrees in education, and for the most part sharing common values and opinions (Feistritzer, 1988). While the majority of respondents were white males, the data regarding personal characteristics of all superintendents sampled in this research do not support such conclusions, even though many commonalities exist among respondents. In some ways, superintendents are a diverse group, especially considering the size and types of districts they serve.

This study, like the one in 1982, found that a greater number of minority and women superintendents are serving in larger districts than in previous surveys. This is especially true in those districts with enrollments of more than 25,000. In the 10 years between the 1982 and 1992 studies, the number of women superintendents edged upward by about 25 percent. Unfortunately, a dramatic underrepresentation of these two groups still exists. For whatever reasons, superintendency preparation programs, state

agencies, school boards, communities, and practicing superintendents have failed to ensure that women and minorities are hired for the superintendency. Of the more than four million professional educators in the nation, only a few women (fewer than 1,000) guide some 15,000-plus school districts in executive leadership positions (NSBA, 1990).

By the year 2020, approximately one in three students will be a member of a minority group. Thus, it is important that well-prepared and experienced minority superintendents be available to serve districts with large numbers of minority children, both as advocates and as role models (Hodgkinson, 1991).

In recent years, many articles have appeared in the media concerning the need for a dramatic increase in the number of minority teachers, and modest federal legislation has been enacted to assist in that objective. While some small federal grant programs and state initiatives have been directed toward the identification, training, and placing of minorities and women in school superintendencies across the nation, the survey results indicate much more needs to be done.

GENDER

Like many other high-profile leadership positions in American society, the American school superintendency is dominated by white males. Of the 1,724 respondents, only 113, or 6.6 percent, were female (see **Table 3.1**). This figure was a slight increase from previous decades. In 1982, using a fairly comparable sample size, 106 women superintendents were sam-

TABLE 3.1 GENDER OF RESPONDENTS

GENDER	GROUP A: 25,000 OR MORE PUPILS		GROUP B: 3,000-24,999 PUPILS		GROUP C: 300-2,999 PUPILS		GROUP D FEWER THAN 300 PUPILS		NATIONAL UNWEIGHTED PROFILE	
	No.	%	No.	%	No.	%	No.	%	No.	%
MALES	131	91.6	574	95.0	675	94.5	220	87.3	1,600	93.4
FEMALES	12	8.4	30	5.0	39	5.5	32	12.7	113	6.6
TOTAL	143	8.3	604	35.3	714	41.7	252	14.7	1,713	100.0

pled, comprising 7 percent of the total. In 1952, 6.7 percent of sampled superintendents were women, but many were located in small rural districts.

Later consolidation of these districts probably reduced the numbers of female superintendents. By 1962, the number of women superintendents was down to 0.06 percent of 1,586 superintendents. Compared to several decades ago, female superintendents are being employed in more populous districts. In districts with 25,000 or more pupils, the percentage of female superintendents, 8.4, is greater than the national average.

RACE

Almost all minority superintendents are black or Hispanic. Most minority superintendents are employed in districts with enrollments of more than 3,000 students. As the 1990s began, blacks or Hispanics served as superintendents in a significant number of the 20 largest school districts in the nation. Few minority superintendents serve in very small districts, and those that do generally are found in the South and Southwest. For instance, Texas has a number of Hispanic superintendents serving in small districts (Collier, 1987).

According to the national profile, about 4 percent of the nation's superintendents are minorities. The total number in the 1992 sample was 66 of 1,714, of whom most led large districts. Of 144 superintendents reporting enrollments in excess of 25,000, 22, or about 15 percent, were minorities (see **Table 3.2**).

Because of shifts of some of racial groups in the nation, minority populations have become majority populations in many large American cities. Thus, many urban school districts have become majority-minority, despite court-imposed desegregation orders and busing programs. There are comparatively few majority-minority medium-size districts with minority superintendents (Rist, 1990).

AGE

The typical career track of teacher, principal, central office administrator, and then superintendent heavily influences the average age of superintendents. Each of these career steps requires training and years of experience. The average entry age for a teacher is 22 or 23. However, a graduate program in school administration (usually taken part time) takes considerable time. So does the certification process in most states, which generally requires a number of years of professional experience both in the principalship and/or at the central office level. Few potential superintendents have completed the progression before age 35.

TABLE 3.2 RACE OF RESPONDENTS

	GROUP A: 25,000 OR MORE PUPILS		GROUP B: 3,000-24,999 PUPILS		GROUP C: 300-2,999 PUPILS		GROUP D: FEWER THAN 300 PUPILS		NATIONAL UNWEIGHTED PROFILE	
	No.	%	No.	%	No.	%	No.	%	No.	%
WHITE	122	84.7	579	95.5	701	98.3	246	98.0	1,648	96.1
MINORITY	22	15.3	27	4.5	12	1.7	5	2.0	66	3.9

TABLE 3.3 AGES OF SUPERINTENDENTS

	GROUP A: 25,000 OR MORE PUPILS		GROUP B: 3,000-24,999 PUPILS		GROUP C: 300-2,999 PUPILS		GROUP D: FEWER THAN 300 PUPILS		NATIONAL UNWEIGHTED PROFILE	
AGE GROUP	No.	%	No.	%	No.	%	No.	%	No.	%
30-35	0	0.0	2	0.3	10	1.4	6	2.4	18	1.0
36-40	2	1.4	18	3.0	48	6.7	37	14.6	105	6.1
41-45	15	10.4	93	15.3	155	21.6	62	24.5	325	18.9
46-50	41	28.5	176	28.9	201	28.1	45	17.8	463	26.9
51-55	38	26.4	165	27.1	159	22.2	55	21.7	417	24.2
56-60	33	22.9	114	18.7	111	15.5	36	14.2	294	17.1
61-65	14	9.7	36	5.9	28	3.9	9	3.6	87	5.1
66+	1	0.7	5	0.8	4	0.6	3	1.2	13	0.8

In the past 60 years, the median age of superintendents has hovered around 48 to 50. In contrast, the 1923 AASA study found a median age of 43.1—the youngest registered in seven studies that have been compiled. Roughly 40 years later in 1960, the median age was 51.8—the oldest among that and six previous studies. In 1992, the median age decreased again to 49.4 (see **Figure 3.1** and **Table 3.4**).

The overall median age of about 50 during the past 60 years is not surprising, considering the typical course of entry as a teacher at 23, a principalship or assistant principalship at 28, a central office position at 33, and the superintendency at age 38 to 40. This seems to be the standard profile of current superintendents with the least years of tenure. Most superintendents enter the position in their early 40s, in a fairly small district, and begin to work their way to larger suburban or urban districts, where salaries and finances generally are more generous. Retirement usually occurs between age 55 and 60, and very few superintendents in any of the previous surveys were older than 60. (See Chapters 4, 5, and 7 of this study.)

In districts with enrollments of more than 25,000 students, nearly 40 percent of the 1992 sample super-intendents were under age 50, meaning many "younger" superintendents are struggling with the immense problems of urban education. On the other hand, a slim majority of superintendents (59.3 percent) from districts with fewer than 300 students were less than 50 years old (see **Table 3.3** and **Figure 3.2**)

Early Retirement

With a median age of 50 and early retirement available at 55 in many states, a majority (50 percent) of superintendents may be retiring in the 1990s. Several studies (Glass, 1989 and Angus, 1986) found that many superintendents do intend to retire early. However, some studies have found that superintendents who declare they will take early retirement hang on for "just one more year." Factors that tend to hasten or delay early retirement might be the financial condition of the district, relations with board members, or collective bargaining pressures (Glass, 1989).

Attrition

A large exodus of superintendents is probably not going to occur in the first half of the 1990s. But by 2000, at least half of the present corps of superinten-

FIGURE 3.1 MEDIAN AGE OF SUPT. 1923-1990

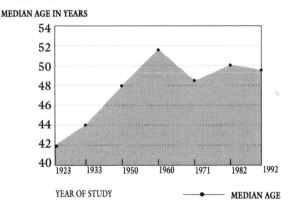

MEDIAN AGE IN YEARS

YEAR OF STUDY   ────•──── MEDIAN AGE

FIGURE 3.2 MEDIAN AGE BY DISTRICT SIZE, 1971, 1982, AND 1992

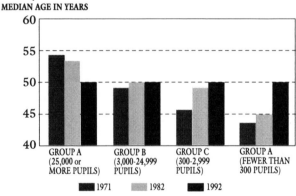

MEDIAN AGE IN YEARS

■ 1971   ■ 1982   ■ 1992

TABLE 3.4 AGE OF SUPERINTENDENTS: 1971, 1982, AND 1992 COMPARISONS

AGE GROUP	GROUP A: 25,000 OR MORE PUPILS			GROUP B: 3,000-24,999 PUPILS			GROUP C: 300-2,999 PUPILS			GROUP D: FEWER THAN 300 PUPILS		
	1971	1982	1992	1971	1982	1992	1971	1982	1992	1971	1982	1992
UNDER 40	3.6	4.5	1.4	7.1	6.3	3.3	21.5	14.8	8.1	46.5	35.3	17.0
40-44	13.9	13.4	10.4	22.2	13.8	15.3	23.5	18.2	21.6	11.3	16.1	24.5
45-49	19.0	21.4	28.5	20.9	22.1	28.9	15.6	21.6	28.1	14.1	14.7	17.8
50-54	19.0	25.0	26.4	21.8	30.3	27.1	15.2	22.3	22.2	2.8	19.2	21.7
55-59	10.7	27.7	18.7	16.7	20.8	18.7	15.9	18.1	15.5	8.5	8.5	14.2
60 +	24.8	7.2	10.4	11.3	6.8	6.8	8.3	4.9	4.5	16.9	6.2	4.8

dents likely will be retired. This comparatively low estimate is predicated upon assumptions that modest inflation will occur in the economy, (lessening worth of retirement annuities) and most districts will be fairly calm in terms of collective bargaining and incursions by special interest groups. Also, turnover depends on whether superintendents will enjoy better health; the status of alternative positions in the private sector may or may not be plentiful, and boards probably will not be so subject to rapid turnover. However, any or all of these assumptions could change without warning.

The pattern of small districts hiring young superintendents before they move "up the ladder" may be changing, however. In the 1970s and 1980s, more superintendents under age 40 were found in very small districts. In 1971, for instance, 46.5 percent of the superintendents in small rural districts with enrollments of fewer than 300 students were under the age of 40. In 1992, that figure was only 17 percent, according to sample data. The same trend is seen to a

lesser degree in districts of 300 to 3,000 students, where 21.5 percent of superintendents were under 40 in 1971, compared to only 8.1 percent in 1990.

These data indicate most superintendents are beginning their careers in their 40s, and serving approximately 15 to 18 years. It appears that most superintendents serve in at least three districts during their superintendency careers (See **Chapter 5**).

MARITAL STATUS

Most superintendents are married. Only about two percent are single, and five to six percent are divorced, separated, or widowed (see **Table 3.5**). Many school board members may expect the superintendent to be a role model in terms of family values. Superintendents are expected to become what authors David Tyack and Elisabeth Hansot call "managers of virtue" in a 1982 book of that title.

The spouses of superintendents often play a big role in the decision to accept new jobs, which in some

TABLE 3.5 MARITAL STATUS OF SUPERINTENDENTS

MARITAL STATUS	GROUP A: 25,000 OR MORE PUPILS		GROUP B: 3,000-24,999 PUPILS		GROUP C: 300-2,999 PUPILS		GROUP D: FEWER THAN 300 PUPILS		NATIONAL UNWEIGHTED PROFILE	
	No.	%	No.	%	No.	%	No.	%	No.	%
SINGLE	8	5.6	8	1.3	13	1.8	8	3.2	37	2.1
MARRIED	126	87.5	565	92.8	671	93.8	227	89.7	1,589	92.3
DIVORCED/SEPARATED	7	4.9	29	4.7	30	4.2	16	6.3	82	4.8
WIDOWED	3	2.1	7	1.1	1	0.1	2	0.8	13	0.8
TOTAL	144	8.4	609	35.4	715	41.5	253	14.7	1,721	100.0

TABLE 3.6 POLITICAL PARTY PREFERENCES OF SUPERINTENDENTS

POLITICAL PARTY PREFERENCE	GROUP A: 25,000 OR MORE PUPILS		GROUP B: 3,000-24,999 PUPILS		GROUP C: 300-2,999 PUPILS		GROUP D: FEWER THAN 300 PUPILS		NATIONAL UNWEIGHTED PROFILE	
	No.	%	No.	%	No.	%	No.	%	No.	%
DEMOCRAT	65	45.1	206	34.3	235	33.1	88	35.3	594	34.8
INDEPENDENT	35	24.3	164	27.3	208	29.3	72	28.9	479	28.1
REPUBLICAN	44	30.6	231	38.4	268	37.7	89	35.7	632	37.1
TOTAL	144	8.4	601	35.2	711	41.7	249	14.6	1,705	100.0

TABLE 3.7 POLITICAL POSTURE OF SUPERINTENDENTS

POLITICAL POSTURE/VIEWS	GROUP A: 25,000 OR MORE PUPILS		GROUP B: 3,000-24,999 PUPILS		GROUP C: 300-2,999 PUPILS		GROUP D: FEWER THAN 300 PUPILS		NATIONAL UNWEIGHTED PROFILE	
	No.	%	No.	%	No.	%	No.	%	No.	%
LIBERAL	26	18.4	69	11.4	63	8.9	28	11.1	186	10.9
MODERATE	98	69.5	386	63.7	420	59.3	137	54.4	1,041	61.0
CONSERVATIVE	17	12.1	151	24.9	225	31.8	87	34.5	480	28.1
TOTAL	141	8.3	606	35.5	708	41.5	252	14.8	1,707	100.0

cases might create a hardship for female superintendents in their 40s or 50s with spouses who are not willing to relocate. Typically, men are less accustomed to the idea of disrupting their professional lives for a spouse (*The School Administrator*, October 1990). Just the opposite has been the case with male superintendents. Traditionally, many male superintendents' wives have been teachers or homemakers who generally believed their roles required participation in school affairs (akin to that of the clergy). This situation may well be changing, along with the number of women in the workplace.

POLITICAL PARTY PREFERENCE

Nationally, very few superintendents are elected on political slates, and very few are appointed by mayors or city councils. Beyond this fact, superintendents respond that they do have political party preferences. Large-city superintendents favor the Democratic party, which agrees with the traditional political voting pattern of their communities. Superintendents serving in smaller districts were more evenly divided between Democrats, Republicans, and Independents (see **Table 3.6**). There is little difference in political party according to age of superintendents (see **Table 3.8**).

A second part of the survey section on political preference asked about political posture. The political party affiliation of superintendents is almost evenly split among Democrats, Republicans, and Independents. The level of activity of superintendents in supporting the political party of their choice is not known, nor is the political affiliation of their spouses. A sizable majority (61 percent) of superintendents, regardless of whether they are Democrat or Republican, perceive themselves as moderates (see **Table 3.7**). Only a small minority see themselves as decidedly liberal or conservative. The political postures of superintendents are fairly typical of the majority of middle-class, college-educated Americans.

The notion that the superintendency is not a political position, however, is naive. While few superintendents are elected, and folklore holds that the superintendency is not a political position, in reality, superintendents are drawn almost daily into contact with elected public officials. In thousands of districts each year, the superintendent, along with the board and community, must organize and lead efforts to obtain voter support at the polls (Blumberg, 1985, p. 45).

COMMUNITY BACKGROUND

The new data show that superintendents are beginning to reflect the contemporary composition of American society in terms of community-size origins. Traditionally, superintendents have reflected the geographical origins of most Americans; specifically, the small town or rural area. This has been true despite the nation's urbanization over the past five decades. Today, however, many more superintendents (44 percent) come from a suburban upbringing than in 1971, when 86.1 percent of them came from rural areas or small towns (see **Table 3.10**). Considering that superintendents' median age was close to 50 in 1971, most of them were born shortly after World War I or just before the Great Depression. At that

TABLE 3.8 POLITICAL PARTY PREFERENCE OF SUPERINTENDENTS, ANALYZED BY AGE

	INDEPENDENT		DEMOCRATIC		REPUBLICAN	
AGE	No.	%	No.	%	No.	%
30-35	6	1.2	3	0.5	8	1.3
36-40	37	7.7	37	6.2	31	4.9
41-45	100	20.7	106	17.8	116	18.2
46-50	121	25.1	161	27.0	181	28.5
51-55	122	25.3	146	24.5	147	23.1
56-60	79	16.4	105	17.6	109	17.1
61-65	17	3.5	33	5.5	36	5.7
66+	0	0.0	5	0.8	8	1.3

TABLE 3.9 POLITICAL PARTY PREFERENCE OF SUPERINTENDENTS, ANALYZED BY AGE– 1992-1982 COMPARISONS

	INDEPENDENT		DEMOCRATIC		REPUBLICAN		OTHER	
	1992	1982	1992	1982	1992	1982	1992	1982
AGE	%	%	%	%	%	%	%	%
30-35	35.3	43.5	17.6	30.4	47.1	23.9	2.2	2.2
35-39	35.2	35.8	35.2	26.5	29.5	37.7	0.0	0.0
40-44	31.1	.35.5	32.9	29.5	36.0	34.6	0.5	0.5
45-49	26.1	32.2	34.8	31.9	39.1	35.5	0.4	0.4
50-54	29.4	33.9	35.2	32.4	35.4	33.6	0.0	0.0
55-59	27.0	33.8	35.8	31.3	37.2	33.8	1.3	1.3
60 +	17.2	25.0	38.4	33.8	44.4	41.2	0.0	0.0

time, America was in the early stages of urbanization. Vocational and professional opportunities were limited in rural and small towns, and graduates often attended "normal" (later state colleges) schools, usually located in small towns. These "colleges" were much less expensive to attend than universities and were more convenient for aspiring educators from rural communities (Tyack and Hansot, 1982).

Exodus

After completing study at the normal schools or state colleges, the most common career path for superintendents of the 1930s-1940s was a teaching position in a small school; a principalship in a small district; and a superintendency. However, after World War II, men graduating from college under the auspices of the GI Bill began to obtain teaching jobs in larger districts in more urban and suburban communities. The growth of the suburbs after World War II provided many of these educators their first superintendency. Indeed, the suburbs probably are responsible for a considerable reduction in the number of superintendents from small-town and rural backgrounds.

Small-Town Roots

In spite of a shift toward urban and suburban backgrounds, 38 percent of superintendents in districts with more than 25,000 students still claim a small-town origin. Half that number, 18.2 percent, say they come from a rural area. In the 3,000 to 25,000 enrollment districts, the superintendents are also predominantly from small-town and rural backgrounds (see **Table 3.12**). Not surprisingly, nearly all of the superintendents in the very small districts come from small towns and rural areas.

The influences of small-town and rural origins on the attitudes and behaviors of superintendents have not been thoroughly studied. But survey responses suggest superintendents as a group are moderately conservative in their social values and lifestyles. This profile matches that of the teaching ranks from which they come (Lortie, 1975).

Large-city superintendents typically come from medium and large communities. Nearly a third are from cities of 100,000 or more in population. Superintendents of small districts generally grew up in very small towns with fewer than 2,500 population.

The 1992 survey indicates an increase in the number of small districts. This is probably due to enrollment declines overall, and not the creation of new communities or school districts. (See **Chapter 2, Tables 2.1** and **2.3**.)

TABLE 3.10 TYPE OF COMMUNITY IN WHICH SUPERINTENDENTS SPENT PRECOLLEGE YEARS: COMPARISONS 1971, 1982, AND 1992

	1971	1982	1992
RURAL/SMALL TOWN	86.1	78.0	56.0
SUBURBAN/URBAN	14.0	22.0	44.0

TABLE 3.11 TYPE OF COMMUNITY LIVED IN BEFORE COLLEGE (ANALYZED BY AGE)

	AGE 45 OR YOUNGER		AGE 46-50		AGE 51-55		AGE 56-60		AGE 61 OR OLDER	
	No.	%	No.	%	No.	%	No.	%	No.	%
RURAL	144	32.3	143	30.8	133	32.0	96	32.9	26	26.0
SMALL TOWN	172	38.6	187	40.3	167	40.1	131	44.9	47	47.0
SUBURBAN	71	15.9	62	13.4	52	12.5	19	6.5	11	11.0
LARGE CITY	59	13.2	72	15.5	64	15.4	46	15.8	16	16.0
TOTAL	446	100.0	464	100.0	416	100.0	292	100.1	100	100.0

TABLE 3.12 TYPE OF COMMUNITY IN WHICH SUPERINTENDENT SPENT PRECOLLEGE YEARS

COMMUNITY TYPE	GROUP A: 25,000 OR MORE PUPILS		GROUP B: 3,000-24,999 PUPILS		GROUP C: 300-2,999 PUPILS		GROUP D: FEWER THAN 300 PUPILS		NATIONAL UNWEIGHTED PROFILE	
	No.	%	No.	%	No.	%	No.	%	No.	%
RURAL	26	18.2	181	29.9	222	31.3	111	44.4	540	31.6
SMALL TOWN	54	37.8	229	37.8	323	45.5	95	38.0	701	41.1
SUBURBAN	20	14.0	95	15.7	82	11.5	15	6.0	212	12.4
LARGE CITY	43	30.1	101	16.7	83	11.7	29	11.6	56	15.0
TOTAL	143	8.4	606	35.5	710	41.5	250	14.6	1709	100.0

FAMILY CHARACTERISTICS

Americans perceive public education as a vehicle for social mobility. The availability of public education traditionally has been one of the most significant differences between European societies and the United States. In many respects superintendents represent this social mobility through education, because so many of them were reared in a blue-collar world and gained entry into the white-collar class through college degrees and teaching positions (Lortie, 1975). According to both 1982 and 1992 data, the average 50-year-old small town superintendent comes from a working-class family.

Parents' Education Level

Father's education. The education level of fathers of superintendents was comparatively low (see **Table 3.14**). In all categories of district size, about 30 percent of the fathers of superintendents possessed only an eighth-grade education. Superintendents' fathers in small districts were slightly more likely to have

high school educations than the fathers of superintendents in the larger school districts. Considering that superintendents in most states must have more than a master's degree, it is remarkable that only 6.2 percent had fathers who graduated from college.

Younger superintendents, however, are more likely to have fathers with more schooling than that of fathers of older superintendents. Ten percent of the fathers of superintendents under 40 years of age had some college education (see **Table 3.15**).

Mother's education. The mothers of superintendents surveyed had slightly higher education levels, which may be attributable to the fact that high schools in historically blue-collar communities typically graduated more girls than boys (see **Table 3.16**).

Presumably, today's superintendents who have risen from working class to professional status will be able to offer even greater opportunities to their offspring. It will be interesting to see whether this new generation chooses education as a profession. Moreover, it will be especially interesting to see whether the children of more white-collar, middle-

TABLE 3.13 SIZE OF COMMUNITY IN WHICH SUPERINTENDENT SPENT PRECOLLEGE YEARS

SIZE OF COMMUNITY	GROUP A: 25,000 OR MORE PUPILS		GROUP B: 3,000-24,999 PUPILS		GROUP C: 300-2,999 PUPILS		GROUP D: FEWER THAN 300 PUPILS		NATIONAL UNWEIGHTED PROFILE	
	No.	%	No.	%	No.	%	No.	%	No.	%
FEWER THAN 2,500	41	28.7	211	34.8	285	39.9	149	58.9	686	40.0
2,500-9,999	25	17.5	139	22.9	192	26.9	33	13.0	389	22.7
10,000-99,999	35	24.5	154	25.4	165	23.1	45	17.8	399	23.3
100,000 OR MORE	42	29.4	102	16.8	72	10.1	26	10.3	242	14.1
TOTAL	143	8.3	606	35.3	714	41.6	253	14.7	716	100.0

TABLE 3.14 EDUCATION LEVEL OF FATHER

FATHER'S EDUCATION LEVEL	GROUP A: 25,000 OR MORE PUPILS		GROUP B: 3,000-24,999 PUPILS		GROUP C: 300-2,999 PUPILS		GROUP D: FEWER THAN 300 PUPILS		NATIONAL UNWEIGHTED PROFILE	
	No.	%	No.	%	No.	%	No.	%	No.	%
8TH GRADE OR LESS	49	34.8	166	27.6	223	31.8	78	32.1	516	30.6
SOME HIGH SCHOOL	17	12.1	122	18.6	109	15.5	34	14.0	272	16.1
COMPLETED HIGH SCHOOL	37	26.2	141	23.5	192	27.4	68	28.0	438	26.0
SOME COLLEGE	17	12.1	55	9.2	63	9.0	22	9.1	157	9.3
TECH/TRADE SCHOOL	1	0.7	10	1.7	16	2.3	9	3.7	36	2.1
GRADUATED COLLEGE	5	3.5	47	7.8	40	5.8	12	4.9	104	6.2
ATTENDED GRAD. SCHOOL	4	2.8	4	0.7	11	1.6	4	1.6	23	1.4
HAVE GRAD. DEGREE	11	7.8	66	11.0	48	6.8	16	6.6	141	8.4
TOTAL	141	8.4	601	35.6	702	41.6	243	14.4	1687	100.0

class families decide to enter teaching with a future career goal of the superintendency.

Parental Activities

The superintendency is a position requiring a great deal of community interaction. However, many superintendents come from families that apparently did not actively participate in community activities.

Involvement in school. Parents of superintendents were not particularly involved in schools, as measured by minimal levels of participation in PTA/PTOs (see **Table 3.17**). These data are consistent with the 1982 study and perhaps with all parents in general.

Involvement in the community. In the area of parent involvement with community groups in general approximately one-third of superintendents indicated

TABLE 3.15 EDUCATION LEVEL OF FATHER BY AGE OF SUPERINTENDENT

FATHER'S EDUCATION LEVEL	30-35 %	36-40 %	41-45 %	46-50 %	51-55 %	56-60 %	61-65 %	66 + %
8TH GRADE OR LESS	11.1	18.3	21.2	23.0	36.2	47.6	37.3	50.0
SOME HIGH SCHOOL	11.1	17.3	14.3	17.3	17.6	14.6	14.2	16.7
COMPLETED HIGH SCHOOL	33.3	26.0	29.3	30.0	20.5	21.9	30.1	16.7
SOME COLLEGE	16.7	12.5	12.5	10.5	7.5	6.3	4.8	8.3
TECH/TRADE SCHOOL	11.1	1.9	3.4	1.1	2.7	1.0	2.4	0.0
GRADUATED COLLEGE	5.6	4.8	8.1	7.9	5.3	4.2	3.6	0.0
ATTENDED GRAD. SCHOOL	0.0	2.9	2.5	1.3	0.5	1.0	1.2	0.0
HAVE GRAD. DEGREE	0.0	16.3	8.7	8.8	9.7	3.5	6.0	8.3

TABLE 3.16 EDUCATION LEVEL OF MOTHER

MOTHER'S EDUCATION LEVEL	GROUP A: 25,000 OR MORE PUPILS No.	%	GROUP B: 3,000-24,999 PUPILS No.	%	GROUP C: 300-2,999 PUPILS No.	%	GROUP D: FEWER THAN 300 PUPILS No.	%	NATIONAL UNWEIGHTED PROFILE No.	%
8TH GRADE OR LESS	37	26.6	111	18.5	143	20.3	56	23.1	347	20.6
SOME HIGH SCHOOL	21	15.1	94	15.7	114	16.2	27	11.2	256	15.2
COMPLETED HIGH SCHOOL	34	24.5	217	36.2	252	35.8	86	35.5	589	35.0
SOME COLLEGE	15	10.8	57	9.5	69	9.8	27	11.2	168	10.0
TECH/TRADE SCHOOL	4	2.9	23	3.8	26	3.7	5	2.1	58	3.4
GRADUATED COLLEGE	18	12.9	56	9.3	70	9.9	24	9.9	168	10.0
ATTENDED GRAD. SCHOOL	4	2.9	10	1.7	6	0.9	9	3.7	29	1.7
HAVE GRAD. DEGREE	6	4.3	31	5.2	24	3.4	8	3.3	69	.1
TOTAL	139	8.3	599	35.6	704	41.8	242	14.4	1,684	100.0

TABLE 3.17 PARENTS ACTIVE IN PTA/PTO

	GROUP A: 25,000 OR MORE PUPILS No.	%	GROUP B: 3,000-24,999 PUPILS No.	%	GROUP C: 300-2,999 PUPILS No.	%	GROUP D: FEWER THAN 300 PUPILS No.	%	NATIONAL UNWEIGHTED PROFILE No.	%
YES	49	34.5	211	35.1	185	26.1	75	29.8	520	30.5
NO	93	65.5	389	64.9	523	73.9	177	70.2	1,182	69.5
TOTAL	142	8.3	600	35.3	708	41.6	252	14.8	1,702	100.0

their parents had been active. This finding is consistent across districts of various sizes, and parallels the 1982 AASA study (see **Table 3.18**).

Involvement in church. In the era when most current superintendents were growing up, the American public attended religious institutions more regularly than is true today. The survey data indicate this is true for superintendents as well: Approximately 60 percent of superintendents' parents were active churchgoers, a higher percentage than is perhaps common in our society today (see **Table 3.19**).

TABLE 3.18 PARENTS ACTIVE IN COMMUNITY GROUPS

	GROUP A: 25,000 OR MORE PUPILS		GROUP B: 3,000-24,999 PUPILS		GROUP C: 300-2,999 PUPILS		GROUP D: FEWER THAN 300 PUPILS		NATIONAL UNWEIGHTED PROFILE	
	No.	%	No.	%	No.	%	No.	%	No.	%
YES	54	38.0	203	33.9	269	38.0	109	43.3	635	37.3
NO	88	62.0	397	66.1	439	62.0	143	56.7	1,067	62.7
TOTAL	142	8.3	600	35.3	708	41.6	252	14.8	1,702	100.0

TABLE 3.19 PARENTS ACTIVE IN RELIGION

	GROUP A: 25,000 OR MORE PUPILS		GROUP B: 3,000-24,999 PUPILS		GROUP C: 300-2,999 PUPILS		GROUP D: FEWER THAN 300 PUPILS		NATIONAL UNWEIGHTED PROFILE	
	No.	%	No.	%	No.	%	No.	%	No.	%
YES	89	62.7	353	58.8	431	60.9	142	56.3	1,015	59.6
NO	53	37.3	247	41.2	277	39.1	110	43.7	687	40.4
TOTAL	142	8.3	600	35.3	708	41.6	252	14.8	1,702	100.0

18

Professional Experiences

During the past half century, professional training for the superintendency has evolved along somewhat the same lines as professions such as law and medicine. Most superintendents must take undergraduate and graduate training and gain experience in teaching and administration. Very few superintendents deviate from this set of pre-superintendency experiences. But the superintendency as a profession is still very much in a developmental state. The current wave of school reform has created a great deal of discussion and some state legislation aimed at improving training and encouraging extensive internships for superintendents. Some states that test teachers for competency now test administrators who want to be certified superintendents, as well.

In the 1990s efforts probably will increase to "professionalize" the superintendency. Currently, greater emphasis is being given by state agencies and professional groups to improve the instructional leadership of principals. The effective and essential school movements have focused significantly on the importance of the principal, but have paid little attention to the role of the superintendent in curriculum development and instructional improvement (Hoyle, 1985). However, many educators believe that as policymakers become frustrated with the slow rate of school restructuring/reform success in the 1990s, there will be renewed and significant attention paid to improving the executive leadership of school districts, namely, the superintendent (Hord, 1990).

ENTRY INTO ADMINISTRATION

School leaders generally obtained their first administrative position in a school district before age 30. This finding also was true in the AASA studies conducted in 1982 and 1971. It is more true in larger districts than in smaller districts. In districts with enrollments of more than 3,000, more than 60 percent of current superintendents obtained their first administrative jobs before age 30. In the very small districts, those with enrollments of fewer than 300 students, only 35.6 percent of current superintendents obtained their first administrative position by age 30. In some cases, that position was a superintendency. In the large urban districts, only 12.6 percent entered administration after the age of 36 (see **Table 4.1**).

It is interesting to reflect on why so many superintendents made an early career decision to seek administrative positions. Were the strongest factors salary, a desire to "make a difference," a need to control, a desire for status, or something else? Individuals' motivations for selecting a career in educational administration needs much more research.

The Dominance of Former Teachers

The superintendency is dominated by former secondary-level teachers. Only 28.5 percent of respondents indicate they had first taught in the elementary grades (see **Table 4.4**). The popular belief that superintendents are former physical education teachers and

TABLE 4.1 AGE AT ENTERING FIRST FULL-TIME ADMINISTRATIVE POSITION OTHER THAN SUPERINTENDENT

AGE GROUP	GROUP A: 25,000 OR MORE PUPILS		GROUP B: 3,000-24,999 PUPILS		GROUP C: 300-2,999 PUPILS		GROUP D: FEWER THAN 300 PUPILS		NATIONAL UNWEIGHTED PROFILE	
	No.	%	No.	%	No.	%	No.	%	No.	%
25-30	100	69.9	376	62.0	377	52.9	90	35.6	943	55.0
31-35	25	17.5	168	27.7	236	33.1	97	38.3	526	30.7
36-40	12	8.4	46	7.6	70	9.8	37	14.6	165	9.6
41-45	6	4.2	12	2.0	25	3.5	16	6.3	59	3.4
46 AND OLDER	0	0.0	4	0.7	5	0.7	13	5.1	22	1.3

coaches is validated neither in the 1992 nor 1982 surveys. Most were social studies teachers, and many others were science, math, or English teachers. The percentages are small enough in each of these teaching fields to prevent predicting which kinds of teachers are most likely to become superintendents in the future.

Conventional wisdom might predict that in very small districts, more elementary teachers might become superintendents, since some of these districts do not have a secondary school. That, however, proved not to be the case . Apparently, teachers of older students in a departmentalized type of instructional environment not only are more familiar with the greater degree of bureaucracy in secondary schools, but also may find administration more alluring than elementary school teachers.

WHAT'S IN A NAME?

The title of the first administrative position held by respondents depends for the most part on the size of school and district. For instance, for superintendents of large districts, the first administrative position usually was assistant principal. The principalship was the

first position for most superintendents of small districts, where it is less likely that the position of assistant principal exists. This is especially true for districts without a secondary school. In 1982, 18.9 percent of superintendents had served as assistant principals, compared to 30.3 percent in 1992 (see **Table 4.5**).

Another increasingly common entry-level position is coordinator or director of a special program. After the emergence of categorical programs in the 1960s, many teachers were able to leave the classroom and become coordinators in remedial or special education. These programs, especially, provided entry-level positions for women administrators. In some cases, however, they created a disadvantage for prospective administrators, because these positions generally do not provide "line" experience, or direct supervision and evaluation of instructional staff.

Where Were They Then?

Many superintendents achieve their first full-time position in education in a secondary school. This finding is consistent for superintendents of districts of all sizes and types. About 19 percent of current superintendents gained their first administrative position in a junior high school, and two percent moved into

TABLE 4.2 AGE AT TIME OF FIRST ADMINISTRATIVE POSITION, ANALYZED BY AGE

	AGE 45 OR YOUNGER		AGE 46-50		AGE 51-55		AGE 56-60		AGE 61 OR OLDER	
AGE	No.	%	No.	%	No.	%	No.	%	No.	%
25-30	282	62.8	291	63.1	209	50.0	126	42.9	39	39.0
31-35	132	29.4	118	25.6	144	34.4	105	35.7	31	31.0
36-40	29	6.5	30	6.5	48	11.5	37	12.6	20	20.0
41-45	5	1.1	18	3.9	8	1.9	21	7.1	7	7.0
46 AND OLDER	1	0.2	4	0.9	9	2.2	5	1.7	3	3.0
TOTAL	449	100.0	461	100.0	418	100.0	294	100.0	100	100.0

TABLE 4.3: TYPE OF SCHOOL DISTRICT WHERE SUPERINTENDENT HELD FIRST FULL-TIME POSITION IN EDUCATION—1992-1982 SUPERINTENDENT COMPARISONS

	GROUP A: 25,000 OR MORE PUPILS		GROUP B: 3,000-24,999 PUPILS		GROUP C: 300-2,999 PUPILS		GROUP D: FEWER THAN 300 PUPILS		NATIONAL UNWEIGHTED PROFILE	
TYPE OF SCHOOL	1992 %	1982 %	1992 %	1982 %	1992 %	1982 %	1992 %	1982 %	1992 %	1982 %
ELEMENTARY	19.4	27.7	25.3	28.2	26.5	27.7	31.2	34.4	26.1	29.0
JUNIOR HIGH/MIDDLE SCHOOL	22.2	23.2	16.9	20.8	13.5	19.0	9.2	11.8	14.9	18.7
HIGH SCHOOL	33.3	36.6	33.6	44.7	37.3	49.1	32.4	47.5	34.9	46.5
COLLEGE/UNIVERSITY	1.4	2.7	1.3	0.0	0.9	0.3	0.0	0.0	1.1	0.4
VOCATIONAL/TECHNICAL	0.0	0.9	1.3	0.3	1.8	0.3	0.8	0.0	1.2	0.3
PAROCHIAL	0.7	0.3	0.1	0.4	0.3	-	-	-	-	-
DISTRICT OFFICE	18.1	14.7	11.7	6.8	12.6	-	-	-	-	-
OTHER	4.9	8.9	6.6	6.1	8.3	3.4	19.2	6.3	9.0	5.2
TOTAL	100.0	100.0	100.0	100.1	100.1	99.8	100.0	100.0	100.1	100.1

administration in a middle school.

Superintendents on average have spent three to five years as classroom teachers before becoming administrators (see **Table 4.11**.) In larger districts, this is true of 63.4 percent of respondents. The relatively few years spent in the classroom reinforce the survey data and indicate that most administrators take their first

job in administration before age 30.

Superintendents in smaller districts typically have more years of experience in the classroom (see **Table 4.5**). This situation might be attributable to the fact that fewer administrative positions are available in small districts. Only about one-third of the superintendents in the 1992 study indicate they had taught in the

TABLE 4.4 SUBJECTS TAUGHT BY SUPERINTENDENT IN FIRST FULL-TIME POSITION IN EDUCATION

SUBJECTS	GROUP A: 25,000 OR MORE PUPILS		GROUP B: 3,000-24,999 PUPILS		GROUP C: 300-2,999 PUPILS		GROUP D: FEWER THAN 300 PUPILS		NATIONAL UNWEIGHTED PROFILE	
	No.	%	No.	%	No.	%	No.	%	No.	%
ELEMENTARY	35	28.7	154	30.6	156	26.4	62	29.7	407	28.5
COUNSELING	0	0.0	0	0.0	3	0.5	0	0.0	3	0.2
FOREIGN LANGUAGE	1	0.8	6	1.2	4	0.7	2	1.0	13	0.9
SOCIAL STUDIES	34	27.9	96	19.1	118	19.9	25	12.0	273	19.1
SPECIAL EDUCATION	1	0.8	16	3.2	5	0.8	17	8.1	39	2.7
P.E./HEALTH	5	4.1	14	2.8	37	6.3	11	5.3	67	4.7
BUSINESS EDUCATION	7	5.7	11	2.2	26	4.4	13	6.2	57	4.0
INDUSTRIAL ARTS	4	3.3	15	3.0	12	2.0	8	3.8	39	2.7
COMPUTER EDUCATION	0	0.0	0	0.0	0	0.0	1	0.5	1	0.1
ART	1	0.8	1	0.2	3	0.5	1	0.5	6	0.4
MATH	11	9.0	46	9.1	57	9.6	18	8.6	132	9.3
MUSIC	2	1.6	11	2.2	9	1.5	9	4.3	31	2.2
ENGLISH	9	7.4	61	12.1	47	7.9	14	6.7	131	9.2
SCIENCE	7	5.7	54	10.7	76	12.8	20	9.6	157	11.0
DRIVER EDUCATION	0	0.0	3	0.6	1	0.2	0	0.0	4	0.3
VOCATIONAL EDUCATION	3	2.5	1	0.2	10	1.7	0	0.0	14	1.0
HOME ECONOMICS	0	0.0	1	0.2	0	0.0	3	1.4	4	0.3
VOCATIONAL AGRICULTURE	0	0.0	4	0.8	16	2.7	4	1.9	24	1.7
OTHER	1	0.8	6	1.2	8	1.4	1	0.5	16	1.1
NO TEACHING EXPERIENCE	1	0.8	3	0.6	4	0.7	0	0.0	8	0.6
TOTAL	122	8.6	503	35.3	592	41.5	209	14.7	1,426	100.0

TABLE 4.5 NATURE OF FIRST ADMINISTRATIVE/SUPERVISORY POSITION

ADMINISTRATIVE/ SUPERVISORY POSITION	GROUP A: 25,000 OR MORE PUPILS		GROUP B: 3,000-24,999 PUPILS		GROUP C: 300-2,999 PUPILS		GROUP D: FEWER THAN 300 PUPILS		NATIONAL UNWEIGHTED PROFILE	
	No.	%	No.	%	No.	%	No.	%	No.	%
ASSISTANT PRINCIPAL	63	43.4	225	37.3	188	26.7	39	16.0	515	30.3
DEAN OF STUDENTS	4	2.8	11	1.8	12	1.7	5	2.0	32	1.9
PRINCIPAL	31	21.4	193	32.0	347	49.2	137	56.1	708	41.7
DIRECTOR-COORDINATOR	26	17.9	96	15.9	76	10.8	22	9.0	220	13.0
ASSISTANT SUPERINTENDENT	3	2.1	10	1.7	18	2.6	4	1.6	35	2.1
STATE AGENCY	3	2.1	7	1.2	2	0.3	3	1.2	15	0.9
BUSINESS OFFICE	1	0.7	8	1.3	6	0.9	1	0.4	16	0.9
OTHER	14	9.7	54	8.9	56	7.9	33	13.5	157	9.2
TOTAL	145	8.5	604	35.6	705	41.5	244	14.4	1,698	100.0

classroom for six to eight years. The data indicate early administrative career choices by respondents who aspired to a principalship or superintendency. Because so many superintendents are former secondary teachers, the position of department chair may be considered a "quasi" administrative role (in some districts, it is classified as a management role) and a stepping stone to the superintendency.

EXTRACURRICULAR ACTIVITIES

In addition, because so many superintendents are former secondary and junior high teachers, the role of extracurricular activities is an important future career indicator. Many extracurricular assignments have responsibilities and experiences that relate directly to administrative leadership.

One example is community interaction between coaches, parents, and community members. In many secondary schools, where athletic offerings have been enlarged since the implementation of Title IX, coaching is almost mandatory as a precursor to the superintendency. **Table 4.7** shows that nearly half of the 1992 respondents (48.8 percent) have coaching experience, with an even greater percentage in smaller school districts.

Other extracurricular assignments such as newspaper advisor, music director, or club advisor are not widely represented in the backgrounds of superintendents. It is likely that many superintendents, during their secondary teaching experiences, found interaction with the community satisfying. That may have helped them in making the decision to seek the secondary principalship and later the superintendency.

CAREER PATTERNS

The career ladder for superintendents historically has been that of teacher, principal, and superintendent. In 1982, 37 percent of respondents followed this track, and 30 percent followed a similar track of teacher, principal, central office administrator, and superintendent. In previous decades (1960 and 1971 studies), most superintendents had not held positions in the central office. Only 14 percent in 1960 and 16 percent in 1971 were central office administrators before becoming superintendents. In 1992, 37.7 percent of the responding superintendents indicated they served as a teacher, principal, and central office administrator (see **Figure 4.1**). In the larger districts, this career track was true about 54 percent of the time (see **Table 4.8**).

In the smaller districts, where central office jobs are few, most superintendents previously had worked

TABLE 4.6 NUMBER OF YEARS SUPERINTENDENT SERVED AS CLASSROOM TEACHER, ANALYZED BY AGE

NO. YEARS	AGE 45 OR YOUNGER No.	%	AGE 46-50 No.	%	AGE 51-55 No.	%	AGE 56-60 No.	%	AGE 61 OR OLDER No.	%
0- 5	217	48.2	246	52.9	181	43.2	138	46.8	46	46.5
6-10	172	38.2	153	32.9	168	40.1	102	34.6	30	30.3
11-15	54	12.0	46	9.9	52	12.4	40	13.6	17	17.2
16-20	6	1.3	15	3.2	14	3.3	10	3.4	3	3.0
21-25	1	0.2	2	0.4	3	0.7	5	1.7	1	1.0
26 AND OLDER	0	0.0	3	0.6	1	0.2	0	0.0	2	2.0
TOTAL	450	99.9	465	99.9	419	99.9	295	100.1	99	100.0

TABLE 4.7 EXTRACURRICULAR ACTIVITY AS A TEACHER

ACTIVITY PARTICIPATION	GROUP A: 25,000 OR MORE PUPILS No.	%	GROUP B: 3,000-24,999 PUPILS No.	%	GROUP C: 300-2,999 PUPILS No.	%	GROUP D: FEWER THAN 300 PUPILS No.	%	NATIONAL UNWEIGHTED PROFILE No.	%
COACHING ATHLETICS	77	44.0	305	43.9	425	52.8	157	51.5	964	48.8
CLUB ADVISOR	41	23.4	178	25.6	148	18.4	44	14.5	411	20.8
CLASS ADVISOR	30	17.1	101	14.5	102	12.7	39	12.9	272	13.8
NEWSPAPER/ANNUAL	7	4.0	31	4.5	38	4.7	18	5.9	94	4.6
MUSIC GROUPS	3	1.7	24	3.6	26	3.2	21	6.9	74	3.7
OTHER	17	9.7	56	8.1	66	8.2	24	7.9	163	8.3
TOTAL	175	8.8	695	35.1	805	40.7	303	15.3	1,978	100.0

only as teachers and principals. Most small-district superintendents also had most of their teaching and principalship experience in small districts. According to some research on the career patterns of women superintendents, women administrators often jump from the classroom to the central office and then to the superintendency (Burnham, 1988). This career track also might be true of minorities who face job bias.

Complexity in the job of superintendent is caused in part by various legislative mandates and legal restrictions. Superintendents must be better versed on personnel and financial matters than in prior decades. It is not always possible, however, for principals to obtain training and experience in these two management areas so critical to current district operations. In the future, a career stop in the central office may be required of superintendents in larger districts in order that they may acquire specialized experience.

At least one study supports this idea. In 1987 and 1988, Joan Burnham at the University of Texas in Austin studied the career patterns of two groups of superintendents. The first group was a random national sample. The second group was composed of superintendents who had been selected as "exemplary." Burnham found that those in the exemplary group had followed the track of teaching, principalship, central office position, and superintendent more often than those in the random sample (Burnham, 1988).

GAINING THE FIRST SUPERINTENDENCY

Most administrators seeking a first superintendency indicated they were able to obtain a position in one year or less. Whether their first superintendency was the size, type, and location of district they most preferred was not asked.

Typically, at least 20-30 administrators apply for each superintendent vacancy; some are seeking a move, while others are trying to enter the superintendency.

The 1992 study asked whether new superintendents were hired from the "inside," meaning already working within the district. About a third of the sample indicated they had been promoted from inside the district (see **Table 4.12**). This is less true in the very small districts. In the larger districts promotions to the superintendency were more common in 1992 than in 1982. Overall, however, the 1982 study indicated 38 percent were promotions; in 1992, 36 percent were promotions. Richard Carlson, in a 1972 study, advanced the reasons for insider selection: primarily district financial problems, elimination of another position, and the fact that superintendents appointed from the inside sometimes will work for less money.

FIGURE 4.1 CAREER PATTERN PRIOR TO SUPERINTENDENCY

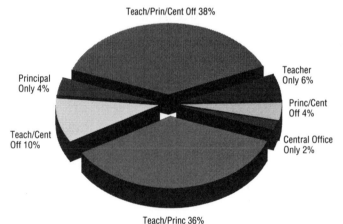

Teach/Prin/Cent Off 38%
Teacher Only 6%
Princ/Cent Off 4%
Central Office Only 2%
Teach/Princ 36%
Teach/Cent Off 10%
Principal Only 4%

TABLE 4.8 CAREER PATTERN PRIOR TO THE SUPERINTENDENCY

CAREER PATTERN	GROUP A: 25,000 OR MORE PUPILS		GROUP B: 3,000-24,999 PUPILS		GROUP C: 300-3,999 PUPILS		GROUP D: FEWER THAN 300 PUPILS		NATIONAL UNWEIGHTED PROFILE	
	No.	%	No.	%	No.	%	No.	%	No.	%
TEACHER ONLY	1	0.7	15	2.7	36	5.4	42	17.7	94	5.9
PRINCIPAL ONLY	1	0.7	15	2.7	38	5.7	11	4.6	65	4.0
CENTRAL OFFICE ONLY	7	5.2	16	2.8	7	1.0	2	0.8	32	2.0
TEACHER & PRINCIPAL	23	17.2	103	18.2	333	49.7	126	53.2	585	36.4
TEACHER & CENTRAL OFFICE	23	17.2	77	13.6	54	8.1	12	5.1	166	10.3
PRINCIPAL & CENTRAL OFFICE	7	5.2	32	5.7	17	2.5	3	1.3	59	3.7
TEACHER, PRINCIPAL, & CENTRAL OFFICE	72	53.7	307	54.3	185	27.6	41	17.3	605	37.7
TOTAL	134	8.3	565	35.2	670	41.7	237	14.8	1,606	100.0

When the Decision Is Made

Typically, a person decides to be a superintendent while serving as a building principal. About one-fourth decide while they are in a central office position. Slightly fewer make that decision as a teacher (see **Table 4.13**). Whether this historical trend will continue into the 1990s is open to question. Many administrators who want to become superintendents are placebound by employed spouses and the substantial expense of relocating. On the other hand, in an era of reform and restructuring many school boards look for "new" faces. Indeed, in some cases, they are willing to offer financial help to make the move possible.

NUMBER OF SUPERINTENDENCIES

The superintendency often is perceived as a position with rapid turnover and mobility. This is not the case, however, since the average superintendent spends half of his or her career in only one superintendency (see also, **Tenure in the Superintendency**, below). As **Table 4.14** indicates, about one-fourth (26) have had two superintendencies, and 11.4 percent have held three. It is a matter of judgment whether this level of mobility is excessive for executive positions. The 1982 study reported that most superintendents held 1.7 superintendencies.

Even in the oldest age groups, 75 percent of respondents had held fewer than three superintendencies (see **Table 4.15**).

Table 4.16 shows only a very small number of superintendents spend their entire teaching and administrative careers in the same district. Those who do tend to be in the larger districts.

TENURE IN THE SUPERINTENDENCY

A common theme in the popular media is that of a board and superintendent falling into conflict, resulting in the superintendent being dismissed. Stories of a superintendent moving on to a new district may

TABLE 4.9 CAREER PATTERN PRIOR TO SUPERINTENDENCY— 1992-1982 COMPARISONS

CAREER PATTERS	GROUP A: 25,000 OR MORE PUPILS 1992 %	1982 %	GROUP B: 3,000-24,999 PUPILS 1992 %	1982 %	GROUP C: 300-2,999 PUPILS 1992 %	1982 %	GROUP D: FEWER THAN 300 PUPILS 1992 %	1982 %	NATIONAL UNWEIGHTED PROFILE 1992 %	1982 %
TEACHER ONLY	0.7	0.0	2.7	5.1	5.4	7.1	17.7	19.4	5.9	7.9
PRINCIPAL ONLY	0.7	0.9	2.7	2.3	5.7	7.4	4.6	5.5	4.0	5.0
CENTRAL OFFICE ONLY	5.2	5.5	2.8	1.8	1.0	0.3	0.8	2.3	2.0	1.5
TEACHER & PRINCIPAL	17.2	12.7	18.2	22.8	49.7	40.3	53.2	47.9	36.4	34.0
TEACHER & CENTRAL OFFICE	17.2	9.1	13.6	11.7	8.1	7.1	5.1	3.2	10.3	8.0
PRINCIPAL & CENTRAL OFFICE	5.2	6.4	5.7	6.9	2.5	2.6	1.3	1.8	3.7	4.1
TEACHER, PRINCIPAL, & CENTRAL OFFICE	53.7	58.2	54.3	43.9	27.6	29.7	17.3	12.4	37.7	33.5
OTHER	7.3	5.6	5.5	7.4	6.0	-	-	-	-	-
TOTAL	99.9	100.1	100.0	100.1	100.0	100.0	100.0	99.9	100.0	100.0

TABLE 4.10 EXPERIENCE COMBINATION DESCRIBING BACKGROUND, ANALYZED BY AGE

	AGE 45 OR YOUNGER No.	%	AGE 46-50 No.	%	AGE 51-55 No.	%	AGE 56-60 No.	%	AGE 61 OR OLDER No.	%
TEACHER ONLY	28	6.5	19	4.4	20	5.2	18	6.6	9	9.6
PRINCIPAL ONLY	9	2.1	21	4.9	21	5.4	11	4.0	3	3.2
CENTRAL OFFICE ONLY	6	1.4	7	1.6	8	2.1	10	3.7	1	1.1
TEACHER & PRINCIPAL	205	47.8	156	36.2	124	32.0	74	27.2	28	29.8
TEACHER & CENTRAL OFFICE	39	9.1	53	12.3	42	10.9	26	9.6	7	7.4
PRINCIPAL & CENTRAL OFFICE	13	3.0	13	3.0	12	3.1	14	5.1	7	7.4
TEACH, PRINCIPAL, & CENTRAL OFFICE	129	30.1	162	37.6	160	41.3	119	43.8	39	41.5
TOTAL	429	100.0	431	100.0	387	100.0	272	100.0	94	100.0

imply that these educators are a highly transitory professional group.

However, data concerning tenure of the survey sample of superintendents show a much different picture. The mean, or average, length of tenure for superintendents was 6.47 years (see **Table 4.16**). Keeping in mind that the typical employment contract for a superintendent is three years, this implies that the average superintendent is in his/her second or third full contract. However, the practice in many states is that of "rollover," which means that each year the board of education may extend the contract of the superintendent for an additional year, thus always keeping the contract at three years.

Big-City Turnover

The reason the superintendency is perceived in turmoil is largely because of rapid turnover in many large urban districts, which makes national news. In

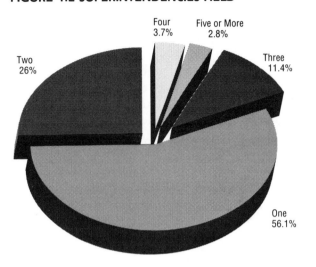

FIGURE 4.2 SUPERINTENDENCIES HELD

Four 3.7%
Five or More 2.8%
Two 26%
Three 11.4%
One 56.1%

TABLE 4.11 LENGTH OF SERVICE AS CLASSROOM TEACHER PRIOR TO ENTERING ADMINISTRATION OR SUPERVISION

YEARS AS TEACHER	GROUP A: 25,000 OR MORE PUPILS		GROUP B: 3,000-24,999 PUPILS		GROUP C: 300-2,999 PUPILS		GROUP D: FEWER THAN 300 PUPILS		NATIONAL UNWEIGHTED PROFILE	
	No.	%	No.	%	No.	%	No.	%	No.	%
0 - 5	92	63.4	352	57.7	306	42.9	75	29.8	825	47.9
6 - 10	44	30.3	191	31.3	292	40.9	94	37.3	621	36.1
11 - 15	6	4.1	60	9.8	88	12.3	55	21.8	209	12.1
16 - 20	3	2.1	6	1.0	21	2.9	18	7.1	48	2.8
21 - 25	0	0.0	1	0.2	6	0.8	5	2.0	12	0.7
26 +	0	0.0	0	0.0	1	0.01	5	2.0	6	0.3

TABLE 4.12 WERE YOU HIRED FROM WITHIN YOUR SCHOOL DISTRICT?

SUCCESSOR TYPE	GROUP A: 25,000 OR MORE PUPILS		GROUP B: 3,000-24,999 PUPILS		GROUP C: 300-2,999 PUPILS		GROUP D: FEWER THAN 300 PUPILS		NATIONAL UNWEIGHTED PROFILE	
	No.	%	No.	%	No.	%	No.	%	No.	%
INSIDE CANDIDATE	62	43.1	256	42.5	258	36.3	40	15.9	616	36.0
OUTSIDE CANDIDATE	82	56.9	347	57.5	453	63.7	212	84.1	1,094	64.0
TOTAL	144	8.4	603	35.3	711	41.6	252	14.7	1,710	100.0

TABLE 4.13 WHEN DID YOU DECIDE TO BE A SUPERINTENDENT?

WHILE HOLDING POSITION AS A	GROUP A: 25,000 OR MORE PUPILS		GROUP B: 3,000-24,999 PUPILS		GROUP C: 300-2,999 PUPILS		GROUP D: FEWER THAN 300 PUPILS		NATIONAL UNWEIGHTED PROFILE	
	No.	%	No.	%	No.	%	No.	%	No.	%
TEACHER	21	16.0	97	17.8	141	21.7	88	37.9	347	22.3
BUILDING ADMINISTRATOR	47	36.9	179	32.9	361	55.6	111	47.8	698	44.9
CENTRAL OFFICE ADMINISTRATOR	49	37.4	223	41.0	109	16.8	15	6.5	396	25.4
OTHER	14	10.7	45	8.3	38	5.9	18	7.8	115	7.4
TOTAL	131	8.4	544	35.0	649	41.7	232	14.9	1,556	100.0

December 1990, for instance, 14 large urban school district superintendencies were vacant (Bradley, 1990). This is not to minimize the effectiveness of short-term superintendents, wherever they occur. However, instability in leadership in districts serving large proportions of at-risk students surely does nothing to advance reform and excellence. (Rist, 1990).

In 1990, Allan Ornstein found in a survey of 86 of the largest district superintendents that 41 had been in their current positions two to five years, 22 less than one year, and 23 had more than five years of tenure (*Education Week*, 1990). In appraising the tenure of large urban districts, the evaluator might ask the question, "How long would big-city mayors last if the city councils appointed them?"

If anything, superintendent tenure has increased during the past decade. Each year, AASA conducts a survey of a statistical sample of its membership regarding their views on current key issues. In the 1989-90 "Opinions and Status" survey, superintendents indicated they had been in their current positions an average of eight years. This is fairly close to *The 1992 Study of the AmericanSchool Superintendency* sample. In the 1982 10-year study, the average length of superinten-

dent tenure was 5.6 years. In the 1971 study, the tenure length was six years.

The probable reason for the increase of superintendent tenure in the 1980s was that most districts already had been through the most severe of enrollment declines and politically divisive activities such as reductions-in-force and school closings.

Size of District

Table 4.16 shows that superintendents of districts of 300 to 3,000 students have the longest tenure (seven years). Superintendents in the largest and smallest districts have the shortest tenure of the four groups, perhaps due to political pressure in large districts, and the entry-level nature of small district superintendencies.

Also, the number of states in which individual superintendents have served is relatively small. Overall, 87.4 percent stayed in one state throughout their careers (see **Table 4.20**). The most-often cited reason for putting down roots was state retirement systems and their lack of pension portability. Of course, some superintendents do make the move to other states, for various reasons, such as better pay in a larger district.

TABLE 4.14 NUMBER OF PUBLIC SCHOOL SUPERINTENDENCIES HELD INCLUDING CURRENT ONE

NUMBER HELD	GROUP A: 25,000 OR MORE PUPILS		GROUP B: 3,000-24,999 PUPILS		GROUP C: 300-2,999 PUPILS		GROUP D: FEWER THAN 300 PUPILS		NATIONAL UNWEIGHTED PROFILE	
	No.	%	No.	%	No.	%	No.	%	No.	%
1	73	50.3	332	54.4	419	58.7	140	56.2	964	56.1
2	24	16.6	167	27.4	187	26.2	69	27.7	447	26.0
3	22	15.2	79	13.0	72	10.1	23	9.2	196	11.4
4	20	13.8	17	2.8	17	2.4	9	3.6	63	3.7
5	5	3.4	9	1.5	14	2.0	5	2.0	33	1.9
6	0	0.0	5	0.8	3	0.4	2	0.8	10	0.6
6 +	1	0.7	1	0.2	2	0.3	1	0.4	5	0.3
TOTAL	145	8.4	610	35.5	714	41.6	249	14.5	1,718	100.0

TABLE 4.15 NUMBER OF PUBLIC SUPERINTENDENCIES HELD, ANALYZED BY AGE

	AGE 45 OR YOUNGER		AGE 46-50		AGE 51-55		AGE 56-60		AGE 61 OR OLDER	
	No.	%	No.	%	No.	%	No.	%	No.	%
1	285	63.6	255	55.1	229	54.5	148	50.3	50	50.0
2	113	25.2	134	28.9	106	25.2	71	24.1	25	25.0
3	43	9.6	45	9.7	51	12.1	45	15.3	14	14.0
4	6	1.3	19	4.1	15	3.6	18	6.1	5	5.0
5	1	0.2	8	1.7	13	3.1	8	2.7	3	3.0
6	0	0.0	2	0.4	3	0.7	2	0.7	3	3.0
7 +	0	0.0	0	0.0	3	0.7	2	0.7	0	0.0
TOTAL	448	99.9	463	99.9	420	99.9	294	99.9	100	100.0

The nation's superintendents for the most part are veterans. The mean number of years in the superintendency is 10.3. Superintendents of the very large districts have held a superintendency an average of 11.3 years. For future superintendents now serving as central office administrators, the average length of leadership probably will be 15-20 years per superintendent. Because the superintendents surveyed have, on average, already served more than six years in the superintendency, these data support the premise that a significant percentage of superintendents could be retiring in five to seven years, especially those in states with early retirement programs.

In summary, when considering that half of superintendents are over age 50, that most states have early retirement programs beginning at age 55, and that most superintendents retire between the ages of 58 and 60, it would not be uncommon to see about eight to 10 percent retire early and another 20 to 25 percent looking for new districts with larger enrollments, greater wealth, and administrator salaries.

MENTORING, DISCRIMINATION, HIRING

Old Boy/Old Girl Network
Researchers such as Feistritzer (1988) claim that the superintendency is dominated by an "old boy/old girl" network. This is supported by the 1992 study, which found that an "old boy" network does exist according to 56.5 percent of superintendents (see Table 4.21). However, these "networks" exsist in many other professions, as well.

Many respondents undoubtedly think that individuals working for superintendent search firms or state school boards associations are part of an informal network. However, in both 1992 and 1982, about 60 percent of superintendents said this so-called network had not helped them.

Gender Discrimination
Considering the small numbers of minority and women superintendents, job discrimination should be a national concern. In 1982, 14 percent of the superintendents said hiring discrimination seriously affected prospective women superintendents. In the 1992 study, 13.7 percent call it a major problem (see Table 4.22). About half of the respondents in 1982 and 1992 thought discrimination against women posed little or no problem.

The question then arises: What deters larger numbers of women from becoming superintendents? It is possible that some sex discrimination in hiring rests with board members, even though women constitute about 35 percent of board membership.

Discrimination Against Minorities
In general, superintendents today think that women have a more difficult time being hired than do minorities. Fewer superintendents think that hiring discrimination against minorities is a major problem. Sixteen percent thought it was a major problem in 1982, while 18.4 percent expressed the same view in 1992, as shown in Table 4.23. Large-district superintendents believed discriminatory hiring is more of a problem than did superintendents in smaller districts.

TABLE 4.16 NUMBER OF YEARS IN CURRENT SUPERINTENDENCY

YEARS	GROUP A: 25,000 OR MORE PUPILS		GROUP B: 3,000-24,999 PUPILS		GROUP C: 300-2,999 PUPILS		GROUP D: FEWER THAN 300 PUPILS		NATIONAL UNWEIGHTED PROFILE	
	No.	%	No.	%	No.	%	No.	%	No.	%
0-3	62	43.2	222	37.4	242	34.8	125	50.0	651	38.8
3.1-6	36	25.2	132	22.3	182	26.2	65	26.4	415	24.7
6.1-9	18	12.6	102	17.2	82	11.8	23	9.3	225	13.4
9.1 AND UP	27	18.9	137	23.1	189	27.2	33	13.4	386	23.0
TOTAL	143	8.5	593	35.4	695	41.4	246	14.7	1,677	100.0

TABLE 4.17 HAVE YOU SPENT YOUR ENTIRE EDUCATIONAL CAREER IN ONE SCHOOL DISTRICT?

	GROUP A: 25,000 OR MORE PUPILS		GROUP B: 3,000-24,999 PUPILS		GROUP C: 300-2,999 PUPILS		GROUP D: FEWER THAN 300 PUPILS		NATIONAL UNWEIGHTED PROFILE	
	No.	%	No.	%	No.	%	No.	%	No.	%
YES	17	12.8	60	11.0	46	7.1	4	1.7	127	8.1
NO	116	87.2	486	89.0	603	92.9	229	98.3	1,434	91.9
TOTAL	133	8.5	546	35.0	649	41.6	233	14.9	1,561	100.0

Recruitment of Women and Minorities

Surprisingly, two-thirds of the superintendents sampled indicated their districts actively recruit women administrators. This finding is especially true in the larger districts. Superintendents in the very large districts indicated this practice is nearly universal. Superintendents in very small districts say this measure is taken only about one-third of the time (see **Table 4.24**).

Only a little more than half of the superintendents indicate their districts actively recruit minorities as administrators. In the very large districts it is a common practice; in districts with fewer than 3,000 students, it is not often a priority.

Whether discrimination in hiring women and minorities exists, the presence of so few women and minority superintendents presents a major challenge to the profession. The compositions of student bodies and teaching staffs, along with community makeup,

TABLE 4.18 HOW MANY YEARS TOTAL HAVE YOU SERVED AS A SUPERINTENDENT?

YEARS	GROUP A: 25,000 OR MORE PUPILS No.	%	GROUP B: 3,000-24,999 PUPILS No.	%	GROUP C: 300-2,999 PUPILS No.	%	GROUP D: FEWER THAN 300 PUPILS No.	%	NATIONAL UNWEIGHTED PROFILE No.	%
0- 4	30	21.0	143	23.4	174	24.4	91	36.5	438	25.6
5- 9	34	23.8	179	29.3	202	28.4	68	27.3	483	28.2
10-14	36	25.2	134	22.0	134	18.8	37	14.9	341	19.9
15-19	26	18.2	82	13.4	120	16.9	28	11.2	256	14.9
20-24	11	7.7	48	7.9	49	6.9	16	6.4	124	7.2
25-29	4	2.8	12	2.0	22	3.1	4	1.6	42	2.5
30-34	2	1.4	11	1.8	6	0.8	5	2.0	24	1.4
35-39	0	0.0	0	0.0	3	0.4	0	0.0	3	0.2
40 +	0	0.0	1	0.2	2	0.3	0	0.0	3	0.2
TOTAL	143	8.3	610	35.6	712	50.4	249	14.5	1,714	100.0

TABLE 4.19 NUMBER OF YEARS SERVED AS SUPERINTENDENT, ANALYZED BY AGE

	AGE 45 OR YOUNGER No.	%	AGE 46-50 No.	%	AGE 51-55 No.	%	AGE 56-60 No.	%	AGE 61 OR OLDER N o.	%
0- 4	200	44.6	115	24.9	72	17.3	37	12.6	11	11.0
5- 9	169	37.7	144	31.2	95	22.8	60	20.4	13	13.0
10-14	61	13.6	114	24.7	96	23.0	63	21.4	11	11.0
15-19	11	2.5	66	14.3	101	24.2	59	20.1	21	21.0
20-24	6	1.3	18	3.9	43	10.3	42	14.3	18	18.0
25-29	0	0.0	2	0.4	6	1.4	22	7.5	12	12.0
30-34	0	0.0	0	0.0	3	0.7	10	3.4	11	11.0
35-40	0	0.0	0	0.0	0	0.0	1	0.3	2	2.0
MORE THAN 40	1	0.2	3	0.6	1	0.2	0	0.0	1	1.0
TOTAL	448	99.9	462	100.0	417	99.9	294	100.0	100	100.0

TABLE 4.20 NUMBER OF STATES SERVED AS A PUBLIC SCHOOL SUPERINTENDENT

NUMBER OF STATES	GROUP A: 25,000 OR MORE PUPILS No.	%	GROUP B: 3,000-24,999 PUPILS No.	%	GROUP C: 300-2,999 PUPILS No.	%	GROUP D: FEWER THAN 300 PUPILS No.	%	NATIONAL UNWEIGHTED PROFILE No.	%
1	96	66.2	524	86.2	651	91.2	231	92.0	1,502	87.4
2	28	19.3	60	9.9	48	6.7	16	6.4	152	8.8
3	13	9.0	17	2.8	11	1.5	1	0.4	42	2.4
4 +	8	5.5	7	1.2	4	0.6	3	1.2	22	1.3
TOTAL	145	8.4	608	35.4	714	41.6	251	14.6	1,718	100.0

challenge the profession to improve its record in preparing and placing women and minority administrators as superintendents. Most minority administrators currently work in majority-minority school districts, often under less than ideal conditions for professional development.

SELECTION TO THE SUPERINTENDENCY

Search Committees

Superintendents are selected for their positions in several ways. The first and most prevalent is that the school board forms its own search committee. One or two members are then designated to work with school staff to draw up a job description, which is forwarded to universities, state associations, and newspapers. The board meets and decides which of the applicants it will interview. The smaller the school district, the more likely this method of superintendent selection is used. In the very small districts, the board acts as its own search agent 76.6 percent of the time. In the very large districts, a private search firm or an agency such as the state school boards association

conducts the search more than 50 percent of the time.

The fees charged by private search firms usually are dictated by the size of the district, the number of services the board wishes, and whether the search is restricted to local candidates. Some search firms are owned and staffed by former superintendents who are retired and have been able to establish a reputation for themselves. Sometimes, professors of educational administration also work as consultants for private search firms or the state school boards associations.

School Board Searches. Most state school boards associations provide some inservice training for board members in superintendent selection. The process is complex, however, and lay persons may be at a disadvantage in assessing whether candidates are fully qualified for the position.

Reasons Why a Superintendent Is Selected

In the 1982 study, two-thirds of the sample superintendents indicated they were hired for their current

TABLE 4.21 IS THERE AN OLD BOY/GIRL NETWORK IN YOUR STATE THAT HELPS INDIVIDUALS GET POSITIONS AS SUPERINTENDENTS?

	GROUP A: 25,000 OR MORE PUPILS		GROUP B: 3,000-24,999 PUPILS		GROUP C: 300-2,999 PUPILS		GROUP D: FEWER THAN 300 PUPILS		NATIONAL UNWEIGHTED PROFILE	
	No.	%	No.	%	No.	%	No.	%	No.	%
YES	86	59.7	339	55.8	404	56.6	141	56.2	970	56.5
NO	44	30.6	194	32.0	211	29.6	69	27.5	518	30.2
DON'T KNOW	14	9.7	74	12.2	99	13.9	41	16.3	228	13.3
TOTAL	144	8.4	607	35.4	714	41.6	251	14.6	1,716	100.0

TABLE 4.22 SEVERITY OF PROBLEM OF DISCRIMINATORY HIRING PRACTICES FOR WOMEN

	GROUP A: 25,000 OR MORE PUPILS		GROUP B: 3,000-24,999 PUPILS		GROUP C: 300-2,999 PUPILS		GROUP D: FEWER THAN 300 PUPILS		NATIONAL UNWEIGHTED PROFILE	
SEVERITY OF PROBLEM	No.	%	No.	%	No.	%	No.	%	No.	%
MAJOR PROBLEM	31	21.5	83	13.7	81	11.4	39	15.7	234	13.7
MINOR PROBLEM	52	36.1	232	38.2	262	36.8	89	35.7	635	37.1
LITTLE OR NO PROBLEM	61	42.3	292	48.1	368	51.8	121	48.6	842	49.2
TOTAL	144	8.4	607	35.5	711	41.6	249	14.6	1,711	100.0

TABLE 4.23 SEVERITY OF PROBLEM OF DISCRIMINATORY HIRING PRACTICES FOR MINORITIES

	GROUP A: 25,000 OR MORE PUPILS		GROUP B: 3,000-24,999 PUPILS		GROUP C: 300-2,999 PUPILS		GROUP D: FEWER THAN 300 PUPILS		NATIONAL UNWEIGHTED PROFILE	
SEVERITY OF PROBLEM	No.	%	No.	%	No.	%	No.	%	No.	%
MAJOR PROBLEM	39	27.3	123	20.3	111	15.6	41	16.5	314	18.4
MINOR PROBLEM	52	36.4	215	35.4	257	36.2	103	41.4	627	36.7
LITTLE OR NO PROBLEM	52	36.4	269	44.4	342	48.1	105	42.2	768	45.0
TOTAL	143	8.4	607	35.5	710	41.5	249	14.6	1,709	100.0

positions because of "personal characteristics." These qualities might include the image or role model they presented during the interview process as well as information the board learned from community members they served in their last district. This factor in superintendent selection may be changing, however. **Table 4.27** shows that in the 1992 sample, only 38.5 percent of superintendents say they were hired by their present board because of personal characteristics. This may reflect a "maturing" of the profession and perhaps the use of more stringent selection criteria by local school boards. Superintendents in the very small districts still are likely to attribute personal characteristics as the reason they were hired, perhaps because of the position's higher visibility in a smaller community.

Movers, Shakers, and Peacekeepers

Change agent. Three roles are typical of the general mission of the superintendency. First, boards may be looking for a change agent, a superintendent who will initiate changes in the district that the board thinks are necessary. School districts sometimes are change-resistant, and superintendents in the role of change agent can start enough conflict and pressure that the board (or a new board) has little choice but to make significant changes. The change-agent role often is sought by school boards that are newly elected or that believe the district is not operating very well. Superintendents in these roles typically are hired from the outside.

Developer. A second role is that of a developer. Superintendents in this role sometimes are required to take over from a change-agent superintendent and build programs once most of the resistance to change has been overcome. This type of superintendency is often one that is secure for a number of years.

Maintaining the status quo. The third role is as maintainer of the status quo. This role is often found in school districts where things have been going well for a number of years. Perhaps an admired superintendent is retiring, and the board is looking for someone of similar personality and program philosophy. Many times these types of superintendent vacancies are filled from within the district (Carlson, 1972).

In **Table 4.26**, more than one-third of the sample superintendents in large school districts indicated they had been hired to be a change agent. The urban superintendency is a difficult position, and boards typically are pressured for improvement in test scores and responsiveness to the community. Here, new superintendents are sought who will correct the ills of their urban school districts. This is the ultimate change-agent role (NSBA, 1992). Still, 29.9 percent of the superintendents of districts with enrollments of 3,000 to 24,999 indicate they were hired for the change-agent role. This in a general way may account for some controversy in many of their districts. Often change-agent roles are assigned to new superintendents moving to districts in turmoil.

In the 1980s, the role of instructional leader was emphasized in the myriad school reform reports. Since the back-to-basics movement of the 1970s, instructional leadership by superintendents and principals has been proffered as a remedy for improving the nation's schools.

To a lesser extent, about 22 percent of superintendents in the 1992 survey said their skills and abilities in instructional leadership were what convinced their

TABLE 4.24 DOES YOUR DISTRICT ACTIVELY RECRUIT WOMEN FOR ADMINISTRATIVE POSITIONS?

	GROUP A: 25,000 OR MORE PUPILS		GROUP B 3,000-24,999 PUPILS		GROUP C: 300-2,999 PUPILS		GROUP D: FEWER THAN 300 PUPILS		NATIONAL UNWEIGHTED PROFILE	
	No.	%	No.	%	No.	%	No.	%	No.	%
YES	127	88.8	491	81.0	439	62.1	91	37.6	1,148	67.6
NO	16	11.2	115	19.0	268	37.9	151	62.4	550	32.4
TOTAL	143	8.4	606	35.7	707	41.6	242	14.3	1,698	100.0

TABLE 4.25 DOES YOUR DISTRICT ACTIVELY RECRUIT MINORITIES FOR ADMINISTRATIVE POSITIONS?

	GROUP A: 25,000 OR MORE PUPILS		GROUP B 3,000-24,999 PUPILS		GROUP C: 300-2,999 PUPILS		GROUP D: FEWER THAN 300 PUPILS		NATIONAL UNWEIGHTED PROFILE	
	No.	%	No.	%	No.	%	No.	%	No.	%
YES	128	88.9	395	65.4	274	38.9	68	28.5	865	51.2
NO	16	11.1	209	34.6	430	61.1	171	71.5	826	48.8
TOTAL	144	8.5	604	35.7	704	41.6	239	14.1	1,691	100.0

present boards to hire them. Certainly, superintendents are concerned about improving instruction and carry that concern into interviews with prospective board employers (Hallinger and Murphy, 1982). A slightly greater number of smaller-district superintendents (enrollments of 300-2,999) indicated they were hired because of their instructional leadership capabilities.

The emphasis on instructional leadership is likely to continue. Laws in states such as Illinois require principals to spend at least 51 percent of their time in instructional leadership. Such reform legislation has helped create a nationwide climate focusing on instruction that has carried over into the superintendency.

SALARIES AND CONTRACTS OF SUPERINTENDENTS

The salaries of superintendents have been examined in each of the previous six studies. The 1992 data may be of limited use since it does not include all or the dollar-value of fringe benefit programs. The 1982 study showed that superintendent salaries had doubled since 1971, when the median salary was $32,592, with 95 percent of salaries below $50,000. According to the 1992 findings, more than half, or 54.7 percent of the sample surveyed, earned salaries above $49,000 annually.

Overall, salaries are higher in larger and more affluent districts, with 70.4 percent of superintendents of districts

with more than 25,000 students earning over $69,000, as opposed to only 6.1 percent of superintendents in smaller (300-2,999 students districts (see **Table 4.28** and **Figure 4.3**). The number of superintendents making more than $69,000 was 21.5 percent, compared to 0.5 percent in 1982 (Heller, 1991).

In a 1990 study, Robert Heller and Associates found superintendent salaries averaged in the $60,000

31

FIGURE 4.3 MEDIAN SALARY BY DISTRICT SIZE

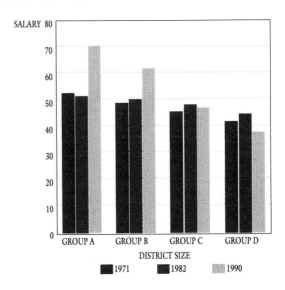

TABLE 4.26 WHAT GROUP/INDIVIDUALS MANAGED THE SEARCH PROCESS FOR CURRENT SUPERINTENDENCY?

GROUP	GROUP A: 25,000 OR MORE PUPILS No.	%	GROUP B: 3,000-24,999 PUPILS No.	%	GROUP C: 300-2,999 PUPILS No.	%	GROUP D: FEWER THAN 300 PUPILS No.	%	NATIONAL UNWEIGHTED PROFILE No.	%
PROFESSIONAL SEARCH FIRM	48	33.6	125	20.8	52	7.3	11	4.4	236	13.9
STATE SCHOOL BOARDS ASSOC.	23	16.1	71	11.8	83	11.7	14	5.6	191	11.2
LOCAL SCHOOL BOARD ASSOC.	54	37.8	310	51.7	508	71.4	190	76.6	1,062	62.4
OTHER	18	12.6	94	15.7	68	9.6	33	13.3	213	12.5
TOTAL	143	8.4	600	35.3	711	41.8	248	14.6	1,702	100.0

TABLE 4.27 REASONS GIVEN BY SUPERINTENDENTS FOR THEIR SELECTION TO CURRENT POSITION

REASON FOR SELECTION	GROUP A: 25,000 OR MORE PUPILS No.	%	GROUP B: 3,000-24,999 PUPILS No.	%	GROUP C: 300-2,999 PUPILS No.	%	GROUP D: FEWER THAN 300 PUPILS No.	%	NATIONAL UNWEIGHTED PROFILE No.	%
PERSONAL CHARACTERISTICS	44	31.7	213	36.4	269	38.9	110	46.6	636	38.5
CHANGE AGENT	50	36.0	175	29.9	180	26.0	47	19.9	452	27.4
MAINTAIN STATUS QUO	1	0.7	5	0.9	17	2.5	12	5.1	35	2.1
INSTRUCTIONAL LEADER	34	24.5	139	23.8	162	23.4	33	14.0	368	22.3
SPECIFIC TASK	3	2.2	14	2.4	9	1.3	4	1.7	30	1.8
NO PARTICULAR REASON	7	5.0	39	6.7	55	7.9	30	12.7	131	7.9
TOTAL	139	8.4	585	35.4	692	41.9	236	14.3	1,652	100.0

to $70,000 range (without fringe benefits). In addition, some school districts pay the portion of the superintendent's salary that is dedicated to the state pension program, as well as social security contributions, auto and travel expenses, professional development expenses, association memberships, tax-free annuities, and term or whole-life insurance policies.

Most superintendents are well-paid professionals in their communities. The down side is that most are on call 24 hours a day and have very long work days, which often don't end until late in the evening. Unlike their counterparts in the private sector, they do not have access to profit-sharing programs, stock options, or end-of-year bonuses. In some districts, considering the time commitment, superintendents and principals are often not paid what they would make as teachers on a daily rate.

Most contracts for superintendents are for a 240- or 248-day year, and often for three years consecutively. Almost half (42 percent) of respondents have multi-year contracts. Another 25.8 percent have contracts of four or more years, indicating a degree of job security for superintendents (see **Table 4.31**).

Considering that superintendents may have as many years in their districts as teachers, a multi-year superintendent contract provides only a portion of the job security that teachers have. The terms of their contracts often are based on recommendations provided by AASA and its affiliates.

The lure of higher salaries in administration apparently is not as great a motivator as in the past for classroom teachers. The collective bargaining process in most states has significantly raised teaching salaries and, in some cases, has helped improve administrative salaries. The usual factors in setting superintendent salaries are the size of the district, what neighboring district superintendents make, the history of the district's superintendent salaries, and the experience of the superintendent being hired. The superintendent's salary usually sets the trend for what central office administrators, and in some cases principals, are paid.

PARTICIPATION IN PROFESSIONAL ORGANIZATIONS

Membership and participation in professional organizations is a common occurrence in the superintendency, and has increased since 1982. For instance, the 1982 sample of superintendents indicated that 66 percent belonged to AASA, which is considered the flagship professional organization for superintendents. In the 1992 study, 76.6 percent of sampled superintendents belong to AASA. In addition, 66.1 percent belong to their state association of school administrators. Also, the 1982 study found that 19.7 percent of respondents belonged to the Association for Supervision and Curriculum Development. In the 1992 survey, 45.3 percent hold ASCD membership (see **Table 4.32**).

Participation of superintendents in professional associations provides opportunities for information sharing and inservice training, as well as the chance to meet with fellow superintendents. The superintendency often is a lonely position, and the opportunity to interact with others in the same role is a welcome change of pace. One of the most important opportunities provided by professional association membership is networking.

TABLE 4.28 SALARIES OF SUPERINTENDENTS

SALARY (IN DOLLARS)	GROUP A: 25,000 OR MORE PUPILS		GROUP B: 3,000-24,999 PUPILS		GROUP C: 300-2,999 PUPILS		GROUP D: FEWER THAN 300 PUPILS		NATIONAL UNWEIGHTED PROFILE	
	No.	%	No.	%	No.	%	No.	%	No.	%
LESS THAN $24,000	0	0.0	14	2.3	73	10.4	21	8.5	108	6.4
$24,000-28,999	2	1.4	23	3.8	38	5.4	27	10.9	90	5.3
$29,000-33,999	0	0.0	12	2.0	44	6.3	35	14.2	91	5.4
$34,000-38,999	2	1.4	22	3.6	62	8.8	52	21.1	138	8.1
$39,000-43,999	9	6.3	33	5.5	75	10.7	49	19.8	166	9.8
$44,000-48,999	6	4.2	38	6.3	105	14.9	27	10.9	176	10.4
$49,000-53,999	5	3.5	58	9.6	86	12.2	19	7.7	168	9.9
$54,000-58,999	3	2.1	67	11.1	81	11.5	11	4.5	162	9.6
$59,000-63,999	6	4.2	61	10.1	67	9.5	2	0.8	136	8.0
$64,000-68,999	9	6.3	55	9.1	29	4.1	3	1.2	96	5.7
GREATER THAN $68,999	100	70.4	22	36.5	43	6.1	1	0.4	364	21.5
TOTAL	142	8.4	603	35.6	703	41.5	247	14.6	1,695	100.0

Many superintendents have their professional organization expenses paid by their districts or from a fund established in their contracts.

MENTORING AND BEING A MENTOR

School superintendents are leaders in their school districts, and many also serve in that role in their peer groups. This is reflected by the fact that 72.2 percent consider themselves mentors to others interested in the superintendency as a career. Some 49.1 percent indicate they were assisted by a mentor in their career development. Also, 88.8 percent of superintendents in larger districts said they have served as mentors, in contrast to 52 to 70 percent of very small to small districts. Superintendents in smaller districts are less likely to receive the help of a mentor (See **Tables 4.33** and **4.34**).

The presence of mentors and the existence of mentoring is an important aspect of any profession. A great deal of professional knowledge is best transferred in a mentoring relationship, rather than in a university classroom or in an inservice workshop. Also, the opportunity for constructive feedback is present in most mentor relationships, which often are outside the supervisor/employee situation (Healy and Welchert, 1990). The superintendency is basically a self-selected profession where principals and central office administrators enroll in a graduate program to earn the superintendency credential, and mentorships are an important link between academic and practical preparation for the job.

FUTURE PLANS OF SUPERINTENDENTS

Even though a significant percentage of superintendents will be eligible for retirement in the 1990s, only 13.6 percent indicated they will seek early retirement, which is available in many states at the age of 55. About two thirds (67.7 percent) indicated they will "soldier on" in the 1990s. A few (2.7 percent) indicated an interest in the professoriate in educational administration and 3.1 percent indicated perference for a position outside the field of education. These data seem to complement the strong indication by superintendents that they receive a good deal of satisfaction from the superintendency and would choose the career over again if given the chance. It seems reasonable to say that superintendents nationwide will not be retiring in large numbers in the next several years.

TABLE 4.30 SALARY AT BEGINNING OF CURRENT POSITION, ANALYZED BY AGE

AGE GROUP	MEAN	STANDARD DEVIATION	NUMBER
45-YOUNGER	$51,118	$17,332	446
46-50	$55,738	$19,397	458
51-55	$53,047	$23,121	413
56-60	$52,875	$25,152	290
61-OLDER	$51,002	$25,309	95
TOTAL	$53,122	$21,335	1,702

TABLE 4.29 SALARIES OF SUPERINTENDENTS—1992-1982 COMPARISONS

PRESENT SALARY (IN DOLLARS)	GROUP A 25,000 OR MORE PUPILS 1992 %	1982 %	GROUP B: 3,000-24,999 PUPILS 1992 %	1982 %	GROUP C: 300-2,999 PUPILS 1992 %	1982 %	GROUP D: FEWER THAN 300 PUPILS 1992 %	1982 %	NATIONAL UNWEIGHTED PROFILE 1992 %	1982 %
LESS THAN $24,000	0.0	3.7	2.3	4.6	10.4	13.6	8.5	13.6	6.4	10.1
$24,000-28,999	1.4	0.0	3.8	5.9	5.4	10.3	10.9	25.0	5.3	10.6
$29,000-33,999	0.0	2.7	2.0	6.9	6.3	16.0	14.2	38.6	5.4	16.0
$34,000-38,999	1.4	7.3	3.6	11.0	8.8	22.7	21.1	15.5	8.1	16.7
$39,000-43,999	6.3	6.4	5.5	13.8	10.7	18.2	19.8	5.0	9.8	13.7
$44,000-48,999	4.2	16.5	6.3	36	14.9	17.2	10.9	0.9	10.4	20.1
$49,000-53,999	3.5	17.4	9.6	11.7	12.2	1.8	7.7	0.9	9.9	5.7
$54,000-58,999	2.1	19.3	11.1	5.9	11.5	0.3	4.5	0.0	9.6	3.5
$59,000-63,999	4.2	13.8	10.1	3.8	9.5	0.0	0.8	0.5	8.0	2.3
$64,000-68,999	6.3	7.3	9.1	0.3	4.1	0.3	1.2	0.0	5.7	0.8
MORE THAN $69,000	70.4	5.5	36.5	0	6.1	0.0	0.4	0.0	21.5	0.5
TOTAL	99.8	99.9	99.9	99.9	99.9	100.4	100.0	100.0	100.1	100.0

TABLE 4.31 LENGTH OF SUPERINTENDENTS' CURRENT CONTRACTS

LENGTH IN YEARS	GROUP A: 25,000 OR MORE PUPILS		GROUP B: 3,000-24,999 PUPILS		GROUP C: 300-2,999 PUPILS		GROUP D: FEWER THAN 300 PUPILS		NATIONAL UNWEIGHTED PROFILE	
	No.	%	No.	%	No.	%	No.	%	No.	%
ONE	9	6.3	36	6.0	124	17.5	130	52.0	299	17.5
TWO	15	10.4	72	12.0	117	16.5	46	18.4	250	14.7
THREE	50	34.7	270	44.9	339	47.9	57	22.8	716	42.0
MORE THAN FOUR	70	48.6	224	37.2	128	18.1	17	6.8	439	25.8
TOTAL	144	8.5	602	35.3	708	41.5	250	14.7	1,704	100.0

TABLE 4.32 MEMBERSHIPS IN PROFESSIONAL ORGANIZATIONS

ORGANIZATIONAL MEMBERSHIP	GROUP A: 25,000 OR MORE PUPILS		GROUP B: 3,000-24,999 PUPILS		GROUP C: 300-2,999 PUPILS		GROUP D: FEWER THAN 300 PUPILS		NATIONAL UNWEIGHTED PROFILE	
	No.	%	No.	%	No.	%	No.	%	No.	%
AASA	135	93.1	519	85.1	537	75.0	130	51.4	1321	76.6
ASBO	18	12.4	37	6.1	59	8.2	10	4.0	124	7.2
NASSP	19	13.1	62	10.2	51	7.1	29	11.5	161	9.3
AFT	0	0.0	4	0.7	3	0.4	3	1.2	10	0.6
AFFILIATE	3	2.1	12	2.0	14	2.0	6	2.4	35	2.0
ASCD	88	60.7	294	48.2	324	45.3	75	29.6	781	45.3
NAESP	4	2.8	21	3.4	25	3.5	21	8.3	71	4.1
NEA	9	6.2	44	7.2	20	2.8	16	6.3	89	5.2
STATE AASA	102	70.3	431	70.7	460	64.2	147	58.1	1,140	66.1
NSPRA	19	13.1	65	10.7	47	6.6	5	2.0	136	7.9
OTHER	22	15.2	121	19.8	145	20.3	55	21.7	343	19.9
TOTAL	145	8.4	610	35.4	716	41.5	253	14.7	1,724	100.0

TABLE 4.33 SUPERINTENDENTS BEING MENTORS FOR SOMEONE ASPIRING TO BE AN ADMINSTRATOR OR SUPERINTENDENT

	GROUP A: 25,000 OR MORE PUPILS		GROUP B: 3,000-24,999 PUPILS		GROUP C: 300-2,999 PUPILS		GROUP D: FEWER THAN 300 PUPILS		NATIONAL UNWEIGHTED PROFILE	
	No.	%	No.	%	No.	%	No.	%	No.	%
YES	127	88.8	477	78.3	505	70.6	132	52.6	1,241	72.2
NO	6	4.2	79	13.0	168	23.5	96	38.2	349	20.3
DON'T KNOW	10	7.0	53	8.7	42	5.9	23	9.2	128	7.5
TOTAL	143	8.3	609	35.4	715	41.6	251	14.6	1,718	100.0

TABLE 4.34 SUPERINTENDENTS HAVING MENTORS FOR THE SUPERINTENDENCY

	GROUP A: 25,000 OR MORE PUPILS		GROUP B: 3,000-24,999 PUPILS		GROUP C: 300-2,999 PUPILS		GROUP D FEWER THAN 300 PUPILS		NATIONAL UNWEIGHTED PROFILE	
	No.	%	No.	%	No.	%	No.	%	No.	%
YES	90	63.4	312	51.3	348	48.7	92	36.5	842	49.1
NO	51	35.9	276	45.4	353	49.4	156	61.9	836	48.7
DON'T KNOW	1	0.7	20	3.3	13	1.8	4	1.6	38	2.2
TOTAL	142	8.3	608	35.4	714	41.6	252	14.7	1,716	100.0

School Boards and Superintendents 5

Early in the history of the superintendency, school boards interacted directly with school employees such as teachers and principals. The superintendent was little more than a supervisor whose position was generally tenuous. During the 19th century, many school boards considered themselves the administrative body of the nation's small and highly localized school districts. Many school boards were quite large and operated on the premise of direct democracy (Griffiths, 1988).

EVOLUTION

The working relationship and lines of authority between school boards and superintendents have evolved over the years in several stages. Before 1900, superintendents, for the most part, were general supervisors, and board members were the primary policy and decision makers. After the turn of the century, many superintendents became advocates of business ideology, which dictated that executives (superintendents) should be highly trained professionals. In each of these stages, their relationships with school board members changed (Callahan, 1966).

During the era of scientific management and efficiency (1900-1930), superintendents in large districts coached board members into adopting a quasi-corporate board model. In a later period, through the 1940s, superintendents changed their self-perceptions to that of "professional educators." This change of identity was accompanied by their viewing boards as interest groups, primarily involved in setting general policy (Tyack and Hansot, 1982).

POWER STRUGGLES

The literature on the superintendency and school boards contains many studies of conflicts between the two groups. Many authors cite the differing job expectations held by boards and superintendents as the root cause of most conflicts. Researchers such as Nancy Pitner and Rodney Ogawa (1981) illustrate this theme in their research on the socio-cultural context in which superintendents work and make decisions about which issues to address. They also suggest that successful superintendents are perceptive and react appropriately to external forces.

Overlapping Roles

Without clear demarcation between roles of superintendents and school boards, tensions in many districts are a given. These tensions in thousands of school districts are minimal and do not seriously interrupt district operations. But role conflict generally is the reason superintendents get into trouble with their school boards and move on to another position (Bevan, 1988).

A study of boards and board members by the Institute for Educational Leadership in 1986 argued that school boards as an institution are in trouble. The IEL study found a great deal of support for the traditional role of the school board as a grass-roots community institution. But, concurrently, it also found apathy and ignorance in the community about what school board members do and the challenges they face in the future (IEL, 1986).

WHO INITIATES POLICY?

Table 5.1 shows that initiation of new policy and direction for school districts usually is considered a function of the superintendent. Two-thirds of the sampled superintendents (66.9 percent) say they are primary initiators of new policy in their school districts. The superintendents indicate that, while board members act on policy, they actually initiate policy decisions less than 4 percent of the time.

Shared Responsibility

In this study, 28.5 percent of superintendents overall say they consider policy initiation a shared responsibility with the board. Shared responsibility is greatest in the larger districts, possibly because many large districts have more board members on standing committees that study issues and recommend new policies to the whole board. In smaller districts with fewer board members, the whole board often makes decisions as one body.

Superintendents in smaller districts say they initiate policy significantly more often than superintendents in larger districts. For instance, 47.6 percent of large-district superintendents took the lead in policy making, compared to 74.5 percent by superintendents in districts of between 300 and 3,000 students.

HOW ARE BOARD MEMBERS ORIENTED?

As district management has become more complex, expectations for board members have become more technical and time consuming. The current interest in school reform and restructuring has put many board members in the "hot seat." (Though some are well-informed, board members may be inexperienced or uninformed in areas such as affirmative action requirements, teacher evaluation statutes, purchasing and bids, collective bargaining, and other very technical concerns.) For this reason many school boards associations conduct orientation sessions for new board members and provide ongoing in-service training. Often, though, the task of initiating new board mem-

bers is left to the superintendent and/or other local board members.

Overall, however, 46.2 percent of superintendents indicated they provide board members their primary orientation. State school boards associations provide primary orientation only 15.6 percent of the time. In addition, 27.4 percent of responding superintendents say primary board member orientation is a shared responsibility between the superintendent and the school boards association. Superintendents apparently believe it is important to provide the primary orientation for new board members since developing good personal and working relationships with the board is a key factor in superintendent employment and success. In the 1992 study, as in 1982, about eight of every 10 superintendents provide the initial orientation of new board members (see **Table 5.2**).

SCHOOL BOARD MEETINGS

School districts put on their public faces whenever they hold school board meetings, and citizens and the media form opinions about the school district from these meetings. The district's image in the community could be the same, regardless of whether the meetings are well-organized and thoughtful or disorganized and chaotic (Anderson, 1989).

TABLE 5.1 WHO TAKES THE LEAD IN DEVELOPING POLICY?

WHO TAKES THE LEAD	GROUP A: 25,000 OR MORE PUPILS		GROUP B: 3,000-24,999 PUPILS		GROUP C: 300-2,999 PUPILS		GROUP D: FEWER THAN 300 PUPILS		NATIONAL UNWEIGHTED PROFILE	
	No.	%	No.	%	No.	%	No.	%	No.	%
SCHOOL BOARD	7	4.8	26	4.3	19	2.7	8	3.2	60	3.5
SCHOOL BOARD CHAIR	0	0.0	4	0.7	2	0.3	1	0.4	7	0.4
SUPERINTENDENT	69	47.6	374	61.6	539	74.5	176	69.6	1,158	66.9
SHARED RESPONSIBILITY	67	46.2	200	32.9	155	21.8	67	26.5	489	28.5
OTHER	2	1.4	3	0.5	5	0.7	1	0.4	11	0.6
TOTAL	145	8.5	607	35.4	720	41.4	253	14.8	1,725	100.0

TABLE 5.2 WHO PROVIDES BOARD MEMBER ORIENTATION?

WHO HANDLES ORIENTATION	GROUP A: 25,000 OR MORE PUPILS		GROUP B: 3,000-24,999 PUPILS		GROUP C: 300-2,999 PUPILS		GROUP D: FEWER THAN 300 PUPILS		NATIONAL UNWEIGHTED PROFILE	
	No.	%	No.	%	No.	%	No.	%	No.	%
SUPERINTENDENT	55	38.2	269	44.8	372	52.9	88	35.3	784	46.2
EXPERIENCED BOARD MEMBERS	5	3.5	11	1.8	21	3.0	21	8.4	58	3.4
SCHOOL BOARDS ASSOCIATION	24	16.7	95	15.8	104	14.8	41	16.5	264	15.6
SHARED RESPONSIBILITY	54	37.5	195	32.5	160	22.8	55	22.1	464	27.4
NOT FORMALLY ORIENTED	3	2.1	21	3.5	37	5.3	36	14.5	97	5.7
OTHER	2	1.4	6	1.0	7	1.0	5	2.0	20	1.2
DO NOT KNOW	1	0.7	3	0.5	2	0.3	3	1.2	9	0.5
TOTAL	144	8.5	600	35.4	703	41.5	249	14.7	1,696	100.0

Who Sets the Agenda?

The development of board meeting agendas is an important school district function usually handled by school superintendents, who plot which items of business must be subject to board discussion and vote. The dominance of superintendents in setting the board meeting agenda has not changed appreciably between the 1971 and 1992 AASA studies. Superintendents in 1971 and 1982 were in control of framing agendas and issues, as they are in 1992 (see **Table 5.3**).

More than 75 percent of responding superintendents said they maintain substantial managerial control over presentation of the board meeting agenda. In very small districts, 85.5 percent of superintendents say they set the agendas.

Another 22.4 percent of superintendents said they share responsibility with the board. In states such as Arizona, where the secretary of the board must sign the agenda, board members have more direct involvement. The survey indicates that superintendents in very large districts share responsibility for agenda planning more often than superintendents in smaller districts.

Most superintendents, after setting the agenda, assemble packages for board members that contain documents and information pertinent to the agenda items. These packages often are forwarded to board members three to four days before the board meeting so they are informed in advance about the agenda items and the positions of the administration. Once posted in public places, agenda items become legal notification and often can be changed only with a 24-hour public notice. Control of the board meeting agenda consequently is an important administrative function for the superintendent (Anderson, 1989).

COMMUNITY PARTICIPATION

School district success depends on community support. An indicator of community support is how actively large numbers of parents and citizens are involved in district activities, especially the decision-making processes. Most school boards and superintendents believe in community participation, but the level of involvement varies from district to district.

School board presidents or chairs indicate that they are fairly well satisfied with the decision-making sources in school districts. However, at the time, they indicate that some empowerment of teachers is needed (Feistritzer, 1989).

Heightened Need

In the 1992 AASA study, the need for community involvement is perceived as more important than in 1982; 71.2 percent of superintendents said it is a very strong need, up from 59.8 percent in 1982. The larger the school district, the more likely are superintendents to indicate that community participation in decisions is needed to ensure continued community support. It is possible these data indicate that districts are feeling the effect of pressures to change and reform. (see **Table 5.4**)

In very large districts, community support includes

TABLE 5.3 WHO PREPARES THE AGENDA FOR BOARD MEETINGS?

SOURCE	GROUP A: 25,000 OR MORE PUPILS		GROUP B: 3,000-24,999 PUPILS		GROUP C: 300-2,999 PUPILS		GROUP D: FEWER THAN 300 PUPILS		NATIONAL UNWEIGHTED PROFILE	
	No.	%	No.	%	No.	%	No.	%	No.	%
SUPERINTENDENT	94	65.3	443	72.9	570	79.8	207	85.5	1,314	76.5
BOARD CHAIRPERSON	0	0.0	1	0.2	2	0.3	1	0.4	4	0.2
SHARED RESPONSIBILITY	50	34.7	159	26.2	137	19.2	39	15.5	385	22.4
OTHER	0	0.0	5	0.8	5	0.7	4	1.6	14	0.8
TOTAL	144	8.4	608	35.4	714	41.6	251	14.6	1,717	100.0

TABLE 5.4 IMPORTANCE OF COMMUNITY PARTICIPATION IN SCHOOL DISTRICT DECISION MAKING

DEGREE OF IMPORTANCE	GROUP A: 25,000 OR MORE PUPILS		GROUP B: 3,000-24,999 PUPILS		GROUP C: 300-2,999 PUPILS		GROUP D: FEWER THAN 300 PUPILS		NATIONAL UNWEIGHTED PROFILE	
	No.	%	No.	%	No.	%	No.	%	No.	%
MORE IMPORTANT IN 1992 THAN 1980	117	81.3	463	76.0	492	69.0	152	60.1	1,224	71.2
ABOUT THE SAME	24	16.7	124	20.4	190	26.6	76	30.0	414	24.1
LESS IMPORTANT IN 1992 THAN 1980	3	2.1	19	3.1	22	3.1	14	5.5	58	3.4
DO NOT KNOW	0	0.0	3	0.5	9	1.3	11	4.3	23	1.3
TOTAL	144	8.4	609	35.4	713	41.5	253	14.7	1,719	100.0

assistance from local property taxpayers, the private sector, and the media. Citizen advisory councils, parent/teacher organizations, and committees to help pass school finance measures were common vehicles of community support during the 1980s.

Increased Willingness

The desire of superintendents to involve citizens in decision-making activities is apparent in the 1992 study data. But how willing are citizens to participate in these activities? Superintendents say citizens are more willing to participate in 1992 than they were in 1982, especially in the large districts. In fact, in many urban school districts, beginning in the 1960s and continuing into the 1990s, parents have demanded they be allowed to participate in the decisions affecting the education of their children. Racial and ethnic conflict in many of these districts has been influential in heightening demands for involvement.

Nearly three-quarters (74.3 percent) of responding superintendents from very large districts (25,000 or more enrollment) think parents and citizens now demand a greater role in district decision making (see Table 5.5). Only 33.6 percent of superintendents in the very small districts think this is true for their districts. Overall, about one-third of superintendents think parents today are just as eager to participate in decision making as in 1982 .

When Is Participation Sought?

How and when do superintendents and boards seek community involvement? Is it sought only before levy or referendum elections, in reaction to some kind of conflict that has occurred or is about to occur in the district? In **Table 5.6**, slightly more than half of the superintendents indicated they frequently seek community participation, and only 16.4 percent indicated they do so only when it is required.

Superintendents can to a limited extent involve the community in district activities without permission of the board. However, when policy is discussed, the superintendent very likely wants board support before initiating projects involving the community.

Superintendents indicate their districts are involving citizens in a planning/advisory capacity, mostly in "general" planning of district priorities and objectives. Also, the areas in which citizens participate appear to involve program/curriculum and efforts to mobilize community support for district funding (see **Table 5.7**).

Do Boards Seek Community Involvement?

Superintendents in 1992 think that board members are more willing to seek parent and community involvement actively in the district's decision making. In 1982, 43.9 percent of surveyed board members indicated a willingness to seek parent and community involvement, compared to 74.7 percent in 1992. Superintendents from large districts were more likely

TABLE 5.5 HOW WILLING ARE PARENTS AND THE COMMUNITY TO PARTICIPATE IN DECISION MAKING?

WILLINGNESS	GROUP A: 25,000 OR MORE PUPILS		GROUP B: 3,000-24,999 PUPILS		GROUP C: 300-2,999 PUPILS		GROUP D: FEWER THAN 300 PUPILS		NATIONAL UNWEIGHTED PROFILE	
	No.	%	No.	%	No.	%	No.	%	No.	%
MORE WILLING TO PARTICIPATE	107	74.3	331	54.4	334	46.8	85	33.6	857	49.9
ABOUT THE SAME	31	21.5	208	34.2	292	41.0	127	50.2	658	38.3
LESS WILLING TO PARTICIPATE	6	4.2	67	11.0	80	11.2	33	13.0	186	10.8
DO NOT KNOW	0	0.0	3	0.5	7	1.0	8	3.2	18	1.0
TOTAL	144	8.4	609	35.4	713	41.5	253	14.7	1,719	100.0

TABLE 5.6 DO YOU ACTIVELY SEEK COMMUNITY PARTICIPATION?

	GROUP A: 25,000 OR MORE PUPILS		GROUP B: 3,000-24,999 PUPILS		GROUP C: 300-2,999 PUPILS		GROUP D: FEWER THAN 300 PUPILS		NATIONAL UNWEIGHTED PROFILE	
	No.	%	No.	%	No.	%	No.	%	No.	%
ALL THE TIME	64	44.4	168	27.7	144	20.3	57	22.5	433	25.2
FREQUENTLY	67	46.5	353	58.2	403	56.7	123	48.6	946	55.2
SELDOM	3	2.1	12	2.0	25	3.5	12	4.7	52	3.0
WHEN REQUIRED	10	6.9	72	11.9	139	19.5	60	23.7	281	16.4
NEVER	0	0.0	2	0.3	0	0.0	1	0.4	3	0.2
TOTAL	144	8.4	607	35.4	711	41.5	253	14.8	1,715	100.0

to perceive the board soliciting community involvement than were small-district superintendents (see **Table 5.8**).

COMMUNITY PRESSURE GROUPS

Most superintendents and school boards see community/school activities basically through a lens of involvement rather than as "pressure" politics. However, for various reasons, some community interest groups become pressure groups. A good example is in communities where the school district relies heavily on local property taxes for funding. In many such communities, local residential taxpayer groups have pressured school boards over budget matters. In other districts, ad hoc pressure groups are formed to question an aspect of curriculum or to urge the board to fire or retain a staff member (often a coach).

The existence of such pressure groups in their school districts is confirmed by 64.5 percent of the superintendents. In the very large districts, where budget and political interests are strong, pressure groups are a reality for 87.3 percent of respondents. Only 31.9 percent of responding superintendents indicate their districts have not been affected by pres-

TABLE 5.7 AREAS IN WHICH SUPERINTENDENTS INVOLVE COMMUNITY IN PLANNING/ADVISORY CAPACITY

AREAS OF INVOLVEMENT	GROUP A: 25,000 OR MORE PUPILS No.	%	GROUP B: 3,000-24,999 PUPILS No.	%	GROUP C: 300-2,999 PUPILS No.	%	GROUP D: FEWER THAN 300 PUPILS No.	%	NATIONAL UNWEIGHTED PROFILE No.	%
OBJECTIVES/PRIORITIES	116	82.3	453	74.5	517	72.9	170	68.8	1,256	73.7
PROGRAM/CURRICULUM	103	73.0	426	70.1	440	62.1	150	60.7	1,119	65.6
STUDENT ACTIVITIES	70	49.6	295	48.5	367	51.8	133	53.8	865	50.7
STUDENT BEHAVIOR/RIGHTS	78	55.3	250	41.1	295	41.6	91	36.8	714	41.9
FINANCE AND BUDGET	70	49.6	218	35.9	194	27.4	57	23.1	539	31.6
EVALUATION OF PROGRAMS	57	40.4	199	32.7	243	34.3	100	40.5	599	35.1
EVALUATION OF PERSONNEL	3	2.1	11	1.8	10	1.4	6	2.4	30	1.8
GENERAL ADMINISTRATION	11	7.8	28	4.6	26	3.7	5	2.0	70	4.1
FUNDRAISING	86	61.0	388	63.8	458	64.6	153	61.9	1,077	63.2
STRATEGIC PLANNING	93	66.0	347	57.1	328	46.3	84	34.0	852	50.0
OTHER	11	7.8	32	5.3	45	6.3	12	4.9	98	5.7
TOTAL	141	8.3	608	35.7	709	41.6	247	14.5	1,705	100.0

TABLE 5.8 DOES THE BOARD ACTIVELY SEEK COMMUNITY PARTICIPATION IN DECISION MAKING AND PLANNING?

	GROUP A: 25,000 OR MORE PUPILS No.	%	GROUP B: 3,000-24,999 PUPILS No.	%	GROUP C: 300-2,999 PUPILS No.	%	GROUP D: FEWER THAN 300 PUPILS No.	%	NATIONAL UNWEIGHTED PROFILE No.	%
ALL THE TIME	73	51.4	198	32.5	198	27.8	68	27.0	537	31.3
FREQUENTLY	48	33.8	280	45.9	318	44.6	100	39.7	746	43.4
SELDOM	19	13.4	128	21.0	193	27.1	81	32.1	421	24.5
NEVER	2	1.4	4	0.7	4	0.6	3	1.2	13	0.8
TOTAL	142	8.3	610	35.5	713	41.5	252	14.7	1,717	100.0

TABLE 5.9 IN LAST 10 YRS HAVE COMMUNITY PRESSURE GROUPS EMERGED TO INFLUENCE THE BOARD?

	GROUP A: 25,000 OR MORE PUPILS No.	%	GROUP B: 3,000-24,999 PUPILS No.	%	GROUP C: 300-2,999 PUPILS No.	%	GROUP D: FEWER THAN 300 PUPILS No.	%	NATIONAL UNWEIGHTED PROFILE No.	%
YES	124	87.3	451	74.1	416	58.3	115	45.6	1,106	64.5
NO	18	12.7	145	23.8	267	37.4	117	46.4	547	31.9
DO NOT KNOW	0	0.0	13	2.1	30	4.2	20	7.9	63	3.7
TOTAL	142	8.3	609	35.5	713	41.6	252	14.7	1,716	100.0

sure groups (see **Table 5.9**).

Included among these pressure groups are employee unions. Common tactics of many pressure groups are to direct their efforts not only toward the superintendent, but also toward individual board members. The result of these efforts is sometimes a "split" board.

The proper handling of pressure groups by the superintendent and the board is, to say the least, a serious task. Some studies of school boards have found that board members themselves often represent special interest or pressure groups. This tends to create board divisiveness and problems in district administration (IEL, 1986).

BOARD ABILITIES

School board members, according to superintendents, are generally "qualified" but not "well-qualified." Superintendents' complaints about uninformed board members and their inappropriate actions crop up frequently in "shop talk" at administrators' meetings. However, when asked on a more formal basis to rate board members' abilities, superintendents give generally positive appraisals though they do not consider many board members particularly "well-qualified."

Fewer superintendents in the very small districts indicated that their board members are "very well qualified" (13.1 percent) than did superintendents in very large districts (23.1). However, for other categories responses were fairly even across the board (see **Table 5.10**).

In the 1990s, the increased complexity of board decisions, the heavy responsibilities, public visibility, and substantial time commitment required have made school board membership less attractive in some communities. Business and professional persons sometimes lose business from school district conflicts that occur during their tenure on the board. Some board members find their employers unhappy with their frequent absences from work caused by school district business. In general, the desirability of being a school board member has declined at a point when high quality lay leadership is most needed for school reform (IEL, 1986; National School Boards Association, 1987).

TABLE 5.10 SUPERINTENDENTS' OPINIONS CONCERNING GENERAL ABILITIES AND PREPARATION OF BOARD MEMBERS TO HANDLE THEIR DUTIES

PREPARATION	GROUP A: 25,000 OR MORE PUPILS		GROUP B: 3,000-24,999 PUPILS		GROUP C: 300-2,999 PUPILS		GROUP D: FEWER THAN 300 PUPILS		NATIONAL UNWEIGHTED PROFILE	
	No.	%	No.	%	No.	%	No.	%	No.	%
VERY WELL QUALIFIED	33	23.1	109	18.0	111	15.6	33	13.1	286	16.7
QUALIFIED	75	52.4	336	55.4	408	57.4	125	49.6	944	55.1
NOT WELL QUALIFIED	31	21.7	152	25.0	179	25.2	89	35.3	451	26.3
INCOMPETENT	4	2.8	10	1.6	13	1.8	5	2.0	32	1.9
TOTAL	143	8.3	607	35.4	711	41.5	252	14.7	1,713	100.0

TABLE 5.11 ARE BOARD MEMBERS APPOINTED OR ELECTED?

	GROUP A: 25,000 OR MORE PUPILS		GROUP B: 3,000-24,999 PUPILS		GROUP C: 300-2,999 PUPILS		GROUP D: FEWER THAN 300 PUPILS		NATIONAL UNWEIGHTED PROFILE	
	No.	%	No.	%	No.	%	No.	%	No.	%
APPOINTED	26	18.1	39	6.4	30	4.2	2	0.8	97	5.7
ELECTED	118	81.9	567	93.6	679	95.8	249	99.8	1,613	94.3
TOTAL	144	8.4	606	35.4	709	41.5	251	14.7	1,710	100.0

TABLE 5.12 DO SUPERINTENDENTS HAVE A FORMAL JOB DESCRIPTION?

	GROUP A: 25,000 OR MORE PUPILS		GROUP B: 3,000-24,999 PUPILS		GROUP C: 300-2,999 PUPILS		GROUP D: FEWER THAN 300 PUPILS		NATIONAL UNWEIGHTED PROFILE	
	No.	%	No.	%	No.	%	No.	%	No.	%
YES	121	88.3	546	91.8	596	86.8	193	80.4	1,456	87.8
NO	16	11.7	49	8.2	91	13.2	47	19.6	203	12.2
TOTAL	137	8.3	595	35.9	687	41.4	240	14.5	1,659	100.0

ELECTED OR APPOINTED?

Almost all superintendents said their board members are elected (94.3 percent). However, in some large districts such as Chicago and Boston, board members are appointed by the mayor or city council (see **Table 5.11**).

EVALUATIONS AND JOB DESCRIPTIONS

The superintendent-board relationship, in most respects, is similar to other executive leadership positions in the public or private sector regarding employment issues. Slightly more than 87 percent of responding superintendents have written job descriptions. This is an increase since 1982, when 75.9 percent of superintendents had written job descriptions. Superintendents in larger districts are more likely to have formal job descriptions then those in smaller districts (see **Table 5.12**).

Only 56.9 percent of the superintendents overall said they actually are evaluated according to the criteria in the job description, and in very small districts, 56.6 percent of superintendents think they are not

evaluated against the job description. In 1982, 59 percent of responding superintendents thought they were being evaluated in accordance with their job descriptions (see **Table 5.13**).

Taking it Personally

This belief by a significant number of superintendents that they are not being evaluated against criteria in their job descriptions reinforces the notion that the quality of the interpersonal relationships between the superintendent and board members is really what counts. It also suggests the possibility that in many districts, job descriptions are taken from books or manuals and used without much thought as to whether the criteria match what the board expects the superintendent to do.

Of the superintendents who are not evaluated, more than half (54.4 percent) do not see a reason to formalize an evaluation process with the board (see **Table 5.14**).

According to **Table 5.15**, almost all superintendents are evaluated annually: 80.6 percent have annual, and only 9.9 percent have semi-annual evaluations.

TABLE 5.13 IF YOU HAVE A FORMAL JOB DESCRIPTION, ARE YOU REALLY EVALUATED AGAINST ITS CRITERIA?

	GROUP A: 25,000 OR MORE PUPILS		GROUP B: 3,000-24,999 PUPILS		GROUP C: 300-2,999 PUPILS		GROUP D: FEWER THAN 300 PUPILS		NATIONAL UNWEIGHTED PROFILE	
	No.	%	No.	%	No.	%	No.	%	No.	%
YES	82	63.6	318	57.7	369	59.6	95	43.4	864	56.9
NO	47	36.4	233	42.3	250	40.4	124	56.6	654	43.1
TOTAL	129	8.5	551	36.3	619	40.8	219	14.4	1,518	100.0

TABLE 5.14 IF YOU ARE NOT EVALUATED, DO YOU SEE A NEED TO DEVELOP A FORMAL PROCEDURE?

	GROUP A: 25,000 OR MORE PUPILS		GROUP B: 3,000-24,999 PUPILS		GROUP C: 300-2,999 PUPILS		GROUP D: FEWER THAN 300 PUPILS		NATIONAL UNWEIGHTED PROFILE	
	No.	%	No.	%	No.	%	No.	%	No.	%
YES	15	48.4	61	41.2	85	45.5	51	51.5	212	45.6
NO	16	51.6	87	58.8	102	54.5	48	48.5	253	54.4
TOTAL	31	6.7	148	31.8	187	40.2	99	21.3	465	100.0

TABLE 5.15 HOW OFTEN DOES THE BOARD EVALUATE YOUR JOB PERFORMANCE?

	GROUP A: 25,000 OR MORE PUPILS		GROUP B: 3,000-24,999 PUPILS		GROUP C: 300-3,999 PUPILS		GROUP D: FEWER THAN 300 PUPILS		NATIONAL UNWEIGHTED PROFILE	
	No.	%	No.	%	No.	%	No.	%	No.	%
ANNUALLY	121	85.8	484	79.7	587	82.1	190	75.4	1,382	80.6
SEMI-ANNUALLY	12	8.5	65	10.7	60	8.4	33	13.1	170	9.9
AT CONTRACT RENEWAL	2	1.4	21	3.5	25	3.5	9	3.6	57	3.3
NEVER	2	1.4	21	3.5	24	3.4	12	4.8	59	3.4
OTHER	4	2.8	16	2.6	19	2.7	8	3.2	47	2.7
TOTAL	141	8.2	607	35.4	715	41.7	252	14.7	1,715	100.0

The Why and How of Evaluation

Superintendents say the major reasons they are evaluated by boards is to ensure systematic accountability and to establish performance goals. Very few superintendents (1.6 percent) think the primary purpose of evaluation is for dismissal (see **Table 5.16**). The data from the 1982 study are very similar to responses in 1992 (First, 1990).

The process by which most superintendents are evaluated usually is a formal one, using an evaluation instrument and often numerical point values. However, approximately one third of superintendents indicated that their boards use both formal and informal methods (see **Table 5.17**.)

Specifically, board members sometimes use a numerical point system in conjunction with an appraisal by board members of communication and other skills that are not easily quantified. Superintendents agree that subjective opinions of board members often enter the informal process. They said they most often are discussed at a meeting with the board (48.4 percent), or evaluated with a rating form (48.2 percent). Approximately one-third of the superintendents said this meeting is in an executive session, meaning closed to the public. More than 18 percent are rated on criteria previously discussed with the board (see **Table 5.18**).

What Counts With the Board?

The most-often-encountered criteria found on 1992 superintendent evaluations is that of "general effectiveness," which echoes the 1982 study. Other top criteria in their evaluations include management functions, board/superintendent relationships, bud-

TABLE 5.16 REASONS BOARD EVALUATES JOB PERFORMANCE

REASONS	GROUP A: 25,000 OR MORE PUPILS		GROUP B: 3,000-24,999 PUPILS		GROUP C: 300-2,999 PUPILS		GROUP D: FEWER THAN 300 PUPILS		NATIONAL UNWEIGHTED PROFILE	
	RANK	%	RANK	%	RANK	%	RANK	%	RANK	%
PERIODIC/SYSTEMATIC ACCOUNTABILITY	1	63.0	1	57.6	1	52.4	1	46.8	1	54.3
EVIDENCE FOR DISMISSAL	10	1.5	12	1.2	11	1.5	10.5	3.0	11	1.6
IDENTIFY AREAS NEEDING IMPROVEMENT	4	19.3	4	19.9	4	27.3	2	30.6	4	24.5
POINT OUT STRENGTHS	10	1.5	7.5	4.5	7	5.6	7	6.4	7	5.0
DOCUMENT DISSATISFACTION	12	0.7	9	3.0	8	3.7	10.5	3.0	8	3.1
ESTABLISH PERFORMANCE GOALS	2	38.5	2	34.9	2	30.7	4	25.5	2	32.1
ASSESS PERFORMANCE WITH STANDARDS	3	33.3	3	28.8	3	28.0	3	28.1	3	29.4
COMPLY WITH BOARD POLICY	5	14.1	5	14.1	5	21.0	5	20.9	5	18.0
DETERMINE QUALIFICATIONS FOR PERMANENT STATUS	10	1.5	13	0.7	13	0.9	12	2.1	13	1.0
TO DETERMINE SALARY	6	7.4	6	12.7	6	13.9	6	13.2	6	12.9
OTHER	8	3.0	10	2.1	9	2.7	8	5.1	10	2.8
DO NOT KNOW	13	0.0	11	1.7	12	1.0	9	3.4	12	1.5
DOES NOT APPLY	7	3.7	7.5	4.5	10	1.9	13	1.7	9	3.0

TABLE 5.17 WHAT KIND OF PROCEDURE DOES BOARD USE TO EVALUATE SUPERINTENDENT'S JOB PERFORMANCE?

PROCEDURE	GROUP A: 25,000 OR MORE PUPILS		GROUP B: 3,000-24,999 PUPILS		GROUP C: 300-2,999 PUPILS		GROUP D: FEWER THAN 300 PUPILS		NATIONAL UNWEIGHTED PROFILE	
	No.	%	No.	%	No.	%	No.	%	No.	%
FORMAL	76	53.9	271	45.3	308	43.1	80	31.9	735	43.1
INFORMAL	13	9.2	76	12.7	108	15.1	63	25.1	260	15.3
BOTH	48	34.0	227	38.0	273	38.2	95	37.8	643	37.7
NOT EVALUATED	4	2.8	24	4.0	25	3.5	13	5.2	66	3.9
TOTAL	141	8.3	598	35.1	714	41.9	251	14.7	1,704	100.0

get development, and educational leadership and knowledge. In the smaller districts, budget development ranks high. Board-superintendent relations is ranked second in almost all categories of district size; in 1982, it ranked fourth (see **Table 5.19**).

According to conventional wisdom, as the district goes, so goes the superintendent's evaluation. Superintendents and professional associations in recent years have emphasized the necessity of developing appropriate evaluation forms for all employees, including superintendents (Robinson and Bickers, 1990). In some states, these efforts have resulted in statutes indicating criteria and modes of evaluation for various educators, which usually exclude superintendents.

BOARD EXPECTATIONS

Superintendents indicated that boards primarily expect superintendents to be general managers. Skills in human relations are ranked second among important expectations, followed closely by instructional leadership. Community relations and planning, while ranking somewhat lower, are crucial skills in many districts. However, many responding superintendents did not think their boards expected a great deal of them in those two areas (see **Table 5.20**).

PROBLEMS BOARD MEMBERS FACE

In the 1982 and 1992 AASA studies, superintendents have perceived similar problems facing board members

TABLE 5.18 PROCEDURES USED IN SUPERINTENDENT'S EVALUATION BY THE BOARD

	GROUP A: 25,000 OR MORE PUPILS		GROUP B: 3,000-24,999 PUPILS		GROUP C: 300-2,999 PUPILS		GROUP D: FEWER THAN 300 PUPILS		NATIONAL UNWEIGHTED PROFILE	
	RANK	%	RANK	%	RANK	%	RANK	%	RANK	%
DISCUSSION AT EXECUTIVE MEETING	3	33.3	3	33.7	3	32.7	3	38.2	3	33.9
DISCUSSION AT MEETING OF BOARD/SUPERINTENDENT	1	55.0	1.5	49.3	2	47.4	1	49.8	1	48.4
RATING FORMS	2	37.2	1.5	49.3	1	51.5	2	42.2	2	48.2
WRITTEN EVALUATION OF SUPERINTENDENT	5	16.3	5	19.4	5	20.3	4	24.0	4	20.2
APPRAISAL CRITERIA DEVELOPED BY BOARD	7	7.8	8	4.3	8	4.4	9	3.6	8	4.5
CRITERIA PREVIOUSLY AGREED UPON	4	24.8	4	22.2	4	18.8	6	7.6	5	18.8
SUPERINTENDENT RATED ON EACH CRITERIA	8	7.0	7	4.7	7	5.5	7.5	6.2	7	5.4
BOARD CONSULTS OTHERS	9	2.3	9.5	1.7	9	2.6	7.5	6.2	9	2.8
OBSERVATION AND ASSOCIATION	6	10.9	6	10.8	6	10.4	5	13.8	6	11.1
ASSESSMENT OF SUPT. BY WRITTEN REPORTS	10	0.8	9.5	1.7	10	0.8	10	1.3	10	1.2

TABLE 5.19 IMPORTANCE OF FACTORS USED IN BOARD EVALUATIONS

	GROUP A: 25,000 OR MORE PUPILS		GROUP B: 3,000-24,999 PUPILS		GROUP C: 300-2,999 PUPILS		GROUP D: FEWER THAN 300 PUPILS		NATIONAL UNWEIGHTED PROFILE	
FACTOR	RANK	%	RANK	%	RANK	%	RANK	%	RANK	%
GENERAL EFFECTIVENESS	1	92.0	1	89.8	1	87.8	1	83.8	1	88.3
PERSONAL CHARACTERISTICS	8	54.4	7	57.3	8	50.6	8	54.0	8	53.8
EDUC. LEADERSHIP/KNOWLEDGE	4	74.6	4	66.8	5	65.8	6	56.9	5	65.6
MANAGEMENT FUNCTIONS	3	75.4	3	73.6	2	76.8	2	73.4	3	75.1
RECRUIT & SUPER. OF PERSONNEL	9	91.6	9	35.1	9	40.0	9	42.0	9	37.9
BUDGET DEVEL./IMPLEMENTATION	6	60.6	8	56.8	3.5	71.5	3	69.6	4	65.8
BOARD/SUPT. RELATIONSHIPS	2	81.8	2	82.8	3.5	71.5	4	65.3	2	75.4
STAFF/SUPT. RELATIONSHIPS	7	55.8	6	58.9	7	51.9	7	56.5	7	55.3
STUDENT/SUPT. RELATIONSHIPS	10	8.1	10	10.2	10	13.2	10	31.7	10	14.5
COMMUNITY/SUPT. RELATIONSHIPS	5	69.6	5	66.6	6	60.3	5	60.3	6	63.2

in fulfilling their duties. In the 1992 instrument, an additional response item asked whether "understanding appropriate role" is a serious problem for boards, and 21.9 percent of the superintendents said it was. In 1992, 39.3 percent of the respondents said finance issues are the most difficult for board members, up from 37.1 percent in 1982. Superintendents indicated community pressure is about the same as in 1982 as a problem for board members. The pattern of responses to these questions is similar across the districts despite enrollment differences (see **Tables 5.21** and **5.22**).

That finance is the biggest problem for superintendents and board members is in line with what was

TABLE 5.20 BOARD'S PRIMARY EXPECTATIONS OF SUPERINTENDENT

EXPECTATION	GROUP A: 25,000 OR MORE PUPILS		GROUP B: 3,000-24,999 PUPILS		GROUP C: 300-2,999 PUPILS		GROUP D: FEWER THAN 300 PUPILS		NATIONAL UNWEIGHTED PROFILE	
	RANK	%	RANK	%	RANK	%	RANK	%	RANK	%
SKILLS IN HUMAN RELATIONS	2	48.8	1	50.7	3	40.9	3	32.8	2	43.8
KNOWLEDGE OF FINANCE/BUDGET	6	11.0	4	22.5	1	53.1	1	55.0	4	39.2
GENERAL MANAGEMENT	1	52.0	3	31.5	2	45.1	2	54.1	1	48.5
COMMUNITY RELATIONS	4	16.5	6	13.8	5	12.1	5	11.8	5	13.0
INSTRUCTIONAL LEADERSHIP DEVELOPMENT	3	38.6	2	32.9	4	28.8	4	28.4	3	40.0
PLANNING STRATEGY	5	15.7	5	14.9	6	9.9	7	3.1	6	11.1
OTHER	7	3.1	7	2.3	7	2.1	6	3.5	7	2.5

TABLE 5.21 WHAT IS THE MOST DIFFICULT PROBLEM BOARD MEMBERS FACE?

PROBLEMS	GROUP A: 25,000 OR MORE PUPILS		GROUP B: 3,000-24,999 PUPILS		GROUP C: 300-2,999 PUPILS		GROUP D: FEWER THAN 300 PUPILS		NATIONAL UNWEIGHTED PROFILE	
	No.	%	No.	%	No.	%	No.	%	No.	%
FINANCIAL ISSUES	44	33.1	221	38.5	282	42.5	84	35.9	631	39.3
COMMUNITY PRESSURE	29	21.8	107	18.6	139	21.0	54	23.1	329	20.5
EMPLOYEE RELATIONS	9	6.8	48	8.4	49	7.4	13	5.6	119	7.4
CURRICULUR ISSUES	0	0.0	6	1.0	10	1.5	3	1.3	19	1.2
INTERNAL BOARD CONFLICT	22	16.5	56	9.8	32	4.8	13	5.6	123	7.7
UNDERSTANDING APPROPRIATE BOARD ROLE	28	21.1	127	22.1	140	21.1	56	23.9	351	21.9
OTHER	1	0.8	9	1.6	11	1.7	11	4.7	32	2.0
TOTAL	133	8.3	574	35.8	663	41.3	234	14.6	1,604	100.0

TABLE 5.22 RANKING OF PROBLEMS BOARD MEMBERS FACE — 1992-1982 COMPARISONS

PROBLEMS	GROUP A: 25,000 OR MORE PUPILS		GROUP B: 3,000-24,999 PUPILS		GROUP C: 300-2,999 PUPILS		GROUP D: FEWER THAN 300 PUPILS		NATIONAL UNWEIGHTED PROFILE	
	1992 RANKING	1982 RANKING	1992 RANKING	1982 RANKING	1992 RANKING	1982 RANKING	1992 RANKING	1982 RANKING	1992 RANKING	1982 RANKING
FINANCIAL ISSUES	1	1	1	1	1	1	1	1	1	1
COMMUNITY PRESSURES	2	2	3	2	3	2	3	2	3	2
UNDERSTANDING AND FULFILLING APPROPRIATE BOARD ROLE	3	4	2	3	2	3	2	3	2	4
INTERNAL BOARD CONFLICT	4	3	4	4	5	4	4.5	4	4	5
EMPLOYEE RELATIONS	5	6	5	5	4	5	4.5	5	5	-
RELATIONS WITH OTHER GOVERNMENTAL UNITS	-	5	-	7	-	6	-	6.5	-	6
CLOSING SCHOOLS	-	7	-	6	-	7	-	6.5	-	7

TABLE 5.23 SUPERINTENDENT RANKING OF ISSUES AND CHALLENGES FACING THE SUPERINTENDENCY

ISSUE AND CHALLENGE	GROUP A: 25,000 OR MORE PUPILS		GROUP B: 3,000-24,999 PUPILS		GROUP C: 300-2,999 PUPILS		GROUP D: LESS THAN 300 PUPILS		NATIONAL UNWEIGHTED PROFILE	
	RANK	%	RANK	%	RANK	%	RANK	%	RANK	%
FINANCING SCHOOLS	1	99.3	1	97.0	1	96.7	1	91.3	1	96.3
ASSESSMENT AND TESTING	2	90.8	2	85.5	3	82.1	6	74.3	2	82.8
ACCOUNTABILITY/CREDIBILITY	3	90.0	4	82.4	2	77.7	5	73.1	3	79.7
CHANGING PRIORITIES IN CURRICULUM	17	76.7	15	75.2	14	83.1	22	80.6	4	79.4
CHANGING SOCIETAL VALUES	7	85.6	7	84.4	5	73.0	10	68.0	5	77.4
ADMINISTRATOR/BOARD REL.	14	78.9	13	80.0	13	76.6	25	72.5	6	77.4
NEW TEACHING DEMANDS	9	82.2	9	76.2	8	76.6	2	71.9	7	76.2
COMPLIANCE WITH MANDATES	19	73.3	16	70.2	15	76.2	11	83.3	8	74.9
PARENT APATHY AND IRRESPONSIBILITY	16	76.9	17	75.8	18	74.1	15	71.7	9	74.5
SPECIAL ED/PL 94.142	18	75.5	18	76.0	17	71.6	28	66.9	10	72.8
OBTAINING INFORMATION	13	79.7	6	73.1	6	70.0	7	75.9	11	72.8
STAFF RECRUITING/SELECTION	6	86.3	5	73.6	9	67.9	9	65.1	12	71.0
DEVELOPING AND FUNDING AT-RISK PROGRAMS	5	87.7	3	79.8	4	64.1	3	44.7	13	68.7
STRATEGIC PLANNING	10	82.0	8	71.5	7	61.7	8	47.1	14	64.6
PERSONAL TIME MANAGEMENT	24	65.3	25	61.6	25	64.0	21	67.3	15	63.7
STAFF & ADMINSTRATOR EVAL.	21	71.2	22	65.8	20	63.7	17	53.6	16	63.5
PROVIDING EARLY CHILD ED.	8	84.2	14	68.6	16	57.8	16	43.0	17	61.6
COMMUNITY INVOLVEMENT	20	73.0	20	63.4	22	60.1	18	54.6	18	61.5
USE OF DRUGS/ALCOHOL IN SCHOOLS	15	77.2	21	66.6	23	56.7	27	46.7	19	60.4
CALIBER OF BOARD PERSONS	25	63.4	27	61.9	26	53.3	35	51.8	20	57.0
SITE-BASED MANAGEMENT	11	81.5	12	61.2	12	53.1	13	43.1	21	56.8
AGING/INADEQUATE FACILITIES	27	60.4	28	58.8	29	56.4	30	50.6	22	56.7
EMPOWERMENT	12	80.1	11	60.3	11	52.1	4	43.1	23	56.0
NEGOTIATIONS, STRIKES, TEACHER MILITANCY	26	62.9	19	56.8	19	53.4	23	35.6	24	52.8
CALIBER OF BOARD RESPONSIBILITY	29	57.0	29	52.9	28	49.1	33	47.8	25	50.9
CHANGING DEMOGRAPHICS	4	88.7	10	62.3	10	36.3	12	31.3	26	49.1
RAPIDLY CHANGING ENROLLMENT	30	50.7	30	47.9	27	47.4	20	49.8	27	48.2
PROVIDING CHILD CARE	23	69.6	23	56.1	24	42.2	31	32.8	28	47.9
DISTRICT RESTRUCTURING	22	70.5	24	47.2	21	43.1	26	37.4	29	47.4
IMPLEMENTING "CHOICE"	31	50.0	31	44.0	30	46.1	19	50.6	30	46.4
DECLINING FEDERAL SUPPORT	32	43.8	32	34.2	32	39.5	29	45.0	31	38.8
STUDENT RIGHTS	33	41.7	35	33.7	34	36.3	32	38.0	32	36.1
GREATER RECOGNITION OF SUPERINTENDENT	36	34.0	33	29.6	33	30.8	34	32.1	33	30.9
INCREASING ATTACKS ON SUPERINTENDENT	35	36.2	38	30.0	36	28.5	37	34.7	34	30.6
CONSOLIDATION	39	11.4	39	17.4	39	29.9	39	59.2	35	28.3
STUDENT DISCIPLINE	28	59.7	26	32.5	31	19.0	24	21.6	36	27.5
PRESSURE TO SUPPORT PRIVATE SCHOOLS	37	29.8	36	21.6	38	24.2	36	19.7	37	23.1
REDUCTION IN FORCE	38	17.0	37	21.0	37	24.6	38	23.6	38	22.5
AFFIRMATIVE ACTION	34	40.0	34	17.4	35	14.3	14	16.9	39	17.9

occurring in many states in the late 1980s and early 1990s, where political support and community priorities for the welfare of children declined. The changing demographics of the 1990s could present an even greater challenge to school boards.

PROBLEMS SUPERINTENDENTS FACE

School finance is viewed by superintendents as the number one problem both they and their school boards face. Fully 96.3 percent of the total sample ranked finance as number one (see **Table 5.23**). Assessment and testing, as well as accountability and credibility, also are critical problems. Time management, according to superintendents, is a primary problem inhibiting their job performance — and one

that could be largely eradicated with additional funding for more support staff.

Superintendents in the largest districts say finance is a more serious problem than do superintendents in smaller districts, while superintendents in smaller districts say they are mired in insignificant details to a greater extent than their counterparts in the largest districts.

Self-Perception

In terms of effectiveness, almost twice as many superintendents in the very large districts rated their effectiveness as "excellent" than did superintendents in small districts (see **Table 5.24**). The probable reasons for this might be they feel trapped in the small district, are expected to do everything, and know that

TABLE 5.24 IN GENERAL, RATE YOUR EFFECTIVENESS AS A SUPERINTENDENT

RATING	GROUP A: 25,000 OR MORE PUPILS		GROUP B: 3,000-24,999 PUPILS		GROUP C: 300-2,999 PUPILS		GROUP D: FEWER THAN 300 PUPILS		NATIONAL UNWEIGHTED PROFILE	
	No.	%	No.	%	No.	%	No.	%	No.	%
EXCELLENT	87	60.4	354	58.5	345	48.5	90	36.1	876	51.2
GOOD	53	36.8	247	40.8	336	47.2	145	58.2	781	45.7
AVERAGE	4	2.8	4	0.7	29	4.1	14	5.6	51	3.0
POOR	0	0.0	0	0.0	2	0.3	0	0.0	2	0.1
INCOMPETENT	0	0.0	0	0.0	0	0.0	0	0.0	0	0.0
TOTAL	144	804.0	605	35.4	712	41.6	249	14.6	1,710	100.0

TABLE 5.25 FACTORS THAT INHIBIT SUPERINTENDENTS' EFFECTIVENESS

RESPONSE CLASSIFICATIONS	GROUP A: 25,000 OR MORE PUPILS		GROUP B: 3,000-24,999 PUPILS		GROUP C: 300-2,999 PUPILS		GROUP D: FEWER THAN 300 PUPILS		NATIONAL UNWEIGHTED PROFILE	
	No.	%	No.	%	No.	%	No.	%	No.	%
INADEQUATE FINANCING	88	60.7	383	62.8	420	58.7	127	50.2	1,018	**59.0**
TOO MANY INSIGNIFICANT DEMANDS	70	48.3	261	42.8	372	52.0	192	75.9	895	**51.9**
STATE REFORM MANDATES	38	26.2	202	33.1	300	41.9	115	45.5	655	**38.0**
COLLECTIVE BARGAINING AGREEMENTS	41	28.3	181	29.7	186	26.0	30	11.9	438	**25.4**
RACIAL/ETHNIC PROBLEMS	11	7.6	22	3.6	4	0.5	1	0.4	38	**22.0**
TOO MUCH ADDED RESPONSIBILITY	14	9.7	59	9.7	161	22.5	72	28.5	306	**17.7**
INSUFFICIENT ADMINISTRATIVE SUPPORT	14	9.7	92	15.1	135	18.9	51	20.2	292	**16.9**
POOR RELATIONS WITH BOARD MEMBERS	29	20.0	113	18.5	71	9.9	30	11.9	243	**14.1**
INEFFECTIVE STAFF MEMBERS	16	11.0	52	8.5	55	7.7	19	7.5	142	**8.2**
DISTRICT TOO SMALL	2	1.4	7	11.5	56	7.8	76	30.0	141	**8.2**
LACK OF COMMUNITY SUPPORT	9	6.2	40	6.6	44	6.1	21	8.3	114	**6.6**
OTHER	10	6.9	36	5.9	43	6.0	13	5.1	102	**5.9**
DRUG PROBLEMS	5	3.4	15	2.5	9	1.3	2	0.8	31	**1.8**

many important tasks are not being completed due to lack of time. More conjecture might be that some feel they are "less" superintendent-effective due to only being able to work in a small, less prestigious district.

Despite the problems with finance and time management, 96.9 percent of sampled superintendents say they think their overall effectiveness level is "good" or "excellent." No superintendents said they are "incompetent."

Factors That Inhibit Effectiveness

Even though superintendents as a group considered themselves quite effective, there are three areas of administration/management they feel inhibit their performance. In **Table 5.25**, again, the first is lack of finances. In 1982, 41.6 percent of superintendents indicated finance was the leading problem in inhibiting their job effectiveness; in 1992, 59 percent identify it as the chief problem (see **Table 5.25**).

The second area is that of having too many insignificant demands placed on them by the board, staff, and community. Of course, this problem might be eased with more support staff, again remembering that most districts are one- or two-person administrative offices.

The third, and more interesting area, is that of compliance with state-mandated reforms. It certainly is true in many states that reform mandates have not been completely state funded, thus causing already scarce district resources to be diverted to implementation of mandates. The strain on the already thin ranks of administrators likely is felt by the superintendents. Unfortunately, many times school boards have not been able to appreciate the need for an adequate

number of administrative staff, especially when implementing new reforms.

Reasons To Leave A District

What reasons do superintendents give for leaving one district for another? The career patterns of superintendents suggest they often begin their superintendency careers in smaller districts and move to larger and better financed ones. This fits with the concept of an upwardly mobile professional. Superintendents of very large districts many times move from a central office position into a medium-sized district.

When asked why they left their last superintendency, 42.8 percent overall said "moving to a larger district." A move to a larger district generally also means an increase in salary and benefits. Often, superintendents believe they have accomplished their goals and seek the challenges of a new job situation.

About 16.7 percent of superintendents indicated a conflict with school boards precipitated their move. Only 9.3 percent of the superintendents in the largest districts said this was the case. Surprisingly, 30.1 percent of superintendents in the smallest districts indicate they had left because of board conflict. In the category of districts with enrollments of 300 to 2,999 enrollment, 14.8 percent of the superintendents say they left due to board conflict. This question was new in 1992 and no comparable data are available from the 1971 or 1982 studies (see **Table 5.26**).

Troubling Issues

Again, the matter or issue superintendents find most troubling is attempting to operate their districts effectively with less than optimum amounts of fund-

TABLE 5.26 REASONS LEFT LAST SUPERINTENDENCY

REASONS	GROUP A: 25,000 OR MORE PUPILS No.	%	GROUP B: 3,000-24,999 PUPILS No.	%	GROUP C: 300-2,999 PUPILS No.	%	GROUP D: FEWER THAN 300 PUPILS No.	%	NATIONAL UNWEIGHTED PROFILE No.	%
LARGER DIST. SUPERINTENDENCY	57	66.3	152	51.4	138	39.3	25	18.4	372	42.8
CONFLICT WITH BOARD MEMBERS	8	9.3	44	14.9	52	14.8	41	30.1	145	16.7
DISTRICT CONSOLIDATION	0	0.0	1	0.3	11	3.1	5	3.7	17	2.0
RETIREMENT	1	1.2	7	2.4	10	2.8	3	2.2	21	2.4
DESEGREGATION CONFLICT	0	0.0	0	0.0	0	0.0	0	0.0	0	0.0
UNION CONFLICT	3	3.5	4	1.4	3	0.9	3	2.2	13	1.5
REDUCTION IN FORCE OF DIST.	0	0.0	1	0.3	2	0.6	0	0.0	3	0.3
FAMILY CONSIDERATIONS	0	0.0	17	5.7	42	12.0	14	10.3	73	8.4
HIGHER EDUC. OPPORTUNITIES	6	7.0	2	0.7	10	2.8	5	3.7	23	2.6
JOB IN "BETTER" FINANCED DIST.	4	4.7	34	11.5	47	13.4	15	11.0	100	11.5
OTHER	7	8.1	34	11.5	36	10.3	25	18.4	102	11.7
TOTAL	86	100.0	296	100.0	351	100.0	136	100.0	869	100.0

TABLE 5.27 EXTENT TO WHICH SUPERINTENDENTS FEEL
SELECTED SITUATIONS ARE SOMETIMES TROUBLESOME

RESPONSE CLASSIFICATIONS	GROUP A: 25,000 OR MORE PUPILS		GROUP B: 3,000-24,999 PUPILS		GROUP C: 300-2,999 PUPILS		GROUP D: FEWER THAN 300 PUPILS		NATIONAL UNWEIGHTED PROFILE	
	No.	%	No.	%	No.	%	No.	%	No.	%
CONCERN OVER GROUP OR INDIVIDUAL REACTIONS TO A CONTRARY DECISION										
VERY FREQUENTLY	6	4.1	20	3.3	27	3.8	16	6.3	69	4.0
FREQUENTLY	31	21.4	120	19.7	144	20.1	63	24.9	358	20.8
SOMETIMES	79	54.5	350	57.4	422	58.9	134	53.0	985	57.1
ALMOST NEVER	26	17.9	103	16.9	107	14.9	35	13.8	271	15.7
NEVER	1	0.7	13	2.1	9	1.3	3	1.2	26	1.5
SELF-CONCERN OVER WHETHER SUPERINTENDENT HAS MADE RIGHT DECISION										
VERY FREQUENTLY	3	2.1	8	1.3	17	2.4	8	3.2	36	2.1
FREQUENTLY	17	11.7	76	12.5	105	14.7	56	22.1	254	14.7
SOMETIMES	72	49.7	310	50.8	397	55.4	124	49.0	903	52.4
ALMOST NEVER	46	31.7	196	32.1	179	25.0	62	24.5	483	28.0
NEVER	5	3.4	15	2.5	13	1.8	1	0.4	34	2.0
CONCERN ABOUT LOCAL POWER STRUCTURE										
VERY FREQUENTLY	8	5.5	18	3.0	24	3.4	11	4.3	61	3.5
FREQUENTLY	44	30.3	128	21.0	154	21.5	46	18.2	372	21.6
SOMETIMES	56	38.6	295	48.4	334	46.6	119	47.0	804	46.6
ALMOST NEVER	229	20.0	140	23.0	169	23.6	62	24.5	400	23.2
NEVER	5	3.4	25	4.1	30	4.2	11	4.3	71	4.1
CONSTANTLY FRUSTRATED WITH BOARD ACTIVITIES/ATTITUDES										
VERY FREQUENTLY	17	11.7	50	8.2	42	5.9	21	8.3	130	7.5
FREQUENTLY	24	16.6	89	14.6	86	12.0	34	13.4	233	13.5
SOMETIMES	51	35.2	203	33.3	232	32.4	69	27.3	555	32.2
ALMOST NEVER	47	32.4	223	36.6	310	43.3	102	40.3	682	39.6
NEVER	4	2.8	42	6.9	42	5.9	25	9.9	113	6.9
CONCERN OVER HOW TO DEAL WITH A NON-PRODUCTIVE/UNCOOPERATIVE STAFF										
VERY FREQUENTLY	13	9.0	49	8.0	63	8.8	18	7.1	143	8.3
FREQUENTLY	31	21.4	158	25.9	221	30.9	72	28.5	482	28.0
SOMETIMES	66	45.5	265	43.4	298	41.6	117	46.2	746	42.2
ALMOST NEVER	32	22.1	120	19.7	117	16.3	37	14.6	306	17.7
NEVER	1	0.7	15	2.5	11	1.5	7	2.8	34	19.7
CONCERN ABOUT COMMUNITY SUPPORT FOR PROGRAMS										
VERY FREQUENTLY	36	24.8	129	21.1	114	15.9	25	9.19	304	17.6
FREQUENTLY	65	44.8	260	42.6	305	42.6	83	32.8	713	41.4
SOMETIMES	30	20.7	164	26.9	210	29.3	103	40.7	507	29.4
ALMOST NEVER	12	8.3	49	8.0	74	10.3	35	13.8	170	9.9
NEVER	0	0.0	5	0.8	9	1.3	5	2.0	19	1.1

TABLE 5.27 (CONTINUED)

RESPONSE CLASSIFICATIONS	GROUP A: 25,000 OR MORE PUPILS		GROUP B: 3,000-24,999 PUPILS		GROUP C: 300-2,999 PUPILS		GROUP D: FEWER THAN 300 PUPILS		NATIONAL UNWEIGHTED PROFILE	
	No.	%	No.	%	No.	%	No.	%	No.	%
CONCERN ABOUT TASK UNDONE OR PROBLEMS UNRESOLVED										
VERY FREQUENTLY	4	2.8	30	4.9	54	7.5	29	11.5	117	6.8
FREQUENTLY	14	9.7	73	12.0	106	14.8	48	19.0	241	14.0
SOMETIMES	34	23.4	169	27.7	224	31.3	85	33.6	512	29.7
ALMOST NEVER	64	44.1	231	37.9	249	34.8	63	24.9	607	35.2
NEVER	27	18.6	101	16.6	79	11.0	25	9.9	232	13.5
CONCERN ABOUT RELATIONS WITH TEACHERS' UNION/ASSOCIATION										
VERY FREQUENTLY	7	4.8	17	2.8	15	2.1	4	1.6	42	2.5
FREQUENTLY	28	19.3	92	15.1	96	13.4	27	10.7	243	14.1
SOMETIMES	70	48.3	261	42.8	320	44.7	73	28.9	724	42.0
ALMOST NEVER	27	18.6	188	30.8	226	31.6	106	41.9	547	31.7
NEVER	11	7.6	49	8.0	55	7.7	40	15.8	155	9.0
CONCERN ABOUT IMPRESSION MADE IN COMMUNITY GROUPS										
VERY FREQUENTLY	14	9.7	42	6.9	51	7.1	12	4.7	119	6.9
FREQUENTLY	32	22.1	171	28.0	186	26.0	73	28.9	462	26.8
SOMETIMES	55	37.9	217	35.6	288	40.2	101	39.9	661	38.3
ALMOST NEVER	31	21.4	138	22.6	152	21.2	51	20.2	372	21.6
NEVER	11	7.6	39	6.4	35	4.9	15	5.9	100	5.8
CONCERN ABOUT FINANCIAL MATTERS AND LEVY ISSUES										
VERY FREQUENTLY	31	21.4	168	27.5	202	28.2	72	28.5	473	227.4
FREQUENTLY	65	44.8	241	39.5	300	41.9	99	39.1	705	40.9
SOMETIMES	38	26.2	163	26.7	176	24.6	59	23.3	436	25.3
ALMOST NEVER	8	5.5	31	5.1	31	4.3	18	7.1	88	5.1
NEVER	1	0.7	5	0.8	4	0.6	3	1.2	13	0.8
FEELING OF NERVOUSNESS WHEN PLANNING OR PARTICIPATING IN BOARD MEETINGS										
VERY FREQUENTLY	4	2.8	10	1.6	20	2.8	14	5.5	48	2.8
FREQUENTLY	8	5.5	58	9.5	85	11.9	34	13.4	185	10.7
SOMETIMES	41	28.3	204	33.4	253	35.3	97	38.3	595	34.5
ALMOST NEVER	62	42.8	263	43.1	265	37.0	85	33.6	675	39.2
NEVER	28	19.3	73	12.0	90	12.6	22	8.7	213	12.4
CONCERN OVER LACK OF CONTROL OVER OVER EVENTS THAT AFFECT SCHOOLS										
VERY FREQUENTLY	14	9.7	59	9.7	77	10.8	46	18.2	196	11.4
FREQUENTLY	36	24.8	163	26.7	201	28.1	72	28.5	472	27.4
SOMETIMES	59	40.7	247	40.5	289	40.4	87	34.4	682	39.6
ALMOST NEVER	28	19.3	112	18.4	132	18.4	46	18.2	318	18.4
NEVER	6	4.1	26	4.3	13	1.8	1	0.4	46	2.7

ing. In the sample group, 27.4 percent indicated they very frequently worry about money issues. And, part of their financial concerns is the apparent lack of community support for schools. Also, they are fairly concerned about the impression they and the district make in the community. This feeling probably results from the negative picture many newspapers paint of schools. Interestingly, superintendents also indicated they do not find their interaction with board members or what their board members do very worrisome. These data seem to contradict some of the recent research concerning board/superintendent relations (NSBA, 1992). In summary, superintendents are worried about financial issues and those activities that tend to discourage community support (see Table 5.27).

Reasons To Leave The Field

Issues superintendents find troubling are the very ones they said might cause them to leave the field. Lack of adequate finances for school district operations is the leading reason 68.7 percent of the respon-

dents said they would leave the superintendency. Second in importance is lack of community support, including the support of the board of education. In the 1971 and 1982 studies, the leading reasons for leaving the field were "attacks on the superintendent" and "negotiations and strikes." Financing of schools was ranked fourth in both of these two previous surveys. Relations with unions and negotiations ranked eleventh out of a possible twelve responses in 1992, indicating that superintendents are not as concerned with negotiations and strikes as they were a decade ago (see Table 5.28).

FULFILLMENT

Despite the problems caused by underfinancing, community pressure groups, and demands for reform, responding superintendents in all district sizes indicate a good deal of satisfaction with their roles as superintendent. Nearly two-thirds indicate considerable satisfaction in their jobs. However, superintendents in smaller districts generally are less satisfied than those in

TABLE 5.28 ISSUES LIKELY TO CAUSE SUPERINTENDENTS TO LEAVE IF NOT CORRECTED

ISSUES	GROUP A: 25,000 OR MORE PUPILS RANK	%	GROUP B: 3,000-24,999 PUPILS RANK	%	GROUP C: 300-2,999 PUPILS RANK	%	GROUP D: FEWER THAN 300 PUPILS RANK	%	NATIONAL UNWEIGHTED PROFILE RANK	%
FINANCIAL MATTERS	2	67.2	1	67.2	1	70.4	1	68.1	1	68.7
LACK OF COMMUNITY SUPPORT	1	70.7	2	64.1	2	58.8	3	43.1	2	59.3
LACK OF CONTROL	4	35.0	3	36.6	4	39.0	2	46.9	3	38.9
NON-PRODUCTIVE STAFF	6	30.8	5	34.1	3	40.0	4	35.9	4	36.6
IMPRESSION I MAKE	5	32.2	4	35.1	5	33.3	5	33.8	5	33.9
RELATIONS/SUPPORT OF LOCAL POWER STRUCTURE	3	36.6	6	24.1	6	25.1	9	22.9	6	25.5
INDIVIDUAL OR GROUP REACTIONS	8	25.9	7	23.1	7	24.1	6	31.5	7	24.9
FRUSTRATED WITH BOARD	7	28.7	8	22.9	9	18.0	10	21.9	8	21.2
TASKS UNDONE/PROBLEMS UNSOLVED	11	12.6	10	17.1	8	22.5	7	30.8	9	20.9
WHETHER I MADE THE RIGHT DECISION	10	14.0	11	13.9	10	17.2	8	25.5	10	17.0
RELATIONS WITH UNIONS	9	24.5	9	18.0	11	15.6	12	12.4	11	16.7
PLANNING/PARTICIPATION IN BOARD MEETINGS	12	8.4	12	11.1	12	14.7	11	19.1	12	13.6

TABLE 5.29 HOW MUCH SELF-FULFILLMENT DOES POSITION OF SUPERINTENDENT PROVIDE?

AMOUNT	GROUP A: 25,000 OR MORE PUPILS No.	%	GROUP B: 3,000-24,999 PUPILS No.	%	GROUP C: 300-2,999 PUPILS No.	%	GROUP D: FEWER THAN 300 PUPILS No.	%	NATIONAL UNWEIGHTED PROFILE No.	%
NONE	0	0.0	2	0.3	3	0.4	1	0.4	6	0.4
LITTLE	3	2.1	12	2.0	20	2.8	14	5.5	49	2.9
MODERATE	30	20.7	174	28.6	271	38.4	112	44.3	587	34.3
CONSIDERABLE	112	77.2	420	69.1	411	58.3	126	49.8	1,069	62.5
TOTAL	145	8.5	608	35.5	705	41.2	253	14.8	1,711	100.0

larger districts. One reason might be that superintendents in smaller districts perform many tasks they believe are inappropriate to their positions, and have little or no help in doing them. Small district superintendents also indicate more stress and tension with board members and the community than their counterparts in larger districts (see **Table 5.29**).

PRESTIGE

Superintendents indicated they think the prestige and status of the position has remained constant in their communities. About one-third indicate they think prestige is increasing, while only 14.7 percent think their position is diminishing in importance and influence (see **Table 5.30**).

STRESS

A certain degree of stress is present in any professional position. This is especially true in the superintendency, where management of fiscal and human resources within a lay governance structure creates unique organizational conditions. Pressures caused by lack of adequate funding, competing community and school groups, employee unions, state legislated mandates, intrusive board members, and the public's dissatisfaction with performance of schools can all cause stress for superintendents (see **Table 5.31**). Stress is not necessarily an unhealthy condition. But if frustrations become too severe, and superintendents have no healthy ways to release them, stress can become disabling. Decisions without benefit of

TABLE 5.30 STATUS/PRESTIGE OF THE SUPERINTENDENCY

STATUS/PRESTIGE	GROUP A: 25,000 OR MORE PUPILS		GROUP B: 3,000-24,999 PUPILS		GROUP C: 300-2,999 PUPILS		GROUP D: FEWER THAN 300 PUPILS		NATIONAL UNWEIGHTED PROFILE	
	No.	%	No.	%	No.	%	No.	%	No.	%
DECREASING IN IMPORTANCE/INFLUENCE	17	11.8	70	11.5	117	16.4	49	19.4	253	14.7
REMAINING THE SAME	41	28.5	235	38.6	327	45.9	109	43.3	712	41.4
INCREASING IN IMPORTANCE/INFLUENCE	80	55.6	261	42.9	216	30.3	62	24.6	619	36.0
DO NOT REALLY KNOW	6	4.2	43	7.1	53	7.4	32	12.7	134	7.8
TOTAL	144	8.4	609	35.4	713	41.5	252	14.7	1,718	100.0

TABLE 5.31 SUPERINTENDENTS' OPINIONS OF THE SUPERINTENDENCY AS A STRESSFUL OCCUPATION

DEGREE OF STRESS	GROUP A: 25,000 OR MORE PUPILS		GROUP B: 3,000-24,999 PUPILS		GROUP C: 300-2,999 PUPILS		GROUP D: FEWER THAN 300 PUPILS		NATIONAL UNWEIGHTED PROFILE	
	No.	%	No.	%	No.	%	No.	%	No.	%
NO STRESS	0	0.0	1	0.2	4	0.6	0	0.0	5	0.3
LITTLE STRESS	20	13.8	41	6.8	53	7.5	20	7.9	134	7.8
MODERATE STRESS	58	40.0	265	43.8	289	40.8	101	40.1	713	41.7
CONSIDERABLE STRESS	54	37.2	256	42.3	311	43.9	103	40.9	724	42.3
VERY GREAT STRESS	13	9.0	42	6.9	51	7.2	28	11.1	134	7.8
TOTAL	145	8.5	605	35.4	708	41.4	252	14.7	1,710	100.0

TABLE 5.32 SUPERINTENDENTS' OPINIONS OF THE SUPERINTENDENCY AS A STRESSFUL OCCUPATION — 1992-1982 COMPARISONS

DEGREE OF STRESS	GROUP A: 25,000 OR MORE PUPILS		GROUP B: 3,000-24,999 PUPILS		GROUP C: 300-2,999 PUPILS		GROUP D: FEWER THAN 300 PUPILS		NATIONAL UNWEIGHTED PROFILE	
	1992 %	1982 %	1992 %	1982 %	1992 %	1982 %	1992 %	1982 %	1992 %	1982 %
NO STRESS	0.0	0.9	0.2	1.0	0.6	0.3	0.0	0.0	0.3	0.5
LITTLE STRESS	13.8	8.1	6.8	6.4	7.5	7.1	7.9	9.0	7.8	7.3
SOME STRESS	40.0	49.5	43.8	45.3	40.8	43.9	40.1	48.2	41.7	45.5
CONSIDERABLE STRESS	37.2	34.2	42.3	40.4	43.9	40.0	40.9	36.9	42.3	39.1
VERY GREAT STRESS	9.0	7.2	6.9	6.9	7.2	8.7	11.1	5.9	7.8	7.5

reflection and rational thought can be made. Interpersonal relations typically suffer when leaders are under extreme stress, and organizations such as school districts, in which leaders constantly are under substantial pressure, generally do not perform well when they are more preoccupied with handling stress than with developing the organization's potential.

In the 1982 AASA study, respondents perceived the superintendency as a moderately stressful occupation. Some 84.6 percent of the sample said that "considerable" or "some" stress was present in the occupation. In 1992, 84 percent say they feel "considerable" or "moderate" stress, and only 7.8 percent indicate "very great stress." There are no significant differences among dis-

tricts according to size. "Very great stress" is indicated a bit more frequently by superintendents of very small school districts (see **Table 5.32**).

Differences in stress perceived by superintendents of differing age groups are not significant. However, superintendents over 60 do indicate lower stress responses than younger superintendents. "Very great stress" is felt more often by superintendents in the 40- to 44-year-old category (see **Table 5.33** and **Table 5.34**).

Some districts and boards encourage "wellness" programs for all employees, a strategy that can help offset the negative aspects of occupational stress. All prospective superintendents should be aware of occupational stress and its causes. Higher education preparation pro-

TABLE 5.33 SUPERINTENDENT'S OPINIONS OF THE SUPERINTENDECY AS A STRESSFULL OCCUPATION BY AGE

DEGREE OF STRESS	UNDER 35 %	35-39 %	40-44 %	45-49 %	50-54 %	55-60 %	60-64 %	65 + %
NO STRESS	0.0	0.0	0.0	0.9	0.0	0.0	1.1	0.0
LITTLE STRESS	0.0	4.8	4.6	7.6	7.2	10.2	18.4	23.1
MODERATE STRESS	50.0	42.3	34.5	38.3	42.4	49.7	52.9	61.5
CONSIDERABLE STRESS	44.4	44.2	48.3	44.0	44.4	35.0	26.4	15.4
VERY GREAT STRESS	5.6	8.7	12.6	9.2	6.0	5.1	1.1	0.0

TABLE 5.34 SUPERINTENDENTS' OPINIONS OF THE SUPERINTENDENCY AS A STRESSFUL OCCUPATION BY AGE 1992-1982 COMPARISON

AGE	UNDER 35		36-39		40-44		45-49		50-54		55-59		60+	
DEGREE OF STRESS	1992 %	1982 %	1992 %	1982 %	1992 %	1982 %	1992 %	1982 %	1992 %	1982 %	1992 %	1982 %	1992 %	1982 %
NO STRESS	0.0	0.0	0.0	0.0	0.0	0.0	0.9	0.4	0.0	0.9	0.0	1.3	1.1	0.0
LITTLE STRESS	0.0	6.5	4.8	10.0	4.6	6.6	7.6	7.8	7.2	5.9	10.2	6.8	18.4	9.0
SOME STRESS	50.0	37.0	42.3	43.3	34.5	46.0	38.3	47.4	42.4	43.5	49.7	47.2	52.9	49.3
CONSIDERABLE STRESS	44.4	43.5	44.2	40.0	48.3	37.9	44.0	35.6	44.4	43.2	35.0	39.1	26.4	34.3
VERY GREAT STRESS	5.6	13.0	8.7	6.7	12.6	9.5	9.2	8.9	6.0	6.5	5.1	5.5	1.1	7.5

TABLE 5.35 SUPERINTENDENTS' SOURCES OF INFORMATION RATED "VERY GREAT" AND "CONSIDERABLE"

SOURCE	GROUP A: 25,000 OR MORE PUPILS RANK	%	GROUP B: 3,000-24,999 PUPILS RANK	%	GROUP C: 300-2,999 PUPILS RANK	%	GROUP D: FEWER THAN 300 PUPILS RANK	%	NATIONAL UNWEIGHTED PROFILE RANK	%
FELLOW SUPERINTENDENTS	5	62.8	4	72.1	3	82.7	2	88.9	4	78.3
CENTRAL OFFICE STAFF	1	100.0	1	97.1	2	85.0	4	57.3	2	86.3
PARENTS	4	69.5	5	61.1	5	57.0	5	56.2	5	59.4
STATE OFFICE STAFF	10	17.2	9	31.8	6	46.8	6	54.7	7	40.2
COMMUNITY GROUPS	7	54.3	6	43.0	7	40.3	9	30.8	6	41.1
PROFFESSIONAL ASSOCIATIONS (AASA, ETC.)	9	23.2	10	30.6	10	31.7	8	36.0	10	31.2
POWER STRUCTURE	6	55.0	7	40.5	9	34.6	10	28.9	8	37.5
TEACHERS	3	77.9	3	78.3	4	78.7	3	78.3	3	78.4
SCHOOL BOARD MEMBERS	2	93.6	2	92.6	1	94.6	1	95.3	1	93.9
CONSULTANTS	8	32.9	8	33.7	8	36.2	7	36.5	9	35.1

grams might consider incorporating stress management training within their educational administration coursework.

COMMUNICATION SOURCES

Sources of information for executive leaders in organizations are vital. Almost 94 percent of superintendents surveyed listed board members as a powerful source of information. Superintendents also say they place great importance on the information they receive from their central office staff. This is natural, since it is the role of these individuals to keep the superintendent informed. Superintendents also value the information they receive from fellow superintendents at informal gatherings and

meetings of professional educational organizations (see **Table 5.35**).

Just as superintendents say they place great importance on information from the school board, they think board members place an equal amount of importance on the information received from them. **Table 5.36** shows superintendents also think central office staff, parents, and teachers are credible sources of information for school board members, as well as special interest groups and local power structures. Between 1982 and 1990 superintendents have lost some "weight" in terms of their degree of worth as a source of information to board members, thought for the most part responses stayed the same (see **Table 5.37**).

TABLE 5.36 BOARD MEMBERS' SOURCES OF INFORMATION RATED "VERY GREAT" AND "CONSIDERABLE"

SOURCE	GROUP A: 25,000 OR MORE PUPILS		GROUP B: 3,000-24,999 PUPILS		GROUP C: 300-2,999 PUPILS		GROUP D: FEWER THAN 300 PUPILS		NATIONAL UNWEIGHTED PROFILE	
	RANK	%	RANK	%	RANK	%	RANK	%	RANK	%
DISTRICT SUPERINTENDENT	1	96.3	1	94.3	1	94.7	1	88.9	1	93.9
CENTRAL OFFICE STAFF	2	81.0	2	80.8	2	67.5	5	40.1	2	70.2
TEACHERS	4	64.8	4	57.2	4	55.6	3	47.4	4	55.7
OTHER EMPLOYEES	7	32.7	7	25.6	7	27.7	9	23.7	7	26.7
PARENTS	3	73.2	3	63.4	3	64.1	2	59.9	3	64.0
STUDENTS	8	20.7	8	18.6	8	25.2	6	27.2	8	22.8
COMMUNITY SPECIAL INTEREST GROUPS	6	46.1	6	35.2	6	31.3	8	25.4	6	33.1
COMMUNITY LOCAL POWER STRUCTURE	5	52.5	5	43.3	5	40.2	4	40.5	5	42.4
NATIONAL SCHOOL BOARD ORGANIZATION	10	6.4	10	6.3	10	6.1	10	9.3	10	6.6
OTHER	11	14.9	9	16.3	9	20.0	7	25.5	9	19.1

TABLE 5.37 BOARD MEMBERS' SOURCES OF INFORMATION — 1992-1982 COMPARISON

	VERY GREAT WEIGHT		CONSIDERABLE WEIGHT		SOME WEIGHT		LITTLE WEIGHT		NO WEIGHT		DON'T KNOW AT ALL	
	1992 %	1982 %	1992 %	1982 %	1992 %	1982 %	1992 %	1982 %	1992 %	1982 %	1992 %	1982 %
DISTRICT SUPERINTENDENT	72.6	76.1	21.3	18.7	3.5	2.8	0.8	0.7	1.2	1.2	0.6	0.4
CENTRAL OFFICE STAFF	22.2	21.2	48.0	45.2	20.9	20.9	3.5	5.4	3.2	4.1	2.2	3.2
PARENTS	13.9	17.9	50.1	48.7	31.4	29.8	3.6	3.3	0.6	0.1	0.4	0.2
LOCAL POWER STRUCTURE	12.3	12.5	30.1	27.1	36.5	36.0	15.4	17.2	3.9	5.0	1.8	2.0
SPECIAL INTEREST GROUPS	8.3	9.0	24.8	23.9	45.7	43.9	17.0	19.6	2.5	2.7	1.6	0.8
SCHOOL BOARD ORGANIZATIONS		6.1		30.5		36.3		19.3		6.7		1.0
STATE SCHOOL BOARD ORGANIZATION	3.3		15.8		37.3		29.6		13.2		0.9	
NATIONAL SCHOOL BOARD ORGANIZATION	0.6		6.0		25.5		40.0		25.9		2.1	
TEACHERS/TEACHER ORGANIZATION	9.8	4.1	45.9	26.1	40.2	47.6	3.9	17.0	0.1	4.3	0.1	0.8
OTHER EMPLOYEES	3.2	2.5	23.5	21.9	55.8	55.2	15.8	18.3	1.3	1.6	0.3	0.5

IF THEY COULD DO IT ALL OVER AGAIN

For the most part, superintendents said they would still be superintendents if they could "do it all over again." Sixty-seven percent gave this answer, with "outside of education" trailing far behind at 14.1 percent (see **Table 5.38**). Obviously, most superintendents feel they are in a worthwhile career.

TABLE 5.38 IF SUPERINTENDENTS HAD TO DO IT ALL OVER AGAIN, WOULD THEY CHOOSE CAREER AS:

CAREER CHOICE	GROUP A: 25,000 OR MORE PUPILS		GROUP B: 3,000-24,999 PUPILS		GROUP C: 300-2,999 PUPILS		GROUP D: FEWER THAN 300 PUPILS		NATIONAL UNWEIGHTED PROFILE	
	No.	%	No.	%	No.	%	No.	%	No.	%
SCHOOL SUPERINTENDENT	104	72.7	435	71.8	476	67.2	141	56.6	1,153	67.7
OTHER CENTRAL OFFICE ADMINISTRATOR	2	1.4	17	2.8	18	2.6	10	4.0	47	2.8
CLASSROOM TEACHER	1	0.7	6	1.0	19	2.7	14	5.6	40	2.4
GUIDANCE COUNSELOR	1	0.7	6	1.0	5	0.7	5	2.0	17	1.0
COLLEGE PROFESSOR	6	4.2	21	3.5	25	3.6	12	4.8	64	3.8
BUSINESS MANAGER	1	0.7	1	0.2	3	0.4	1	0.4	6	0.4
STATE AGENCY EMPLOYEE	0	0.0	1	0.2	3	0.4	1	0.4	5	0.3
INTERMEDIATE SCHOOL DISTRICT ADMINISTRATOR	10	7.0	15	2.5	9	1.3	2	0.8	36	2.1
PRINCIPAL	3	2.1	16	2.6	27	3.8	19	7.6	65	3.8
OUTSIDE OF EDUCATION	13	9.1	80	13.2	110	15.6	37	14.9	240	14.1
OTHER	2	1.4	8	1.3	12	1.7	7	2.8	29	1.7
TOTAL	143	8.4	606	35.6	704	41.4	249	14.6	1,702	100.0

Minority and Women Superintendents

DEMOGRAPHICS

Of the 1,724 superintendents responding to *The 1992 Study of the American School Superintendency*, only 182 are women, minorities or both. A total of 115 women superintendents responded, 6.7 percent of the total, which is an increase from the 1982 and 1971 studies when women respondents represented 1.2 and 1.3 percent of the total. Sixty-seven minority superintendents responded to the survey, compared to the 1,656 nonminority superintendents. (The responses for this chapter are figured two ways and are broken out according to all men, all women, all nonminority, and all minority superintendents responding, as shown in **Table 6.1**.)

Even though some minorities and a few women hold the largest and highest salaried superintendencies in the nation, they are still underrepresented among the ranks of American public school superintendents.

Age

Women superintendents, on the average, are younger than the average male or nonminority superintendent. Nearly 70 percent of women superintendents are younger than the mean national age for superintendents of 49.8 years. Minority superintendents, on the other hand, are very near the mean age of the total respondent group (see **Table 6.2**).

Political Affiliation

As shown in **Table 6.3**, women and minority superintendents more often are Democrats than their nonminority, male colleagues. Fully 66.2 percent of

TABLE 6.1 NUMBERS BY GENDER AND ETHNICITY

		No.	%	%
GENDER	MALES	1,607	92.7	93.3
	FEMALES	115	6.6	6.7
	NO RESPONSE	2	0.7	0.0
	TOTAL	1,724	100.0	100.0
ETHNIC	NONMINORITY	1,656	95.5	96.1
	MINORITY	67	3.9	3.9
	NO RESPONSE	1	0.6	0.0
	TOTAL	1,724	100.0	100.0

TABLE 6.2 AGE OF SUPERINTENDENTS BY GENDER AND MINORITY STATUS

AGE GROUP	GENDER MALE No.	%	GENDER FEMALE No.	%	ETHNIC NONMINORITY No.	%	ETHNIC MINORITY No.	%
30-35	15	0.9	2	1.7	15	0.9	3	4.5
36-40	85	5.3	20	17.4	100	6.0	4	6.0
41-45	296	18.4	30	26.1	312	18.8	12	17.9
46-50	436	27.1	28	24.3	450	27.2	13	19.4
51-55	398	24.8	20	17.4	402	24.3	17	25.4
56-60	282	17.5	9	7.8	280	16.9	14	20.9
61-65	83	5.2	5	4.3	84	5.1	4	6.0
66+	12	0.7	1	0.9	13	0.8	0	0.0
TOTAL	1,607	99.9	115	99.9	1,656	100.0	67	100.1

minority superintendents say they favor the Democratic party, while only 33.6 percent of nonminority superintendents say they are Democrats. Almost half (48.2 percent) of women superintendents indicate they are Democrats. This is probably because many women and minority superintendents hold positions in urban districts where board members and the community at large tend to vote Democrat.

Political Posture

Minority and women superintendents are decidedly more liberal than their nonminority and male counterparts. However, the majority of all groups indicated they view themselves as political moderates (see **Table 6.4**).

Education Level of Parents

Fathers' education. The fathers of minority superintendents had less schooling than their nonminority

counterparts. For instance, 15.4 percent of minority superintendents said their fathers had graduated from high school, as opposed to 26.2 percent of nonminority respondents. Women superintendents report that 27.4 percent of their fathers had graduated from high school, compared to 25.8 percent of fathers of male superintendents (see **Table 6.5**).

Mothers' education. The mothers of minority superintendents also possessed somewhat less education than mothers of their nonminority colleagues. However, fewer mothers of women superintendents had an eighth grade or less education than male superintendents, and more women superintendents' mothers had attended graduate school than male superintendents (See **Table 6.6**).

TABLE 6.3 POLITICAL PARTY AFFILIATION

	GENDER MALE		GENDER FEMALE		ETHNIC NONMINORITY		ETHNIC MINORITY	
	No.	%	No.	%	No.	%	No.	%
DEMOCRAT	535	33.6	55	48.2	552	33.6	43	66.2
INDEPENDENT	453	28.5	28	24.6	465	28.3	13	20.0
REPUBLICAN	603	37.9	31	27.2	624	38.0	9	13.8
TOTAL	1,591	100.0	114	100.0	1,641	99.9	65	100.0

TABLE 6.4 POLITICAL POSTURE/VIEWS

	GENDER MALE		GENDER FEMALE		ETHNIC NONMINORITY		ETHNIC MINORITY	
	No.	%	No.	%	No.	%	No.	%
LIBERAL	159	10.0	26	23.0	166	10.1	19	29.7
MODERATE	969	60.8	70	61.9	1,004	61.0	40	62.5
CONSERVATIVE	466	29.2	18	15.0	475	28.9	5	7.8
TOTAL	1,594	100.0	113	99.9	1,645	100.0	64	100.0

TABLE 6.5 EDUCATION LEVEL OF FATHER

	GENDER MALE		GENDER FEMALE		ETHNIC NONMINORITY		ETHNIC MINORITY	
	No.	%	No.	%	No.	%	No.	%
8TH GRADE OR LESS	492	31.2	24	21.2	489	30.1	27	41.5
SOME HIGH SCHOOL	254	16.1	20	17.7	261	16.1	12	18.5
COMPLETED HIGH SCHOOL	407	25.8	31	27.4	425	26.2	10	15.4
SOME COLLEGE	142	9.0	16	14.2	155	9.6	3	4.6
TECHNICAL/TRADE SCHOOL	34	2.2	1	0.9	35	2.2	1	1.5
GRADUATED COLLEGE	93	5.9	9	8.0	100	6.2	5	7.7
ATTENDED GRADUATE SCHOOL	21	1.3	2	1.8	22	1.4	1	1.5
HAVE GRADUATE DEGREE	132	8.4	10	8.8	136	8.4	6	9.2
TOTAL	1,575	99.9	113	100.0	1623	100.2	65	99.9

Type of Community Lived in Before College

Without question, women and minority superintendents come from more urban backgrounds than nonminority and male superintendents (see **Table 6.7**). More than one-third (34.8 percent) of the minority superintendents lived in cities exceeding 100,000 in population before attending college. By contrast, as shown in **Table 6.8**, 40.7 percent of nonminority superintendents lived in towns with fewer than 2,500 in population before attending college.

CAREER PATHS—THE ROAD MORE TRAVELED

First Administrative Position

A slightly larger percentage of women than men skipped the principalship and went straight from teaching to central office administration. Women superintendents often gained their first administrative positions at the elementary level (29.8 percent), the central-office level (24.6 percent), or in a building-level position not specified as elementary or secondary (see **Table 6.9**).

More women than men began their administrative careers at the elementary level. This was also true for

TABLE 6.6 EDUCATION LEVEL OF MOTHER

	GENDER MALE		GENDER FEMALE		ETHNIC NONMINORITY		ETHNIC MINORITY	
	No.	%	No.	%	No.	%	No.	%
8TH GRADE OR LESS	333	21.2	14	12.4	330	20.4	19	29.7
SOME HIGH SCHOOL	241	15.3	18	15.9	243	15.0	14	21.9
COMPLETED HIGH SCHOOL	549	34.9	42	37.2	573	35.3	15	23.4
SOME COLLEGE	157	10.0	10	8.8	162	10.0	5	7.8
TECHNICAL/TRADE SCHOOL	52	3.3	5	4.4	56	3.5	1	1.6
GRADUATED COLLEGE	153	9.7	11	9.7	164	10.1	4	6.3
ATTENDED GRADUATE SCHOOL	21	1.3	9	8.0	29	1.8	1	1.6
HAVE GRADUATE DEGREE	66	4.2	4	3.5	64	3.9	5	7.8
TOTAL	1,572	99.9	113	99.9	1,621	100.0	64	100.1

TABLE 6.7 WHICH OF THE FOLLOWING BEST DESCRIBES THE TYPE OF THE COMMUNITY IN WHICH YOU LIVED BEFORE COLLEGE?

	GENDER MALE		GENDER FEMALE		ETHNIC NONMINORITY		ETHNIC MINORITY	
	No.	%	No.	%	No.	%	No.	%
RURAL	504	31.6	35	31.0	520	31.6	19	29.2
SMALL TOWN	666	41.7	35	31.0	681	41.4	20	30.8
SUBURBAN	195	12.2	18	15.9	212	12.9	2	3.1
LARGE CITY	231	14.5	25	22.1	232	14.1	24	36.9
TOTAL	1,596	100.0	113	100.0	1645	100.0	65	100.0

TABLE 6.8 WHICH OF THE FOLLOWING BEST DESCRIBES THE SIZE OF THE COMMUNITY IN WHICH YOU LIVED BEFORE COLLEGE?

	GENDER MALE		GENDER FEMALE		ETHNIC NONMINORITY		ETHNIC MINORITY	
	No.	%	No.	%	No.	%	No.	%
UNDER 2,500	644	40.2	42	37.2	672	40.7	16	24.2
2,500-9,999	376	23.5	15	13.3	375	22.7	14	21.2
10,000-99,999	361	22.5	36	31.9	384	23.3	13	19.8
100,000 +	222	13.8	20	17.7	220	13.3	23	34.8
TOTAL	1,603	100.0	113	100.1	1,651	100.0	66	100.0

minority superintendents, who began their administrative careers at the building level even more frequently than women. Minority superintendents also are more likely to have begun their careers at the elementary level than nonminority superintendents.

Length of Classroom Service Before Entering Administration

Women superintendents, on average, spend a longer time as classroom teachers than do men. Almost half of the men surveyed said they spent only about five years as a teacher. Twice as many female as male superintendents have spent 10 or more years in the classroom. Minority superintendents are a bit closer to their nonminority counterparts in classroom teaching experience (see **Table 6.10**).

Age When Appointed to First Administrative Position

Women generally are appointed to their first administrative positions later than men or minorities.

Nearly 60 percent of males were appointed to their first administrative position before age 30. Only 29.6 percent of women superintendents had obtained their first administrative position before age 30. Minority superintendents, on average, received their first administrative positions at about the same age as nonminority superintendents (see **Table 6.11**).

Nature of Superintendents' First Administrative Position

The most common first administrative position women superintendents held is as a coordinator or director of a special program. The second most often held by women starting their administrative careers is assistant principal, also true for other groups. However, 43.6 percent of male superintendents first served in a principalship, while only 11.6 percent of women superintendents gained a principalship as their first administrative position. Many minority superintendents report they started their administrative careers as a coordinator or assistant principal (see **Table 6.12**).

TABLE 6.9 NATURE OF FIRST ADMINISTRATIVE POSITION

	GENDER MALE		GENDER FEMALE		ETHNIC NONMINORITY		ETHNIC MINORITY	
	No.	%	No.	%	No.	%	No.	%
ELEMENTARY SCHOOL	405	25.5	34	29.8	420	25.7	21	32.3
JUNIOR HIGH	207	13.1	7	6.1	204	12.5	9	13.8
HIGH SCHOOL	581	36.6	15	13.2	579	35.4	17	26.2
PAROCHIAL SCHOOL	5	0.3	0	0.0	5	0.3	0	0.0
MIDDLE SCHOOL	36	2.3	4	3.5	40	2.4	0	0.0
COLLEGE	17	1.1	1	0.9	17	1.0	1	1.5
VOCATIONAL	19	1.2	2	1.8	20	1.2	1	1.5
CENTRAL OFFICE	188	11.9	28	24.6	206	12.6	10	15.4
OTHER	128	8.1	23	20.2	145	8.9	6	9.2
TOTAL	1,586	100.1	114	100.1	1,636	100.0	65	99.9

TABLE 6.10 LENGTH OF SERVICE AS CLASSROOM TEACHER BEFORE ENTERING ADMINISTRATION OR SUPERVISION

	GENDER MALE		GENDER FEMALE		ETHNIC NONMINORITY		ETHNIC MINORITY	
YEARS AS TEACHER	No.	%	No.	%	No.	%	No.	%
0 - 5	798	49.8	25	21.7	788	47.7	37	55.2
6 - 10	570	35.5	53	46.1	601	36.4	22	32.8
11 - 15	179	11.2	29	25.2	202	12.2	5	7.5
16 - 20	43	2.7	4	3.5	45	2.7	3	4.5
21 - 25	10	0.6	2	1.7	11	0.7	0	0.0
26 +	4	0.2	2	1.7	6	0.4	0	0.0
TOTAL	1,604	100.0	115	99.9	1,653	100.1	67	100.0

Career Pattern Prior to the Superintendency

The career patterns of women superintendents differ from men in that women more often jump from the classroom past the principalship directly into a central office position before becoming a superintendent. Women are less likely to follow the track of teacher and principal before becoming a superintendent. However, a slightly greater number of women than men follow the track of teacher, principal, and central office employee. On the other hand, minority superintendents are almost twice as likely than nonminorities to follow a career pattern of teacher, principal, central office administrator, and superintendent (see **Table 6.13**).

Place-Bound Succession

Minority and women superintendents succeed to their positions from inside the district about as often as nonminority and male superintendents (group mean: 36.3 percent). The majority in each group

TABLE 6.11 AGE WHEN APPOINTED TO FIRST ADMINISTRATIVE POSITION

AGE	GENDER MALE No.	%	GENDER FEMALE No.	%	ETHNIC NONMINORITY No.	%	ETHNIC MINORITY No.	%
25-30	959	59.9	34	29.6	957	58.0	36	54.5
31-35	463	28.9	40	34.8	484	29.3	18	27.3
35-40	126	7.9	22	19.1	140	8.5	10	15.2
41-50	49	3.1	16	13.9	63	3.8	2	3.0
51+	3	0.2	3	2.6	6	0.4	0	0.0
TOTAL	1,600	100.0	115	100.0	1,650	100.0	66	100.0

TABLE 6.12 NATURE OF SUPERINTENDENTS' FIRST ADMINISTRATIVE POSITION

FIRST ADMINISTRATIVE POSITION	GENDER MALE No.	%	GENDER FEMALE No.	%	ETHNIC NONMINORITY No.	%	ETHNIC MINORITY No.	%
ASSIST. PRINCIPAL	485	30.6	31	27.7	493	29.3	24	35.8
DEAN OF STUDENTS	30	1.9	2	1.8	30	1.8	2	3.0
PRINCIPAL	690	43.6	13	11.6	684	40.6	18	26.9
DIRECTOR-COORDINATOR	186	11.7	36	32.1	260	15.4	17	25.4
ASSISTANT SUPERINTENDENT	32	2.0	3	2.7	34	2.0	1	1.5
STATE AGENCY	11	0.7	3	2.7	14	0.8	1	1.5
BUSINESS OFFICE	16	1.0	0	0.0	16	1.0	0	0.0
OTHER	134	8.5	24	21.4	153	9.1	4	6.0
TOTAL	1,584	100.0	112	100.0	1,684	100.0	67	100.1

TABLE 6.13 CAREER PATTERN PRIOR TO THE SUPERINTENDENCY

CAREER PATTERN	GENDER MALE No.	%	GENDER FEMALE No.	%	ETHNIC NONMINORITY No.	%	ETHNIC MINORITY No.	%
TEACHER ONLY	81	5.4	13	13.1	93	6.0	0	0.0
PRINCIPAL ONLY	62	4.1	3	3.0	62	4.0	3	5.2
CENTRAL OFFICE ONLY	30	2.0	2	2.0	29	1.9	3	5.2
TEACHER & PRINCIPAL	564	37.5	22	22.2	577	37.2	8	13.8
TEACHER & CENTRAL OFFICE	147	9.8	19	19.2	158	10.2	8	13.8
PRINCIPAL & CENTRAL OFFICE	58	3.9	1	1.0	58	3.7	1	1.7
TEACHER, PRINCIPAL,& CENTRAL OFFICE	564	37.5	39	39.4	572	36.9	35	60.3
TOTAL	1,506	100.2	99	99.9	1,549	99.9	58	100.0

came into the superintendency from another district, however (see **Table 6.14**).

Duration of Career in the Same District

Very few women or minority superintendents have spent their entire professional careers in the same district. Minority superintendents, to a very slight degree, have spent more of their careers in the same districts (see **Table 6.15**).

Length of Time Spent Seeking First Superintendency

Women superintendents found their first superintendency faster than minority superintendents or men in general. It is interesting that 67.3 percent of women superintendents say they found their first superintendency in less than a year. Fewer than half (49.2 percent) of minority superintendents say it took less than a year, compared to 53.7 percent of nonminority male superintendents (see **Table 6.16**).

TABLE 6.14 SUCCESSOR TYPES: CAREER OR PLACE-BOUND

SUCCESSOR TYPE	GENDER MALE		GENDER FEMALE		ETHNIC NONMINORITY		ETHNIC MINORITY	
	No.	%	No.	%	No.	%	No.	%
PLACE-BOUND(INSIDE)	566	35.5	44	39.6	590	36.0	23	34.3
CAREER-BOUND(OUTSIDE)	1,029	64.5	67	60.4	1,050	64.0	44	65.7
TOTAL	1,595	100.0	111	100.0	1,640	100.0	67	100.0

TABLE 6.15 HAVE YOU SPENT YOUR ENTIRE EDUCATION CAREER IN ONE SCHOOL DISTRICT?

	GENDER MALE		GENDER FEMALE		ETHNIC NONMINORITY		ETHNIC MINORITY	
	No.	%	No.	%	No.	%	No.	%
YES	121	8.3	6	5.5	122	8.1	6	10.2
NO	1,330	91.7	103	94.5	1,379	91.9	53	89.8
TOTAL	1,451	100.0	109	100.0	1,501	100.0	59	100.0

TABLE 6.16 LENGTH OF TIME SEEKING SUPERINTENDENCY AFTER EARNING CERTIFICATION

LENGTH OF TIME	GENDER MALE		GENDER FEMALE		ETHNIC NONMINORITY		ETHNIC MINORITY	
	No.	%	No.	%	No.	%	No.	%
LESS THAN 1 YR	749	52.5	68	67.3	789	53.7	29	49.2
1 YEAR	210	14.7	7	6.9	210	14.3	7	11.9
2 YEARS	190	13.3	13	12.9	202	13.7	1	1.7
3 YEARS	111	7.8	7	6.9	108	7.3	8	13.6
4 YEARS	39	2.7	2	2.0	38	2.6	2	3.4
5 + YEARS	129	9.0	4	4.0	123	8.4	12	20.3
TOTAL	1,428	100.0	101	100.0	1,470	100.0	59	100.1

TABLE 6.17 WHAT IS THE TOTAL (ALL AGES) POPULATION OF YOUR SCHOOL DISTRICT?

POPULATION	GENDER MALE		GENDER FEMALE		ETHNIC NONMINORITY		ETHNIC MINORITY	
	No.	%	No.	%	No.	%	No.	%
200,000 AND OVER	87	5.5	6	5.4	87	5.3	6	9.2
100,000 TO 199,999	76	4.8	5	4.5	72	4.4	9	13.8
50,000 TO 99,999	159	10.0	8	7.1	154	9.4	15	23.1
30,000 TO 49,999	175	11.0	9	8.0	181	11.0	3	4.6
10,000 TO 29,000	368	23.1	21	18.8	382	23.2	10	15.4
25,000 TO 9,999	407	25.5	25	22.3	415	25.2	15	23.1
FEWER THAN 2,500	324	20.3	38	33.9	353	21.5	7	10.8
TOTAL	1,596	100.2	112	100.0	1,644	100.0	65	100.0

Populations of Communities

Women superintendents for the most part serve in school districts with populations of fewer than 10,000. The majority—56.2 percent—work in districts with fewer than 10,000 students, and 33.9 percent serve districts with populations of fewer than 2,500, compared to 45.8 percent and 20.3 percent, respectively, for male superintendents. Approximately 17 percent of women superintendents serve communities with more than 50,000 people (see **Table 6.17**).

Minority superintendents often serve in communities that are more populous. Some 46 percent of minority superintendents serve districts in which the population exceeds 50,000, according to the 1990 study.

A LEG UP: MENTORING, HIRING PRACTICES

Are Superintendents Mentors?

Nearly all superintendents, including women and minorities, consider themselves mentors. Minority superintendents more often see themselves as mentors than nonminority superintendents. The same is true of women superintendents (see **Table 6.18**).

Do Minority and Women Superintendents Have Mentors?

Women and minority superintendents had mentors more often than did male and nonminority superintendents. However, the differences are not great. As shown in **Table 6.19**, women had mentors 59.1 percent of the time, while men and minority superintendents had mentors 48 percent and 55.2 percent of the time respectively.

Who Manages the Search?

For the most part, local school boards manage the search process for current superintendents. Professional search firms also are likely to have managed searches that result in hiring minority and women superintendents, according to the 1992 survey (see **Table 6.20**). This might be true because higher percentages of minority superintendents serve in larger districts, which might use professional search firms more often than smaller districts.

61

TABLE 6.18 DO YOU CONSIDER YOURSELF A MENTOR?

	GENDER MALE		GENDER FEMALE		ETHNIC NONMINORITY		ETHNIC MINORITY	
	No.	%	No.	%	No.	%	No.	%
YES	1,148	71.7	91	79.1	1,184	71.8	55	82.1
NO	334	20.9	15	13.0	342	20.7	7	10.4
DON'T KNOW	119	7.4	9	7.8	124	7.5	5	7.5
TOTAL	1,601	100.0	115	99.9	1,650	100.0	67	100.0

TABLE 6.19 DO YOU, OR DID YOU EVER, HAVE A MENTOR?

	GENDER MALE		GENDER FEMALE		ETHNIC NONMINORITY		ETHNIC MINORITY	
	No.	%	No.	%	No.	%	No.	%
YES	767	48.0	68	59.1	800	48.5	37	55.2
NO	794	49.7	47	40.9	811	49.2	29	43.3
DON'T KNOW	38	2.4	0	0.0	37	2.2	1	1.5
TOTAL	1,599	100.1	115	100.0	1,648	99.9	67	100.0

TABLE 6.20 WHAT GROUP/INDIVIDUALS MANAGED THE SEARCH PROCESS FOR CURRENT SUPERINTENDENCY?

GROUP	GENDER MALE		GENDER FEMALE		ETHNIC NONMINORITY		ETHNIC MINORITY	
	No.	%	No.	%	No.	%	No.	%
PROFESSIONAL SEARCH FIRM	217	13.7	20	17.9	222	13.6	17	26.2
STATE SCHOOL BOARDS ASSOCIATION	177	11.1	12	10.7	182	11.1	7	10.8
LOCAL SCHOOL BOARD MEMBERS	997	62.8	63	56.3	1,028	62.8	33	50.8
OTHER	197	12.4	17	15.2	204	12.5	8	12.3
TOTAL	1,588	100.0	112	100.1	1,636	100.0	65	100.1

Influence of the Old Boy/Old Girl Network

Women superintendents indicate strongly they had been helped by the "old boy/old girl network." In short, someone made a significant effort to help them get their positions. Fully 80.7 percent of women superintendents say they benefited from this special assistance. Minority superintendents say they received help from a mentor 68.2 percent of the time, compared to 54.9 percent for males and 56 percent of all nonminorities. Very often the "old boy/girl network" is cited as a hindrance for women and minorities in gaining positions, but this appears not to be true in the public school superintendency (see **Table 6.21**).

DISCRIMINATION

Discriminatory Hiring Practices Faced by Women

Women and minority superintendents were much more likely to think that discriminatory hiring practices faced by women are a problem than did male and nonminority superintendents. Women superintendents think that discriminatory hiring practices are a major problem for them almost four times more often (43.8 percent versus 11.7 percent) than men. Minority

superintendents think discrimination against women is a serious problem almost three times more often (35.8 percent versus 12.9 percent) than nonminority superintendents. On the other hand, 40.2 percent of women superintendents and 37.3 percent of minority superintendents think discriminatory hiring practices against women are a minor problem (see **Table 6.22**).

Discriminatory Hiring Practices Faced by Minorities

Similarly, according to the 1992 study, women and minority superintendents think that discriminatory hiring practices against minorities are a major problem, while their nonminority colleagues perceive little difficulty. In fact, 59.7 percent of minority superintendents say hiring discrimination is a major problem compared to only 16.6 percent of nonminority superintendents (see **Table 6.23**).

PRESTIGE, SATISFACTION, FULFILLMENT

Prestige and Influence of the Superintendency

Minority superintendents perceive the prestige and influence of the superintendency increasing more than do nonminorities. As well, more women super-

TABLE 6.21 HAS THE "OLD BOY/OLD GIRL NETWORK" BEEN EFFECTIVE IN ADVANCING YOUR CAREER?

	GENDER MALE		GENDER FEMALE		ETHNIC NONMINORITY		ETHNIC MINORITY	
	No.	%	No.	%	No.	%	No.	%
YES	879	54.9	92	80.7	923	56.0	45	68.2
NO	501	31.3	13	11.4	510	30.9	8	12.1
DO NOT KNOW	220	13.8	9	7.9	216	13.1	13	19.7
TOTAL	1600	100.0	114	100.0	1649	100.0	66	100.0

TABLE 6.22 SEVERITY OF PROBLEM OF DISCRIMINATORY HIRING PRACTICES FOR WOMEN

SEVERITY OF PROBLEM	GENDER MALE		GENDER FEMALE		ETHNIC NONMINORITY		ETHNIC MINORITY	
	No.	%	No.	%	No.	%	No.	%
MAJOR PROBLEM	187	11.7	49	43.8	212	12.9	24	35.8
MINOR PROBLEM	589	36.9	45	40.2	609	37.1	25	37.3
LITTLE PROBLEM	510	31.9	13	11.6	513	31.2	9	13.4
NO PROBLEM	311	19.5	5	4.5	309	18.8	9	13.4
TOTAL	1,597	100.0	112	100.1	1,643	100.0	67	99.9

TABLE 6.23 SEVERITY OF PROBLEM OF DISCRIMINATORY HIRING PRACTICES FOR MINORITIES

SEVERITY OF PROBLEM	GENDER MALE		GENDER FEMALE		ETHNIC NONMINORITY		ETHNIC MINORITY	
	No.	%	No.	%	No.	%	No.	%
MAJOR PROBLEM	266	16.7	48	42.1	272	16.6	40	59.7
MINOR PROBLEM	581	36.5	45	39.5	610	37.2	18	26.9
LITTLE PROBLEM	493	30.9	14	12.3	503	30.7	4	6.0
NO PROBLEM	253	15.9	7	6.1	256	15.6	5	7.5
TOTAL	1,593	100.0	114	100.0	1,641	100.1	67	100.1

intendents than men see it as increasing, but to a lesser degree than do minority superintendents. Male superintendents think levels of prestige and influence remained about the same (see **Table 6.24**).

Who Would "Do It All Over Again"?

The vast majority of superintendents would choose the superintendency again if they had the opportunity. Minority superintendents respond more strongly that they would make the same choice than either nonminorities or women superintendents, even though they see many difficult problems and challenges and endure a substantial amount of stress. The response given second in frequency by all groups was "outside of education" (see **Table 6.25**).

Degree of Fulfillment

Most superintendents—women, minorities, and nonminorities— derive considerable satisfaction from being a superintendent. Minority superintendents feel greater satisfaction than other groups. Approximately

one-third of women, men, and nonminority superintendents indicate they receive moderate fulfillment, and the rest say they get considerable fulfillment. Almost three-quarters of minority superintendents indicate they achieve considerable fulfillment in the superintendency (see **Table 6.26**).

POWER, INFLUENCE, AND DECISION MAKING

Who Takes the Lead in Developing Policy?

About two-thirds of the time, both male and female superintendents take the lead in developing district policy, as shown in **Table 6.27**. Minority superintendents tend to share this responsibility more than other superintendents, very likely because minority superintendents often have large districts with larger boards.

Who Prepares the Agenda for Board Meetings?

Minority and women superintendents prepare the board agenda without participation by board mem-

TABLE 6.24 WHAT IS THE STATUS/PRESTIGE OF THE POSITION OF SUPERINTENDENT?

STATUS/PRESTIGE	GENDER MALE		GENDER FEMALE		ETHNIC NONMINORITY		ETHNIC MINORITY	
	No.	%	No.	%	No.	%	No.	%
DECREASE IN IMPORTANCE/INFLUENCE	245	15.3	9	7.8	245	14.8	8	11.9
REMAINS THE SAME	671	41.9	40	34.8	705	42.7	9	13.4
INCREASE IN IMPORTANCE/INFLUENCE	567	35.4	51	44.3	572	34.7	44	65.7
DO NOT KNOW	118	7.4	15	13.0	128	7.8	6	9.0
TOTAL	1,601	100.0	115	99.9	1,650	100.0	67	100.0

TABLE 6.25 IF YOU HAD THE CHANCE TO START OVER, WOULD YOU CHOOSE A CAREER AS:

	GENDER MALE		GENDER FEMALE		ETHNIC NONMINORITY		ETHNIC MINORITY	
	No.	%	No.	%	No.	%	No.	%
SCHOOL SUPERINTENDENT	1,082	68.2	70	61.4	1,103	67.5	53	79.1
OTHER CENTRAL OFFICE POSITION	41	2.6	6	5.3	45	2.8	2	3.0
CLASSROOM TECHER	34	2.1	6	5.3	38	2.3	1	1.5
GUIDANCE COUNSELOR	15	0.9	1	0.9	16	1.0	0	0.0
COLLEGE PROFESSOR	60	3.8	4	3.5	62	3.8	2	3.0
BUSINESS MANAGER	5	0.3	1	0.9	6	0.4	0	0.0
STATE AGENCY EMPLOYEE	5	0.3	0	0.0	5	0.3	0	0.0
INTERMEDIATE SCHOOL ADMINISTRATOR	34	2.1	2	1.8	35	2.1	1	1.5
PRINCIPAL	61	3.8	4	3.5	63	3.9	1	1.5
PROFESSIONAL OUTSIDE OF EDUCATION	223	14.1	17	14.9	232	14.2	7	10.4
OTHER	26	1.6	3	2.6	29	1.8	0	0.0
TOTAL	1,586	99.8	114	100.1	1,634	100.1	69	100.0

bers somewhat less often than male and nonminority superintendents (see **Table 6.28**).

Parent/Community Participation in Decision Making

Women and minority superintendents often work in districts with greater levels of parent and community involvement in decision making. When asked how willing parents and the community are to participate in decision making, 71.2 percent of minorities, in contrast to 49.1 percent of nonminorities, said they are more willing. This percentage was smaller for female superintendents, but still greater than that of men (see **Table 6.29**). Whether these superintendents foster this kind of behavior is unknown, but the data triggers this interesting question.

Community Group Pressure on the Board

A total of 77.6 percent of minority superintendents report that pressure groups had emerged during the

TABLE 6.26. HOW MUCH SELF-FULFILLMENT DOES YOUR POSITION OF SUPERINTENDENT PROVIDE?

	GENDER MALE		GENDER FEMALE		ETHNIC NONMINORITY		ETHNIC MINORITY	
	No.	%	No.	%	No.	%	No.	%
NONE	6	0.4	0	0.0	6	0.4	0	0.0
LITTLE	49	3.1	0	0.0	45	2.7	3	4.5
MODERATE	550	34.4	38	34.2	571	34.8	14	20.9
CONSIDERABLE	993	62.1	73	65.8	1,021	62.1	50	74.6
TOTAL	1,598	100.0	111	100.0	1,643	100.0	67	100.0

TABLE 6.27 WHO TAKES THE LEAD IN DEVELOPING POLICY?

	GENDER MALE		GENDER FEMALE		ETHNIC NONMINORITY		ETHNIC MINORITY	
	No.	%	No.	%	No.	%	No.	%
SCHOOL BOARD	54	3.4	6	5.2	57	3.5	3	4.5
BOARD CHAIRPERSON	6	0.4	1	0.9	6	0.4	1	1.5
SUPERINTENDENT	1,075	67.3	72	62.6	1,110	67.4	36	53.7
SHARE RESPONSIBILITY	453	28.3	35	30.4	464	28.2	27	40.3
OTHER	10	0.6	1	0.9	10	0.6	0	0.0
TOTAL	1,598	100.0	115	100.0	1,647	100.1	67	100.0

TABLE 6.28 WHO PREPARES THE AGENDA FOR BOARD MEETINGS?

	GENDER MALE		GENDER FEMALE		ETHNIC NONMINORITY		ETHNIC MINORITY	
	No.	%	No.	%	No.	%	No.	%
SUPERINTENDENT	1,242	77.6	72	63.2	1,268	76.9	46	68.7
BOARD CHAIRPERSON	2	0.1	2	1.8	4	0.2	0	0.0
SHARED RESPONSIBILITY	347	21.7	36	31.6	363	22.0	21	31.3
OTHER	10	0.6	4	3.5	14	0.8	0	0.0
TOTAL	1,601	100.0	114	100.1	1,649	99.9	69	100.0

TABLE 6.29 HOW WILLING ARE PARENTS/THE COMMUNITY TO PARTICIPATE IN DECISION MAKING?

	GENDER MALE		GENDER FEMALE		ETHNIC NONMINORITY		ETHNIC MINORITY	
	No.	%	No.	%	No.	%	No.	%
MORE WILLING	788	49.2	67	58.3	811	49.1	47	71.2
ABOUT THE SAME	176	11.0	8	7.0	180	10.9	3	4.5
LESS WILLING	622	38.8	38	33.0	643	38.9	16	24.2
DO NOT KNOW	16	1.0	2	1.7	18	1.1	0	0.0
TOTAL	1,602	100.0	115	100.0	1,652	100.0	66	99.9

past decade to lobby their board members. The same was true for 63.8 percent of nonminority superintendents and 67.5 percent of women superintendents (see **Table 6.30**).

THE MOST DIFFICULT PROBLEMS FACING SCHOOL BOARDS

As perceived by all superintendents, financial issues were the highest ranked problem. Women superintendents were slightly less concerned about their boards facing financial issues. All superintendents have similar opinions on other potential problems listed in the survey. Minority superintendents are slightly more concerned about internal board conflict, probably because they work with larger boards in larger districts and are subject to more pressure groups. "Understanding appropriate board roles" was second in frequency of mention for all groups (see **Table 6.31**).

HIGHEST ACADEMIC DEGREE HELD

A greater percentage of women and minority superintendents hold doctorates than their male and nonminority counterparts. While 41.1 percent of the female respondents hold doctorates, 35.9 percent of the

males hold Ph.D.'s. The disparity was even greater between minorities and nonminorities, with 54.5 percent and 35.4 percent, respectively. Women and minority superintendents also are slightly more supportive of their graduate programs than other superintendents (see **Tables 6.32** and **6.33**).

USEFULNESS OF RESEARCH

Minority and women superintendents are considerably more supportive of educational research than other superintendents. Of women superintendents, 42.5 percent find research highly useful, while only 22.8 percent of males found it highly useful. Among minority superintendents, 49.3 percent found it highly useful, compared to 23.1 percent of nonminority superintendents.

ESSENTIAL RESPONSIBILITIES IN SCHOOL ADMINISTRATION

In general, women and minority superintendents tend to attach greater importance to many responsibilities of the superintendency than do men and nonminorities. In most categories discussed here, women and minorities gave the answer "very essential" more frequently than did the other two groups.

TABLE 6.30 IN LAST 10 YEARS, HAVE COMMUNITY GROUPS EMERGED TO PRESSURE THE BOARD?

	GENDER MALE		GENDER FEMALE		ETHNIC NONMINORITY		ETHNIC MINORITY	
	No.	%	No.	%	No.	%	No.	%
YES	1024	64.0	77	67.5	1051	63.8	52	77.6
NO	516	32.3	33	28.9	536	32.5	13	19.4
DO NOT KNOW	60	3.8	4	3.5	61	3.7	2	3.0

TABLE 6.31 WHAT DO YOU SEE AS THE MOST DIFFICULT PROBLEM YOUR BOARD MEMBERS FACE?

	GENDER MALE		GENDER FEMALE		ETHNIC NONMINORITY		ETHNIC MINORITY	
	No.	%	No.	%	No.	%	No.	%
FINANCIAL ISSUES	591	39.6	38	35.2	608	39.5	24	39.3
COMMUNITY PRESSURE	306	20.5	23	21.3	318	20.6	9	14.8
EMPLOYEE RELATIONS	118	7.9	1	0.9	116	7.5	1	1.6
CURRICULUM ISSUES	19	1.3	0	0.0	18	1.2	1	1.6
INTERNAL BOARD CONFLICT	117	7.8	6	5.6	115	7.5	9	14.8
UNDERSTANDING APPROPRIATE BOARD ROLES	319	21.4	32	29.6	334	21.7	17	27.9
OTHER	24	1.6	8	7.4	32	2.1	0	0.0
TOTAL	1,494	100.1	108	100.0	1,541	100.1	61	100.0

Area 1: District Climate

Women and minority superintendents are more likely to say "establishing a district climate conducive to instruction and a high level of staff performance" are more essential than either male or nonminority superintendents are. Seventy-two percent of women superintendents, compared to 52.8 percent of male superintendents; and 69.2 percent of minority, compared to 53.5 percent of nonminority superintendents, said this type of environment is very essential (see **Table 6.35**).

Area 2: Obtaining Support for Education

At 43 and 40 percent respectively, women and minority superintendents essentially share the opinion that this performance area is "very essential." They also are more likely to say obtaining support for education is critical than their male and nonminority counterparts (see **Table 6.36**)

Area 3: Providing an Effective Curriculum Program

Similarly, women and minority superintendents think that the establishment of an effective, nonbiased curriculum that expands the definitions of literacy is more essential to their effectiveness as superintendents than do either nonminority or male superintendents (see **Table 6.37**).

Area 4: Effective Instructional Programs

Without a doubt, women and minority superintendents think that instructional program leadership by the superintendent is even more essential than do other superintendents. More than 70 percent of women superintendents listed this performance area as "very essential," in contrast to 50.9 percent of male superintendents (see **Table 6.38**).

Area 5: Continuous Improvement and Evaluation

Women and minority superintendents think evaluations are more essential than do other superintendents (see **Table 6.39**). When asked how essential it is to create a program of continuous improvement and evaluation, 71 percent of women and 65.2 percent of minorities sampled, as opposed to 48.9 percent of men, said it was "very essential."

TABLE 6.32 HIGHEST DEGREE HELD

	GENDER MALE		GENDER FEMALE		ETHNIC NONMINORITY		ETHNIC MINORITY	
	No.	%	No.	%	No.	%	No.	%
BA OR BS	4	0.3	4	3.6	8	0.5	0	0.0
BACHELOR'S DEGREE	1	0.1	4	3.6	5	0.3	0	0.0
MASTER'S IN EDUCATION	70	4.4	4	3.6	67	4.1	8	12.1
MASTER'S NOT IN EDUCATION	1	0.1	1	0.9	2	0.1	0	0.0
MASTER'S + GRADUATE WORK	392	24.7	17	15.2	400	24.5	9	13.6
MASTER'S + DOCTORAL WORK	142	9.0	15	13.4	153	9.4	5	7.6
SPECIALIST DEGREE	257	16.2	8	7.1	262	16.1	3	4.5
DOCTORATE	568	35.9	46	41.1	577	35.4	36	54.5
BEYOND DOCTORATE	129	8.1	12	10.7	136	8.3	5	7.6
SOME OTHER DEGREE	20	1.3	1	0.9	21	1.3	0	0.0
TOTAL	1,584	100.1	112	100.1	1,631	100.0	66	99.9

TABLE 6.33 EVALUATION OF YOUR PROGRAM OF GRADUATE STUDIES AS PREPARATION FOR SUPERINTENDENCY?

	GENDER MALE		GENDER FEMALE		ETHNIC NONMINORITY		ETHNIC MINORITY	
	No.	%	No.	%	No.	%	No.	%
EXCELLENT	418	26.5	32	30.8	428	26.5	25	37.9
GOOD	760	48.2	38	36.5	773	47.8	23	34.8
FAIR	350	22.2	23	22.1	359	22.2	14	21.2
POOR	50	3.2	11	10.6	57	3.5	4	6.1
NO OPINION	0	0.0	0	0.0	0	0.0	0	0.0
TOTAL	1,578	100.1	104	100.0	1,617	100.0	66	100.0

Area 6: Financial and Budget Management

Women and minority superintendents list management of fiscal resources as "very essential" more often than male and nonminority superintendents, but the difference is not as pronounced as their views on responsibility in areas such as curriculum and instruction (see **Table 6.40**).

Area 7: Operations Management

Women and minority superintendents also listed operations management — or, skillfully managing school system operations and facilities to enhance student learning — as more essential than did nonminority superintendents. The difference was greatest between women and men; while 64.2 percent of women deemed this area of responsibility "very essential," 45.8 percent of men gave this response (see **Table 6.41**).

Area 8: Using Research

Women and minority superintendents think that using research in the superintendency is more essential than either male or nonminority superintendents, by substantial margins. Specifically, half of the minority superintendents said they thought this was very important, while a quarter of the men and nonminorities, and 41.5 percent of the women, saw this area as vital (see **Table 6.42**).

STRESS

In terms of "very great stress," at 11.6 percent women seem to feel this more often than do men, at 7.5 percent. More than 42 percent of women, male, and nonminority superintendents say they feel "considerable" stress, compared to 38.8 percent of minority respondents. Interestingly, the greatest difference occured in the response "little stress," where 19.4 percent of minorities gave this response, as opposed to 7.3 percent of nonminorities (See **Table 6.43**).

TABLE 6.34 OPINION OF USEFULNESS OF EDUCATIONAL RESEARCH?

	GENDER MALE		GENDER FEMALE		ETHNIC NONMINORITY		ETHNIC MINORITY	
	No.	%	No.	%	No.	%	No.	%
HIGHLY USEFUL	366	22.8	48	42.5	381	23.1	33	49.3
USUALLY USEFUL	663	41.4	41	36.3	688	41.7	16	23.9
OCCASIONALLY USEFUL	544	33.9	24	21.2	551	33.4	18	26.9
IS NOT USEFUL	24	1.5	0	0.0	24	1.5	0	0.0
NO OPINION	6	0.4	0	0.0	6	0.4	0	0.0

TABLE 6.35 AREA 1. ESTABLISHES AND MAINTAINS A POSITIVE AND OPEN LEARNING ENVIRONMENT

	GENDER MALE		GENDER FEMALE		ETHNIC NONMINORITY		ETHNIC MINORITY	
	No.	%	No.	%	No.	%	No.	%
VERY ESSENTIAL	836	52.8	77	72.0	869	53.5	45	69.2
ESSENTIAL	549	34.7	21	19.6	556	34.2	14	21.5
SOMEWHAT ESSENTIAL	178	11.3	8	7.5	179	11.0	6	9.2
ALMOST NEVER ESSENTIAL	19	1.2	1	0.9	20	1.2	0	0.0
NEVER ESSENTIAL	0	0.0	0	0.0	1	0.1	0	0.0
TOTAL	1,582	100.0	107	100.0	1,625	100.0	65	99.9

.TABLE 6.36 AREA 2. BUILDS STRONG LOCAL, STATE, AND NATIONAL SUPPORT FOR EDUCATION

	GENDER MALE		GENDER FEMALE		ETHNIC NONMINORITY		ETHNIC MINORITY	
	No.	%	No.	%	No.	%	No.	%
VERY ESSENTIAL	525	33.1	46	43.0	545	33.5	26	40.0
ESSENTIAL	677	42.7	38	35.5	684	42.0	27	41.5
SOMEWHAT ESSENTIAL	337	21.2	21	19.6	351	21.5	11	16.9
ALMOST NEVER ESSENTIAL	46	2.9	1	0.9	46	2.8	1	1.5
NEVER ESSENTIAL	1	0.1	1	0.9	3	0.2	0	0.0
TOTAL	1,586	100.0	107	99.9	1,629	100.0	65	99.9

TABLE 6.37 AREA 3. DEVELOPS AND DELIVERS AN EFFECTIVE CURRICULUM THAT EXPANDS THE DEFINITIONS OF LITERACY

	GENDER MALE		GENDER FEMALE		ETHNIC NONMINORITY		ETHNIC MINORITY	
	No.	%	No.	%	No.	%	No.	%
VERY ESSENTIAL	927	58.5	75	70.1	956	58.8	46	69.7
ESSENTIAL	513	32.4	24	22.4	519	31.9	18	27.3
SOMEWHAT ESSENTIAL	136	8.6	8	7.5	142	8.7	2	3.0
ALMOST NEVER ESSENTIAL	9	0.6	0	0.0	10	0.6	0	0.0
NEVER ESSENTIAL	0	0.0	0	0.0	0	0.0	0	0.0
TOTAL	1,585	100.1	107	100.0	1,627	100.0	66	100.0

TABLE 6.38 DEVELOPS AND IMPLEMENTS EFFECTIVE MODELS/MODES OF INSTRUCTIONAL DELIVERY THAT MAKE THE BEST USE OF TIME, STAFF, ADVANCED TECHNOLOGIES, COMMUNITY RESOURCES, AND FINANCIAL MEANS TO MAXIMIZE STUDENT OUTCOMES

	GENDER MALE		GENDER FEMALE		ETHNIC NONMINORITY		ETHNIC MINORITY	
	No.	%	No.	%	No.	%	No.	%
VERY ESSENTIAL	806	50.9	75	70.1	840	51.7	43	65.2
ESSENTIAL	599	37.9	25	23.4	604	37.2	19	28.8
SOMEWHAT ESSENTIAL	164	10.4	7	6.5	166	10.2	4	6.1
ALMOST NEVER ESSENTIAL	13	0.8	0	0.0	14	0.9	0	0
NEVER ESSENTIAL	0	0.0	0	0.0	0	0.0	0	0.0
TOTAL	1,582	100.0	107	100.0	1,624	100.0	66	100.1

TABLE 6.39 AREA 5. CREATES PROGRAM OF CONTINUOUS IMPROVEMENT AND EVALUATION

	GENDER MALE		GENDER FEMALE		ETHNIC NONMINORITY		ETHNIC MINORITY	
	No.	%	No.	%	No.	%	No.	%
VERY ESSENTIAL	773	48.9	76	71.0	809	49.8	43	65.2
ESSENTIAL	667	42.2	28	26.2	670	41.3	22	33.3
SOMEWHAT ESSENTIAL	134	8.5	2	1.9	135	8.3	1	1.5
ALMOST NEVER ESSENTIAL	8	0.5	1	0.9	10	0.6	0	0.0
NEVER ESSENTIAL	0	0.0	0	0.0	0	0.0	0	0.0
TOTAL	1,582	100.1	107	100.0	1,624	100.0	66	100.0

TABLE 6.40 AREA 6. MAINTAINS AND IS RESPONSIBLE FOR ALL SCHOOL FINANCE ISSUES

	GENDER MALE		GENDER FEMALE		ETHNIC NONMINORITY		ETHNIC MINORITY	
	No.	%	No.	%	No.	%	No.	%
VERY ESSENTIAL	757	48.0	71	67.0	790	48.8	38	57.6
ESSENTIAL	630	39.9	28	26.4	635	39.2	24	36.4
SOMEWHAT ESSENTIAL	167	10.6	6	5.7	169	10.4	4	6.1
ALMOST NEVER ESSENTIAL	22	1.4	1	0.9	23	1.4	0	0.0
NEVER ESSENTIAL	1	0.1	0	0.0	1	0.1	0	0.0
TOTAL	1,577	100.0	106	100.0	1,618	99.9	66	100.1

TABLE 6.41 AREA 7. SKILLFULLY MANAGES SCHOOL SYSTEM OPERATIONS AND FACILITIES TO ENHANCE STUDENT LEARNING

	GENDER MALE		GENDER FEMALE		ETHNIC NONMINORITY		ETHNIC MINORITY	
	No.	%	No.	%	No.	%	No.	%
VERY ESSENTIAL	725	45.8	68	64.2	754	46.5	39	59.1
ESSENTIAL	686	43.4	29	27.4	695	42.8	22	33.3
SOMEWHAT ESSENTIAL	150	9.5	9	8.5	153	9.4	5	7.6
ALMOST NEVER ESSENTIAL	21	1.3	0	0.0	21	1.3	0	0.0
NEVER ESSENTIAL	0	0.0	0	0.0	0	0.0	0	0.0
TOTAL	1,582	100.0	106	100.1	1,623	100.0	66	100.0

69

TABLE 6.42 AREA 8. CONDUCTS AND USES RESEARCH IN PROBLEM SOLVING AND PROGRAM PLANNING OF ALL KINDS

	GENDER MALE		GENDER FEMALE		ETHNIC NONMINORITY		ETHNIC MINORITY	
	No.	%	No.	%	No.	%	No.	%
VERY ESSENTIAL	402	25.4	44	41.5	414	25.5	33	50.0
ESSENTIAL	699	44.2	42	39.6	721	44.5	21	31.8
SOMEWHAT ESSENTIAL	422	26.7	16	15.1	425	26.2	12	18.2
ALMOST NEVER ESSENTIAL	55	3.5	4	3.8	59	3.6	0	0.0
NEVER ESSENTIAL	3	0.2	0	0.0	3	0.2	0	0.0
TOTAL	1,581	100.0	106	100.0	1,622	100.0	66	100.0

TABLE 6.43 AMOUNT OF STRESS IN YOUR SUPERINTENDENCY

	GENDER MALE		GENDER FEMALE		ETHNIC NONMINORITY		ETHNIC MINORITY	
	No.	%	No.	%	No.	%	No.	%
NO STRESS	5	0.3	0	0.0	5	0.3	0	0.0
LITTLE STRESS	129	8.1	5	4.5	120	7.3	13	19.4
MODERATE STRESS	666	41.7	47	42.0	690	42.0	24	35.8
CONSIDERABLE STRESS	676	42.4	47	42.0	698	42.5	26	38.8
VERY GREAT STRESS	120	7.5	13	11.6	129	7.9	4	6.0
TOTAL	1,596	100.0	112	100.0	1,642	100.0	67	100.0

70

Professional Preparation And Training 7

The content and quality of training is an important part of any profession, especially the superintendency. Preparation of American school superintendents is not always an orderly and well-defined process as in professions such as law, medicine, dentistry, and accounting, which have national and state boards that heavily influence content, process, and licensing. The American school superintendent's professional career generally begins as a classroom teacher, later moving up through building-level administration, and then often into a central office position or directly into the superintendency. The first steps on the professional ladder in many ways complement those skills and competencies required in the superintendency.

Preparation varies. Professional training standards on a national basis do not currently exist for the formal preparation of superintendents. Instead, preparation and training is, for the most part, dictated by state teacher/administration certification codes. These state certification codes vary from one state to another. In addition, most superintendents are recommended for certification in their respective states after completing "approved" programs of study sponsored by institutions of higher education. These higher education programs themselves have no standard course of study and vary greatly in subject content, degree of difficulty, and required field/clinical experiences.

PAST HISTORY

All of the previous 10-year studies of the American superintendency have explored the training and preparation of administrators. Since 1923, the various studies have collected information about the number of degrees, years of experience, major fields of study in college, and types of graduate programs taken for degrees and state certification. Several of the studies posed value questions, such as whether practicing superintendents thought that training programs were adequately preparing them for their jobs. In the 1982

study, new questions were introduced concerning challenges and issues superintendents thought should be covered in their training and preparation. Questions also were asked about superintendents' needs for continuing education, an important concern in the development of the profession.

HOW THE 1992 STUDY DIFFERS

The 1992 study introduces another topic area for discussion regarding the training and preparation of superintendents: performance areas. In 1982, an AASA task force completed a report entitled, *Guidelines for the Preparation of School Administrators.* The *Guidelines* have served as the basis for several doctoral dissertation studies and books focusing on what superintendents should know and be able to do. The 1992 study asks superintendents to indicate which of the eight "performance areas" contained in the guidelines are "most essential" to effective performance in the superintendency.

For those interested in a closer examination of these performance areas and specific skills needed to be an effective superintendent, we recommend AASA's publication, *Skills for Successful School Leaders,* written by John Hoyle, Fenwick English, and Betty Steffy. It contains valuable information on skills of educational leaders.

FORMAL ACADEMIC TRAINING AND DEGREES

Administrators enter the superintendency through academic degrees and state certification. State certification requires at least one academic degree; entry into teaching in all states requires at least a bachelor's degree, and a master's degree is required for administrative certification in nearly all states except several that do not have administrative certificate programs.

Meeting needs. In some states, continuing professional development needs are partially met by state-sponsored "academies," which offer inservice programs often mandated by state school-reform legislation. Many continuing education programs for superintendents are offered through workshops and seminars sponsored by state and national associations, such as AASA, colleges and universities, and the private sector.

SCHOOLING PRIOR TO THE SUPERINTENDENCY

Degrees Held

About 96 percent of superintendents in the 1990 sample hold a combination of a master's degree, specialist certificate, or doctorate. The number of degrees possessed by superintendents has increased since the 1971 and 1982 studies. One reason is that many older superintendents who had been "grandfathered" in state certificate programs had retired by

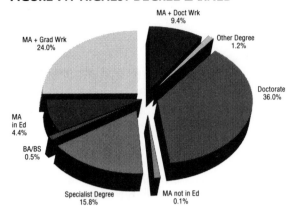

FIGURE 7.1 HIGHEST DEGREE EARNED

MA + Doct Wrk 9.4%
Other Degree 1.2%
MA + Grad Wrk 24.0%
Doctorate 36.0%
MA in Ed 4.4%
BA/BS 0.5%
Specialist Degree 15.8%
MA not in Ed 0.1%

TABLE 7.1 HIGHEST DEGREE HELD BY SUPERINTENDENT

	GROUP A: 25,000 OR MORE PUPILS		GROUP B: 3,000-24,999 PUPILS		GROUP C: 300-2,999 PUPILS		GROUP D: FEWER THAN 300 PUPILS		NATIONAL UNWEIGHTED PROFILE	
	No.	%	No.	%	No.	%	No.	%	No.	%
BA OR BS	0	0.0	0	0.0	1	0.1	7	2.8	8	0.5
BACHELOR'S DEGREE	0	0.0	0	0.0	0	0.0	5	2.0	5	0.3
MASTER'S IN EDUCATION	8	5.6	15	2.5	34	4.8	18	7.2	75	4.4
MASTER'S NOT IN EDUCATION	0	0.0	1	0.2	1	0.1	0	0.0	2	0.1
MASTER'S + GRADUATE WORK	12	8.5	101	16.8	198	28.1	97	38.6	408	24.0
MASTER'S + DOCTORATE WORK	8	5.6	40	6.7	81	11.5	30	12.0	159	9.4
SPECIALIST DEGREE	5	3.5	59	9.8	138	19.6	64	25.5	266	15.8
DOCTORATE	88	62.0	295	49.2	208	29.5	20	8.0	611	36.0
BEYOND DOCTORATE	21	14.8	83	13.8	32	4.5	7	2.8	143	8.4
SOME OTHER DEGREE	0	0.0	6	1.0	12	1.7	3	1.2	21	1.2
TOTAL	142	8.4	600	35.3	705	41.5	251	14.8	1,698	100.0

TABLE 7.2 UNDERGRADUATE MAJOR OF SUPERINTENDENTS

	GROUP A: 25,000 OR MORE PUPILS		GROUP B: 3,000-24,999 PUPILS		GROUP C: 300-2,999 PUPILS		GROUP D: FEWER THAN 300 PUPILS		NATIONAL UNWEIGHTED PROFILE	
	No.	%	No.	%	No.	%	No.	%	No.	%
AGRICULTURE	1	0.7	9	1.5	28	4.1	9	3.7	47	2.9
BUSINESS	7	5.1	24	4.1	38	5.6	18	7.4	87	5.3
EDUCATION (NOT PHYS. EDUCATION)	35	25.7	158	26.9	166	24.3	58	23.9	417	25.3
FINE ARTS	3	2.2	14	2.4	15	2.2	10	4.1	42	2.5
HUMANITIES	20	14.7	49	8.3	56	8.2	19	7.8	144	8.7
MATHEMATICS	9	6.6	45	7.7	53	7.8	20	8.2	127	7.7
PHYSICAL EDUCATION	14	10.3	34	5.8	81	11.9	35	14.4	164	9.9
PHYSICAL OR BIOLOGICAL SCIENCES	6	4.4	72	12.3	71	10.4	22	9.1	171	10.4
SOCIAL SCIENCES	36	26.5	147	25.0	152	22.3	38	15.6	373	22.6
OTHER	5	3.7	35	6.0	23	3.4	14	5.8	77	4.7
TOTAL	136	8.2	587	35.6	683	41.4	243	14.7	1,649	100.0

1992. Many older, practicing superintendents hold a master's degree and have completed course credits beyond that advanced degree which qualifies them for their certificates. Most states now require about 30 semester hours of course work beyond the master's degree to qualify for the superintendent's credential.

In 1982, 28 percent of sampled superintendents indicated they possessed a doctoral degree. In 1992, this proportion has risen to 36 percent. The larger the district, the more likely the superintendent is to have a doctoral degree (See **Table 7.1** and **Figure 7.1**).

Undergraduate degrees. Undergraduate academic majors for superintendents are generally education (25.3 percent), social sciences (22.6 percent), biological/physical sciences (10.4 percent), or physical education (9.9 percent). The nature of many responsibilities in the superintendency focuses on areas usually associated with business management. However, only 5.3 percent of superintendents had business as an undergraduate major (See **Table 7.2**).

Master's degrees. As would be expected because it is usually required by state certification agencies, the prevalent master's degree major for superintendents is educational administration/supervision. Almost 60 percent of reporting superintendents possess a master's degree in educational administration. Secondary education majors are reported by 11.7 percent, which is not unusual since such a large number of superintendents are former secondary teachers (See **Table 7.3**).

Certificates. The specialist certificate (CAS or EDS) is a mid-range program between the master's and doctorate levels. Typically, it consists of 30 semester hours of study in the field of educational administration or closely aligned subjects. In many states, certification requirements for the superintendency include 30 semester hours beyond the master's degree. These 30 hours often are packaged in a specialist degree. As shown in **Table 7.4**, of those superintendents possessing this degree (765), 90.2 percent had taken the degree in the field of educational administration/supervision.

Doctorates. At the doctorate level, almost all (88.9 percent) superintendents major in educational administration. None of the sampled superintendents indicated they had taken a business doctorate. From this data it is apparent the superintendency is dominated by degree holders in education (See **Table 7.5**).

Full-Time Vs. Part-Time
One of the criticisms often made about academic programs in educational administration is that they are so largely composed of part-time students (Finn and Petersen, 1985; [and] Clark, 1989). For most administrators to attend graduate school on a full-time basis would require giving up their full-time positions as teachers or administrators. Only 12.8 percent indicate they had been a graduate assistant while completing their master's degree (See **Table 7.6**). This low per-

TABLE 7.3 MAJOR OF SUPERINTENDENT'S MASTER'S DEGREE

	GROUP A: 25,000 OR MORE PUPILS		GROUP B: 3,000-24,999 PUPILS		GROUP C: 300-2,999 PUPILS		GROUP D: FEWER THAN 300 PUPILS		NATIONAL UNWEIGHTED PROFILE	
	No.	%	No.	%	No.	%	No.	%	No.	%
EDUCATIONAL ADMIN./ SUPERVISION	73	51.4	334	56.0	427	61.6	156	64.5	990	59.2
SECONDARY EDUCATION	15	10.6	73	12.2	83	12.0	24	9.9	195	11.7
PHYSICAL EDUCATION	1	0.7	9	1.5	20	2.9	6	2.5	36	2.2
HUMANITIES/FINE ARTS	11	7.7	35	5.9	27	3.9	11	4.5	84	5.0
SCIENCE OR ENGINEERING	2	1.4	14	2.3	12	1.7	3	1.2	31	1.9
BUSINESS	2	1.4	7	1.2	2	0.3	2	0.8	13	0.8
MATHEMATICS	3	2.1	7	1.2	11	1.6	2	0.8	23	1.4
ELEMENTARY EDUCATION	10	7.0	26	4.4	27	3.9	13	5.4	76	4.5
OTHER	25	17.6	91	15.3	84	12.1	25	10.3	225	13.4
TOTAL	142	8.5	596	35.6	693	41.4	242	14.5	1,673	100.0

TABLE 7.4 MAJOR OF SUPERINTENDENT'S SPECIALIST CERTIFICATE

	GROUP A: 25,000 OR MORE PUPILS		GROUP B: 3,000-24,999 PUPILS		GROUP C: 300-2,999 PUPILS		GROUP D: FEWER THAN 300 PUPILS		NATIONAL UNWEIGHTED PROFILE	
	No.	%	No.	%	No.	%	No.	%	No.	%
EDUCATIONAL ADMIN./SUPERVISION	41	91.1	24	90.3	328	90.1	117	90.0	690	90.2
SECONDARY EDUCATION	1	2.2	4	1.8	8	2.2	4	3.1	17	2.2
PHYSICAL EDUCATION	0	0.0	0	0.0	0	0.0	0	0.0	0	0.0
HUMANITIES/FINE ARTS	2	4.4	0	0.0	1	0.3	3	2.3	6	0.8
SCIENCE OR ENGINEERING	0	0.0	1	0.4	0	0.0	1	0.8	2	0.3
BUSINESS	0	0.0	1	0.4	3	0.8	1	0.8	5	0.7
MATHEMATICS	0	0.0	2	0.9	0	0.0	0	0	2	0.3
ELEMENTARY EDUCATION	0	0.0	3	1.3	9	2.5	3	2.3	15	2.0
OTHER	1	2.2	11	4.9	15	4.1	1	0.8	28	3.7
TOTAL	45	5.9	46	29.5	364	47.6	130	17.0	765	100.0

TABLE 7.5 MAJOR OF SUPERINTENDENT'S DOCTORATE

	GROUP A: 25,000 OR MORE PUPILS		GROUP B: 3,000-24,999 PUPILS		GROUP C: 300-2,999 PUPILS		GROUP D: FEWER THAN 300 PUPILS		NATIONAL UNWEIGHTED PROFILE	
	No.	%	No.	%	No.	%	No.	%	No.	%
EDUCATIONAL ADMIN./SUPERVISION	100	88.5	349	86.8	266	93.0	40	83.3	755	88.9
SECONDARY EDUCATION	3	2.7	5	1.2	3	1.0	0	0.0	11	1.3
PHYSICAL EDUCATION	0	0.0	0	0.0	0	0.0	0	0.0	0	0
HUMANITIES/FINE ARTS	0	0.0	1	0.2	0	0.0	2	4.2	3	0.4
SCIENCE OR ENGINEERING	0	0.0	2	0.5	1	0.3	1	2.1	4	0.5
BUSINESS	0	0.0	0	0.0	0	0.0	0	0.0	0	0
MATHEMATICS	0	0.0	1	0.2	0	0.0	0	0.0	1	0.1
ELEMENTARY EDUCATION	0	0.0	5	1.2	4	1.4	0	0.0	9	1.1
OTHER	10	8.8	39	9.7	12	4.2	5	10.4	66	7.8
TOTAL	113	13.3	402	47.3	286	33.7	48	5.7	849	100.0

TABLE 7.6 SUPERINTENDENTS RECEIVING FELLOWSHIPS OR ASSISTANTSHIPS WHILE WORKING ON MASTER'S DEGREES

	GROUP A: 25,000 OR MORE PUPILS		GROUP B: 3,000-24,999 PUPILS		GROUP C: 300-2,999 PUPILS		GROUP D: FEWER THAN 300 PUPILS		NATIONAL UNWEIGHTED PROFILE	
	No.	%	No.	%	No.	%	No.	%	No.	%
YES	22	17.1	78	14.7	72	11.5	19	9.1	191	12.8
NO	107	82.9	453	85.3	553	88.5	190	90.9	1,303	87.2
TOTAL	129	8.6	531	35.5	625	41.8	209	14.0	1,494	100.0

TABLE 7.7 SUPERINTENDENTS RECEIVING SABBATICALS OR OTHER FINANCIAL SUPPORT FROM DISTRICT WHILE WORKING ON MASTER'S DEGREES

	GROUP A: 25,000 OR MORE PUPILS		GROUP B: 3,000-24,999 PUPILS		GROUP C: 300-2,999 PUPILS		GROUP D: FEWER THAN 300 PUPILS		NATIONAL UNWEIGHTED PROFILE	
	No.	%	No.	%	No.	%	No.	%	No.	%
YES	7	5.5	18	3.4	42	6.7	12	5.7	79	5.3
NO	121	94.5	513	96.6	581	93.3	199	94.3	1,414	94.7
TOTAL	128	8.6	531	35.6	623	41.7	211	14.1	1,493	100.0

centage was similar to responses received in both the 1982 and 1971 studies of the superintendency.

Financial Support
School districts provided financial support for attaining new degrees only 5.3 percent of the time. A few superintendents were assisted financially by the GI Bill (See **Table 7.7**).

Age and Experience
Most administrators began their master's degree programs after only two or three years of teaching (See **Table 7.8**). A frequently asked question is whether, after such a short time, a teacher has sufficient knowledge of teaching and the schooling process to profit from advanced-level study in management. The mean age of superintendents finishing master's degree programs was 29. The young superintendents (45 and younger at the time of the survey) finished at 28, on the average (See **Table 7.9**).

In general, teachers aspiring to be superintendents decide on their own to enroll in graduate-level educational administration courses. Typically, they begin these programs after several years of teaching. Teachers often bear the costs for graduate school without district monies or release time to attend on a full-time basis (Clark, 1989).

Specialist Level
The specialist level offers those courses required for the superintendency certificate. Here again, the majority of respondents (93.2 percent) received no help in the form of a graduate assistantship(See **Table 7.10**). Most completed work for this degree, which usually qualifies them for the superintendency credential, by age 35 (See **Table 7.11**).

Sabbatical Leave
To reinforce the data that superintendents do not attend graduate programs full-time or receive financial assistance is the fact that, of the sampled superintendents, only 9 percent received sabbatical leave or district support in pursuing their specialist certificate (See **Table 7.12**).

TABLE 7.9 AGE AT COMPLETION OF MASTER'S DEGREE BY SUPERINTENDENTS' AGE GROUPS

GROUP (BY AGE OF RESPONDENT)	MEAN AGE	STANDARD DEVIATION	NUMBER
45-UNDER	28.39	5.84	356
46-50	28.36	5.01	384
51-55	29.23	4.63	365
56-60	26.67	4.85	246
61-ABOVE	32.62	7.08	91
TOTAL	29.08	5.36	1442

TABLE 7.8 LENGTH OF SERVICE AS CLASSROOM TEACHER PRIOR TO ENTERING ADMINISTRATION OR SUPERVISION

YEARS AS TEACHER	GROUP A: 25,000 OR MORE PUPILS No.	%	GROUP B: 3,000-24,999 PUPILS No.	%	GROUP C: 300-2,999 PUPILS No.	%	GROUP D: FEWER THAN 300 PUPILS No.	%	NATIONAL UNWEIGHTED PROFILE No.	%
0 - 5	92	63.4	352	57.7	306	42.9	75	29.8	825	47.9
6 - 10	44	30.3	191	31.3	292	40.9	94	37.3	621	36.1
11 - 15	6	4.1	60	9.8	88	12.3	55	21.8	209	12.1
16 - 20	3	2.1	6	1.0	21	2.9	18	7.1	48	2.8
21 - 25	0	0.0	1	0.2	6	0.8	5	2.0	12	0.7
26 +	0	0.0	0	0.0	1	0.01	5	2.0	6	0.3
TOTAL	145	0.0	610	0.0	714	0.0	252	0.0	1,721	100.0

TABLE 7.10 SUPERINTENDENTS RECEIVING FELLOWSHIPS OR ASSISTANTSHIPS WHILE WORKING ON SPECIALIST DEGREES

	GROUP A: 25,000 OR MORE PUPILS No.	%	GROUP B: 3,000-24,999 PUPILS No.	%	GROUP C: 300-2,999 PUPILS No.	%	GROUP D: FEWER THAN 300 PUPILS No.	%	NATIONAL UNWEIGHTED PROFILE No.	%
YES	6	14.6	16	7.8	23	6.8	3	2.5	48	6.8
NO	35	85.4	188	92.2	316	93.2	115	97.5	654	93.2
TOTAL	41	5.8	204	29.1	339	48.3	118	16.8	702	100.0

Method of Payment

Self-financed. Most superintendents indicated they financed their schooling themselves. Few superintendents (12.5 percent), during their specialist programs, relied on loans to finance their educational costs. This fact further indicates that most superintendents did not leave their full-time employment to study for a degree that would qualify them for the superintendent's credential (See **Table 7.13**).

Doctoral level. Many more superintendents received sabbaticals and financial assistance from their districts at the doctoral level. While 38 percent received financial assistance, 26.5 percent received some type of sabbatical leave (See **Tables 7.14** and **7.15**).

Approximately one in four superintendents attended graduate school on a full-time basis for a period of time during their residencies. Some higher education doctoral programs require at least one year of full-time residency. Also, colleges of education sometimes reserve positions in student teaching supervision and similar kinds of activities for doctoral students with experience in public school teaching or administration.

About one-quarter of superintendents received sabbaticals and obtained graduate assistantships and still had to borrow funds (See **Table 7.16**).

In the future, it is likely that a greater percentage of superintendents will be acquiring doctorates in educational administration—at a younger age and with fewer years of experience (seven years at present) in administration/supervision. (This has been a trend for the past 20 years, and there is no indication that it will be reversed.) (See **Tables 7.17** and **7.18**) Competition for higher-paying superintendencies in wealthier districts generally draws pools of candidates with doctoral degrees.

TABLE 7.11 AGE AT WHICH SUPERINTENDENTS RECEIVED SPECIALIST DEGREE

GROUP (BY AGE OF RESPONDENTS)	AGE	STANDARD DEVIATION	NUMBER
45-UNDER	33.02	7.07	189
46-50	34.91	7.58	188
51-55	35.50	6.05	136
56-60	37.22	6.00	99
61-ABOVE	38.39	8.37	31
TOTAL	35.00	7.10	643

TABLE 7.12 SUPERINTENDENTS RECEIVING SABBATICALS OR OTHER FINANCIAL SUPPORT FROM DISTRICT WHILE WORKING ON SPECIALIST DEGREE

	GROUP A: 25,000 OR MORE PUPILS		GROUP B: 3,000-24,999 PUPILS		GROUP C: 300-2,999 PUPILS		GROUP D: FEWER THAN 300 PUPILS		NATIONAL UNWEIGHTED PROFILE	
	No.	%	No.	%	No.	%	No.	%	No.	%
YES	6	15.0	16	7.9	30	8.7	11	9.5	63	9.0
NO	34	85.0	187	92.1	313	91.3	105	90.5	639	91.0
TOTAL	40	5.7	203	28.9	343	48.9	116	16.5	702	100.0

TABLE 7.13 DID SUPERINTENDENTS SEEK LOANS TO COMPLETE STUDY ON SPECIALIST DEGREE?

	GROUP A: 25,000 OR MORE PUPILS		GROUP B: 3,000-24,999 PUPILS		GROUP C: 300-2,999 PUPILS		GROUP D: FEWER THAN 300 PUPILS		NATIONAL UNWEIGHTED PROFILE	
	No.	%	No.	%	No.	%	No.	%	No.	%
YES	13	10.7	49	9.4	82	13.4	39	18.8	183	12.5
NO	109	89.3	470	90.6	532	86.6	169	81.2	1,280	87.5
TOTAL	122	8.3	519	35.5	614	42.0	208	14.2	1,463	100.0

TABLE 7.14 DID SUPERINTENDENTS RECEIVE FELLOWSHIPS OR ASSISTANTSHIPS WHILE WORKING ON DOCTORATE?

	GROUP A: 25,000 OR MORE PUPILS		GROUP B: 3,000-24,999 PUPILS		GROUP C: 300-2,999 PUPILS		GROUP D: FEWER THAN 300 PUPILS		NATIONAL UNWEIGHTED PROFILE	
	No.	%	No.	%	No.	%	No.	%	No.	%
YES	45	42.1	154	40.4	94	33.9	15	33.3	308	38.0
NO	62	57.9	227	59.6	183	66.1	30	66.7	502	62.0
TOTAL	107	13.2	381	47.0	277	34.2	45	5.6	810	100.0

QUALITY OF EDUCATIONAL ADMINISTRATION PROGRAMS

Critics of educational administration programs often claim that many educational administration programs lack serious academic vigor (Finn and Peterson, 1985). The establishment in the late 1980s of the National Policy Board for Educational Administration signaled that preparation of administrators does indeed fit into the school reform movement and that policymakers will pay attention to this activity. However, David Clark, writing in the first report of the National Policy Board For Educational Administration (1989), said programs in educational administration were noted more for their weaknesses than their strengths.

Different Strokes

There are between 400 and 500 educational administration programs that vary greatly in their curriculums, requirements, and degree of academic integrity. In reality, generalizations about such a diverse group of programs are hard to make. Many of these programs may be approved by state certification agencies and have only one or even no full-time faculty members in education. The course and credit requirements imposed by state agencies largely determine the content and the experiences administrators receive in their graduate programs in educational administration. Therefore, if the state does not require important experiences such as full-time or at least part-time internships, then they usually do not appear in the graduate program requirements (Clark, 1989).

Quality of Programs

The 1990 study asked respondents to indicate their overall appraisal of the graduate program that prepared them for the superintendency. A similar question was asked in 1982. About one-quarter (26.8 percent) said their preparation program was "excellent." About half (47.4 percent) said it was "good." The remaining 25.8 percent said their program was "fair" or "poor." No one said "no opinion."

TABLE 7.15 SUPERINTENDENTS RECEIVING SABBATICALS OR OTHER FINANCIAL SUPPORT FROM DISTRICT WHILE WORKING ON DOCTORATE

	GROUP A: 25,000 OR MORE PUPILS		GROUP B: 3,000-24,999 PUPILS		GROUP C: 300-2,999 PUPILS		GROUP D: FEWER THAN 300 PUPILS		NATIONAL UNWEIGHTED PROFILE	
	No.	%	No.	%	No.	%	No.	%	No.	%
YES	31	29.2	95	25.0	76	27.4	12	26.7	214	26.5
NO	75	70.8	285	75.0	201	72.6	33	73.3	594	73.5
TOTAL	106	13.1	380	47.0	277	34.3	45	5.6	808	100.0

TABLE 7.16 DID SUPERINTENDENTS SEEK LOANS TO COMPLETE STUDY ON DOCTORATE?

	GROUP A: 25,000 OR MORE PUPILS		GROUP B: 3,000-24,999 PUPILS		GROUP C: 300-2,999 PUPILS		GROUP D: FEWER THAN 300 PUPILS		NATIONAL UNWEIGHTED PROFILE	
	No.	%	No.	%	No.	%	No.	%	No.	%
YES	27	26.2	74	20.1	71	25.7	16	37.2	188	23.8
NO	76	73.8	295	79.9	205	74.3	27	62.8	603	76.2
TOTAL	103	13.0	369	46.6	276	34.9	43	5.4	791	100.0

TABLE 7.17 AGE AT WHICH SUPERINTENDENTS FINISHED THEIR DOCTORATE

GROUP (BY AGE OF RESPONDENT)	MEAN AGE	STANDARD DEVIATION	NUMBER
45-UNDER	32.00	5.21	208
46-50	32.56	5.91	224
51-55	34.49	5.58	205
56-60	35.62	6.47	130
61-ABOVE	36.96	7.99	45
TOTAL	33.39	6.06	812

TABLE 7.18 DOCTORATE-YEARS OF ADMINISTRATIVE EXPERIENCE WHEN RECEIVED, ANALYZED BY AGE

GROUP (BY AGE OF RESPONDENT)	MEAN YEARS	STANDARD DEVIATION	NUMBER
45-UNDER	7.71	4.57	180
46-50	7.39	5.65	204
51-55	7.41	5.48	190
56-60	9.54	6.08	128
61-ABOVE	9.72	6.24	43
TOTAL	7.82	5.55	745

Superintendents under the age of 45 are somewhat more critical of their graduate programs than other age groups (See **Tables 7.19** and **7.20**).

When individuals completing professional programs are asked to evaluate the quality of those programs, their typical response is "good" or "excellent" regardless of other indicators. Many link their own self-worth with their professional preparation program, and most would not like to admit they made a mistake in choosing a given program.

This behavioral trend may be reflected in the question of how sampled superintendents appraise educational administration programs in general. In this case, responses are much more critical. Fully 44.2 percent say the programs were only "fair." Another 43.9 percent say they were "good" and 7.9 percent indi-

cate the programs were "poor" (See **Table 7.21**).

By age. Superintendents younger than age 45 are more critical of educational administration programs, with 58.2 percent indicating they were only "fair" or "poor." In the 46- to 50-year-old age group, 52.6 percent of the respondents gave the same response (See **Table 7.22**).

By district size. Superintendents in large districts are more critical of graduate programs than are those in smaller districts (See **Table 7.23**). The only difference was that superintendents in very small districts were more critical in 1982 than those responding in 1992.

TABLE 7.19 SUPERINTENDENT'S EVALUATION OF GRADUATE PROGRAMS AS PREPARATION FOR SUPERINTENDENCY

	GROUP A: 25,000 OR MORE PUPILS		GROUP B: 3,000-24,999 PUPILS		GROUP C: 300-2,999 PUPILS		GROUP D: FEWER THAN 300 PUPILS		NATIONAL UNWEIGHTED PROFILE	
	No.	%	No.	%	No.	%	No.	%	No.	%
EXCELLENT	39	27.7	186	31.1	182	26.0	44	18.0	451	26.8
GOOD	63	44.7	268	44.7	341	48.7	127	52.0	799	47.4
FAIR	34	24.1	126	21.0	154	22.0	60	24.6	374	22.2
POOR	5	3.5	19	3.2	23	3.3	13	5.3	60	3.6
NO OPINION	0	0.0	0	0.0	0	0.0	0	0.0	0	0.0
TOTAL	141	8.4	599	35.6	700	41.6	244	14.5	1,684	100.0

TABLE 7.20 EVALUATION OF GRADUATE PROGRAMS FOR SUPERINTENDENCY, ANALYZED BY AGE

	AGE 45-UNDER		AGE 46-50		AGE 51-55		AGE 56-60		AGE 61-ABOVE	
	No.	%	No.	%	No.	%	No.	%	No.	%
EXCELLENT	109	24.5	103	22.8	119	29.0	92	32.2	32	32.0
GOOD	194	43.7	240	53.2	190	46.3	127	44.4	51	51.0
FAIR	117	26.4	96	21.3	92	22.4	54	18.9	14	14.0
POOR	24	5.4	12	2.7	9	2.2	13	4.5	3	3.0
TOTAL	444	100.0	451	100.0	410	99.9	286	100.0	100	100.0

TABLE 7.21 EVALUATION OF GRADUATE PROGRAMS NATIONWIDE IN EDUCATIONAL ADMINISTRATION

	GROUP A: 25,000 OR MORE PUPILS		GROUP B: 3,000-24,999 PUPILS		GROUP C: 300-2,999 PUPILS		GROUP D: FEWER THAN 300 PUPILS		NATIONAL UNWEIGHTED PROFILE	
	No.	%	No.	%	No.	%	No.	%	No.	%
EXCELLENT	4	3.1	26	4.8	22	3.6	8	3.8	60	4.0
GOOD	38	29.5	224	41.0	290	47.3	107	50.5	659	43.9
FAIR	63	48.8	257	47.0	262	42.7	82	38.7	664	44.2
POOR	24	18.6	40	7.3	39	6.4	15	7.1	118	7.9
NO OPINION	0	0.0	0	0.0	0	0.0	0	0.0	0	0.0
TOTAL	129	8.6	547	36.4	613	40.8	212	14.1	1,501	100.0

Quality of Instructors

Most educational administration professors were rated "good" or "fair," no matter what the ages of the respondent (See **Table 7.24**). Educational administration professors often are accused by practitioners as being too "theoretical" and removed from the realities of operating school districts. In a 1989 study, Michael Sass found in a sample of 480 professors of educational administration, exactly two-thirds had never served in the superintendency. Of the third who had been superintendents, a large majority were between 50 and 65 years of age, meaning that very few younger professors have ever been superintendents (Sass, 1989).

Future superintendents may not be trained in higher education programs by former superintendents if this trend continues. Exactly how preparation programs will incorporate field training components

using practitioners is yet to emerge on a broad basis.

What Counts in Preparation Programs?

Strengths. Superintendents indicated that professors and their courses in educational administration are the strongest part of their preparation programs (See **Table 7.25**). It should be noted that few programs have extensive, practical field work (paid, full-time internships). In all likelihood, if educational administration programs had more extensive internships and practicums, superintendents might have given this category a much higher rating.

Weaknesses. The major weakness of educational administration programs, according to superintendents, is poor and irrelevant course work (see **Table 7.26**). In 1982, 21 percent of the superintendents said

TABLE 7.22 EVALUATION OF GRADUATE PROGRAMS NATIONWIDE IN EDUCATIONAL ADMINISTRATION, ANALYZED BY AGE

	AGE 45-UNDER		AGE 46-50		AGE 51-55		AGE 56-60		AGE 61-ABOVE	
	No.	%	No.	%	No.	%	No.	%	No.	%
EXCELLENT	14	3.6	15	3.8	15	4.1	10	3.8	6	6.9
GOOD	150	38.3	172	43.7	160	43.2	132	50.4	49	56.3
FAIR	188	48.0	178	45.2	175	47.3	96	36.6	27	31.0
POOR	40	10.2	29	7.4	20	5.4	24	9.2	5	5.7
TOTAL	392	100.1	394	100.1	370	100.0	262	100.0	87	99.9

TABLE 7.23 EVALUATION OF CREDIBILITY OF EDUCATIONAL ADMINISTRATION PROFESSORS

	GROUP A: 25,000 OR MORE PUPILS		GROUP B: 3,000-24,999 PUPILS		GROUP C: 300-2,999 PUPILS		GROUP D: FEWER THAN 300 PUPILS		NATIONAL UNWEIGHTED PROFILE	
	No.	%	No.	%	No.	%	No.	%	No.	%
EXCELLENT	10	6.9	53	8.8	68	9.6	18	7.3	149	8.8
GOOD	56	38.9	274	45.4	307	43.6	107	43.7	744	43.8
FAIR	52	36.1	229	37.9	261	37.0	102	41.6	644	37.9
POOR	26	18.1	48	7.9	69	9.8	18	7.3	161	9.5
NO OPINION	0	0.0	0	0.0	0	0.0	0	0.0	0	0.0
TOTAL	144	8.5	604	35.6	705	41.6	245	14.4	1,698	100.0

TABLE 7.24 EVALUATION OF CREDIBILITY OF EDUCATIONAL ADMINISTRATION PROFESSORS, ANALYZED BY AGE

	AGE 45-UNDER		AGE 46-50		AGE 51-55		AGE 56-60		AGE 61-OLDER	
	No.	%	No.	%	No.	%	No.	%	No.	%
EXCELLENT	40	9.0	44	9.6	28	6.8	27	9.3	12	11.9
GOOD	171	38.4	189	41.4	195	47.1	137	47.2	57	56.4
FAIR	182	40.9	174	38.2	158	38.2	103	35.5	28	27.7
POOR	52	11.7	49	10.7	33	8.0	23	7.9	4	4.0
TOTAL	445	100.0	456	99.9	414	100.1	290	99.9	101	100.0

this was the greatest weakness, very close to the 20.4 percent in 1992. In fact, about the same response pattern is seen in both studies. The "quality of professors" category dropped by 5 percent from 1982 to 1992.

EDUCATIONAL RESEARCH

Education is an important social endeavor. However, less than one percent of education spending is dedicated to research. The 1980s saw a considerable reduction in educational research funds available at the federal and state levels. Introduction of new program initiatives, materials, and techniques in public education frequently originate in federally sponsored projects or at projects affiliated with a college or university. Little research that is widely disseminated originates at the local school level, since most districts do not have a research staff.

Most superintendents believe that educational research is useful. While 24.2 percent said it is "highly useful," 41 percent said it is "usually useful," and 33.1 percent said it is "occasionally useful" (See **Table 7.27**). This might mean that dissemination efforts are improving and that superintendents are interested in using research or that some research is becoming more relevant to their needs.

RATING PERFORMANCE AREAS

The 1992 sample of superintendents was asked to rate the eight performance areas most important to the superintendency as developed by AASA in 1982 (see Chapter 6 for a breakout of sexes and races). Other groups of superintendents, selected on a national and state basis, were asked to perform a similar task in the late 1980s. Their responses might signal the "most essential" areas or functions of the superintendency in the 1990s.

TABLE 7.25 MAJOR STRENGTHS OF SUPERINTENDENTS GRADUATE STUDY PROGRAMS

	GROUP A: 25,000 OR MORE PUPILS		GROUP B: 3,000-24,999 PUPILS		GROUP C: 300-2,999 PUPILS		GROUP D: FEWER THAN 300 PUPILS		NATIONAL UNWEIGHTED PROFILE	
	No.	%	No.	%	No.	%	No.	%	No.	%
HIGH-QUALITY PROFESSORS	38	28.4	167	29.3	147	22.3	45	19.6	397	24.9
HIGH-CALIBER FELLOW STUDENTS	20	14.9	63	11.1	99	15.0	32	13.9	214	13.4
QUALITY OF EDUCATIONAL ADMINISTRATION COURSES	13	9.7	116	20.4	164	24.9	60	26.1	353	22.2
QUALITY OF OTHER COURSES IN EDUCATION	1	0.7	8	1.4	14	2.1	1	0.4	24	1.5
AVAILABILITY OF NONEDUCATION/COGNATES	9	6.7	14	2.5	12	1.8	7	3.0	42	2.6
FIELD CONTACT/PRACTICAL WORK	29	21.6	77	13.5	99	15.0	32	13.9	237	14.9
LIBRARY OR OTHER FACILITIES	0	0.0	8	1.4	6	0.9	9	3.9	23	1.4
INDEPENDENT/INDIVIDUAL STUDY & INSTRUCTION	8	6.0	63	11.1	40	6.1	9	3.9	120	7.5
INTERNSHIP	7	5.2	25	4.4	29	4.4	16	7.0	77	4.8
OTHER	5	3.7	13	2.3	11	1.7	6	2.6	35	2.2
NO STRENGTHS	4	3.0	16	2.8	37	5.6	13	5.7	70	4.4
TOTAL	134	8.4	570	35.8	658	41.3	230	14.4	1,592	100.0

Curriculum director. The performance area named most often by superintendents as being "very essential" is number 3, (see Chapter 6, **Tables 6.35-6.42** for a listing of all eight areas) "developing an effective curriculum" (see **Table 7.28**). Of those responding, 59.3 percent indicated this performance area is "very essential." Superintendents in the larger districts said this performance area is more essential than did superintendents in small districts.

Climate control. Performance Area 1, "Establishes and maintains a positive learning environment," is "very essential," according to 54.1 percent of respondents (See **Table 7.29**). Close behind is the performance area of developing and implementing effective methods of instruction. Fifty-two (52.2) percent of superintendents

rated this item "very essential" (See **Table 7.30**).

Evaluating for quality. Another performance area rated "very essential" by more than 50 percent of superintendents is creating effective evaluation programs for students and staff to ensure quality performance (See **Table 7.31**).

Money matters. Just below the 50 percent category in terms of being rated "very essential" is the performance area of managing district finances (49.3 percent). Superintendents from small and very small school districts listed this area as very essential even more often. Another 38.9 percent of superintendents said it is "essential" but not "very essential." (See **Table 7.32**).

TABLE 7.26 MAJOR WEAKNESSES OF SUPERINTENDENTS' GRADUATE STUDY PROGRAMS

	GROUP A: 25,000 OR MORE PUPILS		GROUP B: 3,000-24,999 PUPILS		GROUP C: 300-2,999 PUPILS		GROUP D: FEWER THAN 300 PUPILS		NATIONAL UNWEIGHTED PROFILE	
	No.	%	No.	%	No.	%	No.	%	No.	%
LOW-QUALITY PROFESSORS	12	8.8	42	7.2	59	8.8	29	12.5	142	8.8
POOR/IRRELEVANT COURSE OFFERINGS	26	19.0	118	20.2	146	21.9	41	17.7	331	20.4
LACK OF SPECIFIC COURSES	8	5.8	50	8.6	73	10.9	25	10.8	156	9.6
LACK OF QUALITY INTERNSHIP	10	7.3	45	7.7	56	8.4	20	8.6	131	8.1
POOR EDUCATIONAL ADMINISTRATION COURSES	22	16.1	59	10.1	58	8.7	22	9.5	161	9.9
LACK OF OTHER DEPARTMENTAL SUPPORT	7	5.1	28	4.8	19	2.8	4	1.7	58	3.6
POOR LIBRARY OR FACILITIES	2	1.5	6	1.0	3	0.4	4	1.7	15	0.9
LACK OF OPPORTUNITIES FOR FULL-TIME STUDY	11	8.0	52	8.9	57	8.5	20	8.6	140	8.6
STUDENTS WITH INADEQUATE ADMINISTATIVE EXPERIENCE	5	3.6	15	2.6	14	2.1	3	1.3	37	2.3
EXCESSIVE TENSION	3	2.2	11	1.9	12	1.8	10	4.3	36	2.2
OTHER	3	2.2	26	4.5	28	4.2	11	4.7	68	4.2
NO WEAKNESSES	24	17.5	109	18.7	112	16.8	39	16.8	284	17.5
NO OPINION	4	2.9	22	3.8	31	4.6	4	1.7	61	3.8
TOTAL	137	8.5	583	36.0	668	41.2	232	14.3	1,620	100.0

TABLE 7.27 OPINION OF USEFULNESS OF EDUCATIONAL RESEARCH

	GROUP A: 25,000 OR MORE PUPILS		GROUP B: 3,000-24,999 PUPILS		GROUP C: 300-2,999 PUPILS		GROUP D: FEWER THAN 300 PUPILS		NATIONAL UNWEIGHTED PROFILE	
	No.	%	No.	%	No.	%	No.	%	No.	%
HIGHLY USEFUL	46	31.7	178	29.2	148	20.8	43	17.0	415	24.2
USUALLY USEFUL	59	40.7	227	37.3	332	46.7	86	34.0	704	41.0
OCCASIONALLY USEFUL	39	26.9	197	32.3	219	30.8	114	45.1	569	33.1
IS NOT USEFUL	1	0.7	6	1.0	10	1.4	7	2.8	24	1.4
NO OPINION	0	0.0	1	0.2	2	0.3	3	1.2	6	0.3
TOTAL	145	8.4	609	35.4	711	41.4	253	14.7	1,718	100.0

Operations and facilities. The allied performance area of managing district operations and facilities is rated as "very essential" by 47 percent of responding superintendents. Superintendents in very large districts indicate this area is slightly more essential than do their colleagues in smaller districts. This response is perhaps due to the substantial amount of funds needed by large districts to replace aging infrastructures. This somewhat "hidden" crisis in American

public schools was recently pointed out by an AASA study entitled *Schoolhouse in the Red* (1992). (See **Table 7.33**).

Rallying support. Superintendents apparently believe the most important tasks associated with being an effective superintendent are those closest to home. However, 75.9 percent rate the performance area of building strong support for education at the

TABLE 7.28 AREA 3
DEVELOPS AND DELIVERS AN EFFECTIVE CURRICULUM THAT EXPANDS THE DEFINITIONS OF LITERACY, COMPETENCY, AND CULTURAL INTEGRATION TO INCLUDE ADVANCED TECHNOLOGIES,PROBLEM SOLVING, CRITICAL THINKING, AND CULTURAL ENRICHMENT FOR ALL STUDENTS

	GROUP A: 25,000 OR MORE PUPILS		GROUP B: 3,000-24,999 PUPILS		GROUP C: 300-2,999 PUPILS		GROUP D: FEWER THAN 300 PUPILS		NATIONAL UNWEIGHTED PROFILE	
	No.	%	No.	%	No.	%	No.	%	No.	%
VERY ESSENTIAL	93	64.1	401	66.1	374	53.8	136	55.1	1,004	59.3
ESSENTIAL	42	29.0	157	25.9	260	37.4	77	31.2	536	31.6
SOMEWHAT ESSENTIAL	10	6.9	43	7.1	58	8.3	33	13.4	144	8.5
ALMOST NEVER ESSENTIAL	0	0.0	6	1.0	3	0.4	1	0.4	10	0.6
NEVER ESSENTIAL	0	0.0	0	0.0	0	0.0	0	0.0	0	0.0
TOTAL	145	8.6	607	35.8	695	41.0	247	14.6	1,694	100.0

TABLE 7.29 AREA 1
ESTABLISHES AND MAINTAINS A POSITIVE AND OPEN LEARNING ENVIRONMENT TO BRING ABOUT MOTIVATION AND SOCIAL INTEGRATION OF STUDENTS AND STAFF

	GROUP A: 25,000 OR MORE PUPILS		GROUP B: 3,000-24,999 PUPILS		GROUP C: 300-2,999 PUPILS		GROUP D: FEWER THAN 300 PUPILS		NATIONAL UNWEIGHTED PROFILE	
	No.	%	No.	%	No.	%	No.	%	No.	%
VERY ESSENTIAL	85	58.6	347	57.5	341	49.0	142	57.5	915	54.1
ESSENTIAL	41	28.3	191	31.7	262	37.6	75	30.4	569	33.6
SOMEWHAT ESSENTIAL	17	11.7	56	9.3	84	12.1	28	11.3	185	10.9
ALMOST NEVER ESSENTIAL	2	1.4	8	1.3	9	1.3	2	0.8	21	1.2
NEVER ESSENTIAL	0	0.0	1	0.2	0	0.0	0	0.0	1	0.1
TOTAL	145	8.6	603	35.7	696	41.2	247	14.6	1,691	100.0

TABLE 7.30 AREA 4
DEVELOPS AND IMPLEMENTS EFFECTIVE MODELS/MODES OF INSTRUCTIONAL DELIVERY THAT MAKE THE BEST USE OF TIME, STAFF, ADVANCED TECHNOLOGIES, COMMUNITY RESOURCES, AND FINANCIAL MEANS TO MAXIMIZE STUDENT OUTCOMES

	GROUP A: 25,000 OR MORE PUPILS		GROUP B: 3,000-24,999 PUPILS		GROUP C: 300-2,999 PUPILS		GROUP D: FEWER THAN 300 PUPILS		NATIONAL UNWEIGHTED PROFILE	
	No.	%	No.	%	No.	%	No.	%	No.	%
VERY ESSENTIAL	84	57.9	354	58.4	339	48.9	105	42.5	882	52.2
ESSENTIAL	46	31.7	197	32.5	277	40.0	103	41.7	623	36.8
SOMEWHAT ESSENTIAL	15	10.3	50	8.3	69	10.0	38	15.4	172	10.2
ALMOST NEVER ESSENTIAL	0	0.0	5	0.8	8	1.2	1	0.4	14	0.8
NEVER ESSENTIAL	0	0.0	0	0.0	0	0.0	0	0.0	0	0.0
TOTAL	145	8.6	606	35.8	693	41.0	247	14.6	1,691	100.0

local, state, and national levels as "very essential" or "essential" (See **Table 7.34**).

Research for improvement. The last performance area is that of conducting and using research as a basis for problem solving and program improvement. Of those responding, 26.3 percent said it is a "very essential" performance area for the superintendency, and 43.9 percent rated it "essential" (See **Table 7.35**). Superintendents in other AASA-sponsored studies were also asked to rank the eight performance areas (See **Table 7.36** for data and explanation).

When considering the companion studies on the AASA performance areas, an inference can be made that indicates that superintendents are becoming more concerned about professional expertise in the area of instructional and organizational leadership and a bit less concerned about financial management. Even though they are very concerned about the financing of schools, the actual day-to-day management of those funds does not seem to be an absolutely essential performance area for effective superintendents.

TABLE 7.31: AREA 5
CREATES PROGRAMS OF CONTINUOUS IMPROVEMENT AND EVALUATION OF BOTH STAFF AND PROGRAM EFFECTIVENESS AS KEYS TO STUDENT LEARNING AND DEVELOPMENT

	GROUP A: 25,000 OR MORE PUPILS		GROUP B: 3,000-24,999 PUPILS		GROUP C: 300-2,999 PUPILS		GROUP D: FEWER THAN 300 PUPILS		NATIONAL UNWEIGHTED PROFILE	
	No.	%	No.	%	No.	%	No.	%	No.	%
VERY ESSENTIAL	82	56.6	324	53.5	331	47.7	112	45.5	849	50.2
ESSENTIAL	53	36.6	230	38.0	307	44.2	106	43.1	696	41.2
SOMEWHAT ESSENTIAL	10	6.9	47	7.8	52	7.5	27	11.0	136	8.0
ALMOST NEVER ESSENTIAL	0	0.0	5	0.8	4	0.6	1	0.4	10	0.6
NEVER ESSENTIAL	0	0.0	0	0.0	0	0.0	0	0.0	0	0.0
TOTAL	145	8.6	606	35.8	694	41.0	246	14.5	1,691	100.0

TABLE 7.32 AREA 6
MANAGES AND IS RESPONSIBLE FOR ALL SCHOOL FINANCE ISSUES OF THE SCHOOL DISTRICT

	GROUP A: 25,000 OR MORE PUPILS		GROUP B: 3,000-24,999 PUPILS		GROUP C: 300-2,999 PUPILS		GROUP D: FEWER THAN 300 PUPILS		NATIONAL UNWEIGHTED PROFILE	
	No.	%	No.	%	No.	%	No.	%	No.	%
VERY ESSENTIAL	64	44.1	273	45.3	361	52.2	133	53.8	831	49.3
ESSENTIAL	60	41.4	261	43.4	248	35.9	86	34.8	655	38.9
SOMEWHAT ESSENTIAL	20	13.8	56	9.3	77	11.1	21	8.5	174	10.3
ALMOST NEVER ESSENTIAL	0	0.0	12	2.0	5	0.7	7	2.8	24	1.4
NEVER ESSENTIAL	1	0.7	0	0.0	0	0.0	0	0.0	1	0.1
TOTAL	145	8.6	602	35.7	691	41.0	247	14.7	1,685	100.0

TABLE 7.33 AREA 7
SKILLFULLY MANAGES SCHOOL SYSTEM OPERATIONS AND FACILITIES TO ENHANCE STUDENT LEARNING

	GROUP A: 25,000 OR MORE PUPILS		GROUP B: 3,000-24,999 PUPILS		GROUP C: 300-2,999 PUPILS		GROUP D: FEWER THAN 300 PUPILS		NATIONAL UNWEIGHTED PROFILE	
	No.	%	No.	%	No.	%	No.	%	No.	%
VERY ESSENTIAL	74	51.0	275	45.5	326	47.0	119	48.4	794	47.0
ESSENTIAL	59	40.7	257	42.5	299	43.1	100	40.7	715	42.3
SOMEWHAT ESSENTIAL	11	7.6	63	10.4	63	9.1	22	8.9	159	9.4
ALMOST NEVER ESSENTIAL	1	0.7	10	1.7	6	0.9	5	2.0	22	1.3
NEVER ESSENTIAL	0	0.0	0	0.0	0	0.0	0	0.0	0	0.0
TOTAL	145	8.6	605	35.8	694	41.1	246	14.6	1,690	100.0

SUMMARY

Thousands of new superintendents will be prepared to lead American school districts in the 1990s. Current certification programs that now drive the content and activities of most educational administration programs will, in many cases, need to be redefined to meet new leadership and reform challenges.

Perhaps the most serious problem facing the super-intendency in the 1990s is not lack of funding, relations with school boards, or pressures for accountability or reform, but is instead the creation of appropriate preparation and training programs.

It is quite clear that superintendents feel much improvement could be made in preparation programs, which is corroborated by research and the school reform press.

TABLE 7.34 AREA 2
BUILDS STRONG LOCAL, STATE, AND NATIONAL SUPPORT FOR EDUCATION

	GROUP A: 25,000 OR MORE PUPILS		GROUP B: 3,000-24,999 PUPILS		GROUP C: 300-2,999 PUPILS		GROUP D: FEWER THAN 300 PUPILS		NATIONAL UNWEIGHTED PROFILE	
	No.	%	No.	%	No.	%	No.	%	No.	%
VERY ESSENTIAL	57	39.3	223	36.8	211	30.3	80	32.4	571	33.7
ESSENTIAL	63	43.4	250	41.3	309	44.3	93	37.7	715	42.2
SOMEWHAT ESSENTIAL	22	15.2	113	18.6	158	22.7	66	26.7	359	21.2
ALMOST NEVER ESSENTIAL	3	2.1	17	2.8	19	2.7	8	3.2	47	2.8
NEVER ESSENTIAL	0	0.0	3	0.5	0	0.0	0	0.0	3	0.2
TOTAL	145	8.6	606	35.8	697	41.1	247	14.6	1,695	100.0

TABLE 7.35 AREA 8
CONDUCTS AND USES RESEARCH AS A BASIS OF PROBLEM SOLVING AND PROGRAM PLANNING

	GROUP A: 25,000 OR MORE PUPILS		GROUP B: 3,000-24,999 PUPILS		GROUP C: 300-2,999 PUPILS		GROUP D: FEWER THAN 300 PUPILS		NATIONAL UNWEIGHTED PROFILE	
	No.	%	No.	%	No.	%	No.	%	No.	%
VERY ESSENTIAL	55	37.9	164	27.1	176	25.4	49	20.0	444	26.3
ESSENTIAL	60	41.4	271	44.8	309	44.5	102	41.6	742	43.9
SOMEWHAT ESSENTIAL	29	20.0	152	25.1	181	26.1	78	31.8	440	26.1
ALMOST NEVER ESSENTIAL	1	0.7	18	3.0	25	3.6	16	6.5	60	3.6
NEVER ESSENTIAL	0	0.0	0	0.0	3	0.4	0	0.0	3	0.2
TOTAL	145	8.6	605	35.8	694	41.1	245	14.5	1,689	100.0

TABLE 7.36 IMPORTANCE OF PERFORMANCE GOAL AREAS FOR VARIOUS SAMPLE GROUPS

GROUPS	STUDY	RANK CLIMATE	RANK SUPPORT	RANK CURRICULUM	RANK INSTRUCTION	RANK EVALUATION	RANK FINANCE	RANK MANAGEMENT	RANK RESEARCH
ILLINOIS SUPERINTENDENTS	DROZONICK	2	7	5	6	3	1	4	8
NATIONAL SAMPLE OF SUPERINTENDENTS	SCLAFANI	1	7	3	6	4	2	5	8
EFFECTIVE SUPERINTENDENT SAMPLE	BURNHAM	1	7	2	3	4	5	6	8
EDUCATIONAL ADMINISTRATION PROFESSORS	SASS	1	7	2	4	3	6	5	8
TEXAS SUPERINTENDENTS	COLLIER	2	7	3	6	5	1	4	8
1992 NATIONAL SAMPLE	AASA	2	7	1	3	4	5	6	8

The above studies, completed in the 1980s, asked various groups of superintendents to rank identical sets of performance goals found in AASA's *Guidelines for the Preparation of Educational Administrators.* All preceding studies are unpublished dissertations.

District Characteristics

There are many differences among American school districts, ranging from size to state-mandated structures (grade configurations). For instance, Hawaii traditionally has only one statewide district; Nevada has 17 districts; while Illinois has 951, and Texas more than 1,000. Within some states, such as Florida, county school superintendents administer schools located in more than one community. In other states, intermediate school districts provide local school district supervision and technical assistance. The amount of state education department involvement also varies greatly from state to state.

Asked in *The 1992 Study of the American School Superintendency* to describe the nature of their jobs, 88.6 percent of superintendents indicated they are "general" superintendents, which implies they are chief executive officers of their districts, directly responsible to the local school boards. Only 6.4 percent indicate they serve in the role of a county superintendent, and another 2.6 percent say they are intermediate district superintendents (see **Table 8.1**).

TYPES OF SCHOOL DISTRICTS

School districts across America do not always provide comprehensive elementary through high school pro-grams. Some districts provide only elementary services, and others serve only secondary students. However, the most common district organization is kindergarten through the 12th grade (K-12). Consequently, most superintendents serve in districts offering 13 grades of instruction.

Of superintendents sampled in 1992, a vast majority (81.1 percent) serve in K-12 districts. Just over 10 percent are superintendents in elementary districts (defined here as K-6 or K-8), and only 2.8 percent are in districts with grade spans of 7 to 12 or 9 to 12 (see **Table 8.2**).

AGE OF SUPERINTENDENTS

In AASA's 1971 and 1982 studies, the percentage of smaller districts with young superintendents was quite high. Similarly, the 1992 data show that the majority of superintendents age 45 and younger work in districts with fewer than 3,000 students enrolled.

Districts with between 1,000 and 3,000 students have a high percentage of superintendents who are older than 50, indicating that many superintendents may complete their career in districts of this size (see **Table 8.3**).

TABLE 8.1 WHICH OF THE FOLLOWING TITLES BEST DESCRIBES YOUR PRESENT POSITION?

	GROUP A: 25,000 OR MORE PUPILS		GROUP B: 3,000-24,999 PUPILS		GROUP C: 300-2,999 PUPILS		GROUP D: FEWER THAN 300 PUPILS		NATIONAL UNWEIGHTED PROFILE	
	No.	%	No.	%	No.	%	No.	%	No.	%
GENERAL SUPERINTENDENT(CEO)	114	79.7	494	81.9	676	94.5	234	92.9	1,518	88.6
AREA OR SUBDISTRICT SUPERINTENDENT	0	0.0	5	0.8	5	0.7	1	0.4	11	0.6
COUNTY SUPERINTENDENT	12	8.4	78	12.9	17	2.4	3	1.2	110	6.4
VOCATIONAL/TECHNICAL SUPERINTENDENT	0	0.0	0	0.0	12	1.7	1	0.4	13	0.8
INTERMEDIATE UNIT SUPERINTENDENT	16	11.2	25	4.1	1	0.1	2	0.8	44	2.6
OTHER	1	0.7	1	0.2	4	0.6	11	4.4	17	1.0
TOTAL	143	8.3	603	35.2	715	41.7	252	14.7	1,713	100.0

SCHOOL REFORMS

During the 1980s, school reformers recommended various programs to make America's schools more competitive in the world and remedy some of the social ills afflicting the nation, such as crime, poverty, and a rapidly deteriorating workforce. One such program is early childhood education, which has proven in some cases to assist "at-risk" children in overcoming the effects of poverty, inadequate language skills, and other handicaps. Pioneering programs such as Head Start have led the way for the development of early childhood and prekindergarten programs.

Early Childhood Education

In the 1992 study, 52.4 percent of superintendents reported their districts sponsor prekindergarten programs. These programs were much more likely to be in place in the very large districts (enrollments greater than 25,000), which tend to have large numbers of "at-risk" children. Fewer prekindergarten programs existed in districts with smaller enrollments (see **Table 8.4**). However, during the 1990s, with additional assistance from the federal and state governments, the number of prekindergarten programs may well increase.

Day-care programs. Many parents asked their school districts to provide day-care services during the 1980s, as the number of working mothers increased and two-career families became more common.

In the 1992 study, one in four superintendents (25.7 percent) reported that day-care programs are offered in their districts (see **Table 8.5**). Again, the very large districts are more likely to have these programs than smaller districts. In more affluent districts, private child-care programs may be more common.

TABLE 8.2 WHAT GRADE LEVELS ARE INCLUDED IN YOUR DISTRICT?

GRADE LEVELS	GROUP A: 25,000 OR MORE PUPILS		GROUP B: 3,000-24,999 PUPILS		GROUP C: 300-2,999 PUPILS		GROUP D: FEWER THAN 300 PUPILS		NATIONAL UNWEIGHTED PROFILE	
	No.	%	No.	%	No.	%	No.	%	No.	%
K OR 1-12	118	84.3	525	87.4	577	81.2	162	64.0	1,382	81.1
K OR 1- 9	0	0.0	1	0.2	0	0.0	1	0.4	2	0.1
K OR 1- 8	1	0.7	20	3.3	72	10.1	67	26.5	160	9.4
K OR 1- 6	0	0.0	2	0.3	7	1.0	12	4.7	21	1.2
10-12	0	0.0	0	0.0	2	0.3	0	0.0	2	0.1
9-12	1	0.7	13	2.2	22	3.1	3	1.2	39	2.3
7-12	2	1.4	4	0.7	3	0.4	0	0.0	9	0.5
OTHER	17	12.1	32	5.3	22	3.1	8	3.2	79	4.6
VOCATIONAL/TECHNICAL	1	0.7	4	0.7	6	0.8	0	0.0	11	0.6
TOTAL	140	8.2	601	35.2	711	41.7	253	14.8	17.5	100.0

TABLE 8.3 SIZE OF SCHOOL DISTRICT ANALYZED BY SUPERINTENDENTS' AGE

ENROLLMENT	AGE 45-YOUNGER		AGE 46-50		AGE 51-55		AGE 56-60		AGE 61-OLDER	
	No.	%	No.	%	No.	%	No.	%	No.	%
100,000 OR MORE	0	0.0	7	1.5	5	1.2	4	1.4	3	3.0
50,000-99,999	4	0.9	8	1.7	11	2.6	14	4.8	3	3.0
25,000-49,999	13	2.9	26	5.6	22	5.3	15	5.1	9	9.0
10,000-24,999	18	4.0	53	11.4	30	7.2	31	10.5	14	14.0
5,000- 9,999	38	8.5	58	12.5	67	16.1	38	12.9	11	11.0
3,000- 4,999	57	12.7	65	14.0	68	16.3	45	15.3	16	16.0
1,000- 2,999	109	24.3	118	25.5	101	24.2	73	24.8	25	25.0
300-999	104	23.2	83	17.9	58	13.9	38	12.9	7	7.0
300 OR FEWER	105	23.4	45	9.7	55	13.2	36	12.2	12	12.0
TOTAL	448	99.9	463	99.8	417	100.0	294	99.9	100	100.0

Given that school readiness was listed as the first of the nation's goals for education in 1991, it is likely that significant political pressure will be placed on school districts during the 1990s to provide further child-care services encompassing educational activities.

School-Business Partnerships

Another popular reform agenda item is the creation of school-business partnerships. Historically, relations between schools and the private sector have been informal. During the 1980s, many executives in the private sector complained about the quality of the emerging workforce and suggested that private businesses and schools begin to form working partnerships. These partnerships, they hoped, would improve the quality of education and better prepare high school students for entry into the world of work. In a few isolated cases, private sector organizations actually took over the operation of school programs.

With nearly half (47.1 percent) of the sampled superintendents in the 1990 study indicating their district had a school/business partnership in operation, the gap between the schools and the private sector might well be drawing much closer. Once again, the larger districts are much more likely to have partnership programs than the very small districts (see **Table 8.6**).

School Volunteers

School volunteers increasingly are used in school districts to assist the instructional programs and improve school/community relations. Most school districts are eager to have assistance in academic tutoring, extracurricular activities, and many other important tasks. Eight out of 10 school districts currently use community volunteers in the schools (see **Table 8.7**).

TABLE 8.4 DOES YOUR SCHOOL DISTRICT PROVIDE PREKINDERGARTEN EDUCATION?

	GROUP A: 25,000 OR MORE PUPILS		GROUP B: 3,000-24,999 PUPILS		GROUP C: 300-2,999 PUPILS		GROUP D: FEWER THAN 300 PUPILS		NATIONAL UNWEIGHTED PROFILE	
	No.	%	No.	%	No.	%	No.	%	No.	%
YES	117	81.8	389	64.1	311	43.7	82	32.4	899	52.4
NO	26	18.2	218	35.9	401	56.3	171	67.6	816	47.6
TOTAL	143	8.3	607	35.4	712	41.5	253	14.8	1,715	100.0

TABLE 8.5 DOES YOUR SCHOOL DISTRICT PROVIDE CHILD/DAY-CARE?

	GROUP A: 25,000 OR MORE PUPILS		GROUP B: 3,000-24,999 PUPILS		GROUP C: 300-2,999 PUPILS		GROUP D: FEWER THAN 300 PUPILS		NATIONAL UNWEIGHTED PROFILE	
	NO.	%	NO.	%	NO.	%	NO.	%	NO.	%
YES	88	62.0	242	40.0	103	14.4	8	3.2	441	25.7
NO	54	38.0	363	60.0	611	85.6	245	96.8	1,273	74.3
TOTAL	142	8.3	605	35.3	714	41.7	253	14.8	1,714	100.0

TABLE 8.6 DOES YOUR DISTRICT CURRENTLY HAVE A SCHOOL-BUSINESS PARTNERSHIP?

	GROUP A: 25,000 OR MORE PUPILS		GROUP B: 3,000-24,999 PUPILS		GROUP C: 300-2,999 PUPILS		GROUP D: FEWER THAN 300 PUPILS		NATIONAL UNWEIGHTED PROFILE	
	NO.	%	NO.	%	NO.	%	NO.	%	NO.	%
YES	136	95.8	434	71.4	213	29.8	26	10.3	809	47.1
NO	6	4.2	174	28.6	502	70.2	227	89.7	909	52.9
TOTAL	142	8.3	608	35.4	715	41.6	253	14.7	1,718	100.0

TABLE 8.7 DOES YOUR DISTRICT HAVE A VOLUNTEER PROGRAM?

	GROUP A: 25,000 OR MORE PUPILS		GROUP B: 3,000-24,999 PUPILS		GROUP C: 300-2,999 PUPILS		GROUP D: FEWER THAN 300 PUPILS		NATIONAL UNWEIGHTED PROFILE	
	NO.	%	NO.	%	NO.	%	NO.	%	NO.	%
YES	130	90.3	520	85.8	559	79.4	152	61.3	1,361	80.0
NO	14	9.7	86	14.2	145	20.6	96	38.7	341	20.0
TOTAL	144	8.5	606	35.6	704	41.4	248	14.6	1,702	100.0

CHANGING DEMOGRAPHICS

One of the most dramatic changes in America's schools in the 1970s and 1980s was in community demographics. As the baby boom came to a close in the 1960s, many school districts began suffering effects of declining enrollment. Despite a "baby boomlet" in the 1980s, some areas of the country continued to lose enrollment during the decade.

Decreasing Enrollments

Of the 1,689 superintendents responding in 1992 to this AASA survey item, 860 indicated their districts had lost enrollment since 1980. This was especially true for superintendents in very small districts with enrollments of fewer than 300. Fully 17 percent of very small dis-

tricts indicated a decrease in enrollment of 25 percent or more (see **Table 8.8**).

Also, the number of districts in this smallest enrollment category grew by nearly 1,700 over the 10-year period. In short, during the 1980s, many districts in the 300 to 2,999 enrollment category dropped down to the category of fewer than 300 (Cunningham, 1982, p. 28). Many of these districts have found it increasingly difficult to maintain a comprehensive instructional program and adequate services.

Geographical distribution. The geographical distribution of responding superintendents was fairly comparable to the distribution of the general population with no one geographical area overrepresented (see **Table 8.9**).

TABLE 8.8 HOW DOES YOUR PRESENT ENROLLMENT COMPARE WITH THAT OF JANUARY 1980?

	GROUP A: 25,000 OR MORE PUPILS		GROUP B: 3,000-24,999 PUPILS		GROUP C: 300-2,999 PUPILS		GROUP D: FEWER THAN 300 PUPILS		NATIONAL UNWEIGHTED PROFILE	
	No.	%	No.	%	No.	%	No.	%	No.	%
INCREASE OF 25% OR MORE	20	14.3	83	13.9	56	7.9	19	7.8	178	10.5
INCREASE OF 20 TO 24%	9	6.4	26	4.3	25	3.5	10	4.1	70	4.1
INCREASE OF 15 TO 19%	6	4.3	18	3.0	28	4.0	8	3.3	60	3.6
INCREASE OF 10 TO 14%	15	10.7	40	6.7	57	8.1	8	3.3	120	7.1
INCREASE OF 5 TO 9%	12	8.6	58	9.7	60	8.5	15	6.1	145	8.6
INCREASE OF LESS THAN 5%	19	13.6	101	16.9	98	13.9	38	15.5	256	15.2
DECREASE OF 25% OR MORE	6	4.3	36	6.0	61	8.7	42	17.1	145	8.6
DECREASE OF 20 TO 24%	11	7.9	40	6.7	45	6.4	12	4.9	108	6.4
DECREASE OF 15 TO 19%	8	5.7	40	6.7	67	9.5	16	6.5	131	7.8
DECREASE OF 10 TO 14%	10	7.1	66	11.0	87	12.3	31	12.7	194	11.5
DECREASE OF 5 TO 9%	24	17.1	91	15.2	121	17.2	46	18.8	282	16.7
TOTAL	140	8.3	599	35.5	705	41.7	245	14.5	1,689	100.0

TABLE 8.9 IN WHICH GEOGRAPHICAL REGION IS YOUR SCHOOL DISTRICT LOCATED?

	GROUP A: 25,000 OR MORE PUPILS		GROUP B: 3,000-24,999 PUPILS		GROUP C: 300-2,999 PUPILS		GROUP D: FEWER THAN 300 PUPILS		NATIONAL UNWEIGHTED PROFILE	
	No.	%	No.	%	No.	%	No.	%	No.	%
NEW ENGLAND	5	3.4	52	8.5	114	16.0	5	2.0	176	10.2
ROCKY MOUNTAINS	7	408.0	15	2.5	32	4.5	40	15.9	94	5.5
SOUTHEAST	41	28.3	113	18.6	53	7.4	4	1.6	211	12.3
GREAT LAKES	17	11.7	139	22.8	140	19.6	25	9.9	321	18.7
MIDEAST	16	11.0	75	12.3	82	11.5	21	8.3	194	11.3
SOUTHWEST	27	18.6	65	10.7	66	9.3	27	10.7	185	10.8
PLAINS	6	4.1	40	6.6	118	16.5	68	27.0	232	13.5
FAR WEST	20	13.8	83	13.6	72	10.1	55	21.8	230	13.4
ALASKA	3	2.1	6	1.0	12	1.7	4	1.6	25	1.5
OTHER	3	2.1	21	3.4	24	3.4	3	1.2	51	3.0
TOTAL	145	8.4	609	35.4	713	41.5	252	14.7	1,719	100.0

Total school population. Nearly half (46.4 percent) of reporting school districts are located in communities of fewer than 10,000 in general population. This fits well with other study data indicating the presence of many very small districts in small communities across the nation. The superintendents responding from districts in communities with populations of more than 200,000 constitute only 5.4 percent of the sample, but serve a majority of the nation's school children (see **Table 8.10**).

An important question. Are superintendents being adequately prepared to administer both the very large and the very small districts? The lack of fit between the number and size of school districts and the distribution of schools and the general population might be an important issue on the school reform agenda during the 1990s.

CENTRAL OFFICE ADMINISTRATORS

The number of central office administrators has increased during the past 10 years. This study shows, moreover, that more superintendents served in central office positions before obtaining a superintendency. The increasing complexity of district management has made the creation of central office administrative positions a necessity in most districts. For instance, legal requirements related to personnel have made it necessary for many districts to have a personnel administrator. The same is true for finance, budget, and other areas, such as communications, curriculum, and instruction.

Number of Central Office Personnel
The survey data indicate quite predictably there are more central office administrators in larger districts than in smaller ones (see **Table 8.12**). A typical district of 3,000 students has two or three central office administrators, including assistant superintendents for finance, personnel, and instruction. Smaller districts generally do not have a second central office administrator until they reach perhaps an enrollment of 1,000 students; indeed, 79.3 percent of school superintendents from districts with fewer than 300 pupils said they have no central office personnel.

Women and Minorities
Women are slightly more likely than men to gain administrative experience through central office positions (See **Table 8.13**). In fact, as noted in the 1982

TABLE 8.10 THE TOTAL (ALL AGES) POPULATION OF SUPERINTENDENTS' SCHOOL DISTRICT

	GROUP A: 25,000 OR MORE PUPILS		GROUP B: 3,000-24,999 PUPILS		GROUP C: 300-2,999 PUPILS		GROUP D: FEWER THAN 300 PUPILS		NATIONAL UNWEIGHTED PROFILE	
	No.	%	No.	%	No.	%	No.	%	No.	%
200,000 AND ABOVE	78	54.5	13	2.1	2	0.3	0	0.0	93	5.4
100,000 TO 199,999	30	21.0	41	6.7	9	1.3	1	0.4	81	4.7
50,000 TO 99,999	14	9.8	147	24.2	9	1.3	0	0.0	170	9.9
30,000 TO 49,999	12	8.4	152	25.0	19	2.7	2	0.8	185	10.8
10,000 TO 29,999	8	5.6	201	33.1	180	25.3	1	0.4	390	22.8
2,500 TO 9,999	1	0.7	52	8.6	358	50.4	21	8.3	432	25.2
FEWER THAN 2,500	0	0.0	2	0.3	134	18.8	227	90.1	363	21.2
TOTAL	143	8.3	608	35.5	711	41.5	252	14.7	1,714	100.0

TABLE 8.11 WHICH OF THE FOLLOWING BEST DESCRIBES YOUR SCHOOL DISTRICT?

	GROUP A: 25,000 OR MORE PUPILS		GROUP B: 3,000-24,999 PUPILS		GROUP C: 300-2,999 PUPILS		GROUP D: FEWER THAN 300 PUPILS		NATIONAL UNWEIGHTED PROFILE	
	No.	%	No.	%	No.	%	No.	%	No.	%
MAJOR URBAN CENTER	56	39.7	7	1.2	2	0.3	1	0.4	66	3.9
CITY DISTRICT	39	27.7	80	13.3	8	1.1	1	0.4	128	7.5
SUBURBAN	29	20.6	277	45.9	143	20.2	19	7.6	468	27.5
RURAL	17	12.1	239	39.6	556	78.4	230	91.6	1,042	61.2
TOTAL	141	8.3	603	35.4	709	41.6	251	14.7	1,704	100.0

study, women and minority superintendents often have an added career stop before the superintendency (Cunningham, 1982). Women, in fact, are more likely than men to bypass a principalship in reaching the superintendency. The 1992 study indicates that women are much better represented in central office administrative positions than in the superintendency. Whether this factor will result in more women entering the superintendency during the next decade is a question that needs further study.

The racial composition of central office administrators is consistent with the superintendency, as shown in **Table 8.14**. Black central office administrators are found in greater numbers and percentages in larger school districts (see **Table 8.15**). The number of Hispanic central office administrators is quite small, except in a few districts with large numbers of Hispanic children (see **Table 8.16**). Both Hispanics and blacks, as well as other ethnic/racial groups, are seriously underrepresented in the central office administrative positions, as they are in the superinten-

dency.

Active recruitment and hiring of women and minority central office administrators will be essential if proportional representation of these groups is to be attained. It is from these ranks that superintendents emerge.

CHAIN OF COMMAND

Superintendents face extensive demands to spend time in the community, with the board, in the schools with principals and teachers, and with state/local educational agency personnel. They often have little time to supervise central office administrators directly, though supervision of these administrators is a necessary part of district management. The 1992 data indicate that superintendents directly supervise more administrators than the typical CEO in the private sector (Glaub, 1988). More than 30 percent indicated they supervise more than 10 people. This is especially true in districts in the two medium enrollment

TABLE 8.12 NUMBER OF CENTRAL OFFICE ADMINISTRATORS

No. OF CENTRAL OFFICE ADMINISTRATORS	GROUP A: 25,000 OR MORE PUPILS		GROUP B: 3,000-24,999 PUPILS		GROUP C: 300-2,999 PUPILS		GROUP D: FEWER THAN 300 PUPILS		NATIONAL UNWEIGHTED PROFILE	
	No.	%	No.	%	No.	%	No.	%	No.	%
0	0	0.0	5	0.8	257	36.2	195	79.3	457	27.0
1-5	11	8.4	290	48.0	436	61.5	51	20.7	788	46.6
6-10	21	16.0	174	28.8	12	1.7	0	0.0	207	12.2
11-15	9	6.9	60	9.9	1	0.1	0	0.0	70	4.1
16-20	9	6.9	25	4.1	3	0.4	0	0.0	37	2.2
21-25	5	3.8	15	2.5	0	0.0	0	0.0	20	1.2
26 OR MORE	76	58.0	35	5.8	0	0.0	0	0.0	111	6.6
TOTAL	131	7.8	604	35.7	709	42.0	246	14.6	1,690	100.0

TABLE 8.13 NUMBER OF FEMALE CENTRAL OFFICE ADMINISTRATORS

No. OF CENTRAL OFFICE ADMINISTRATORS	GROUP A: 25,000 OR MORE PUPILS		GROUP B: 3,000-24,999 PUPILS		GROUP C: 300-2,999 PUPILS		GROUP D: FEWER THAN 300 PUPILS		NATIONAL UNWEIGHTED PROFILE	
	No.	%	No.	%	No.	%	No.	%	No.	%
0	7	5.4	106	17.7	420	63.4	200	87.3	733	45.2
1-5	33	25.6	399	66.5	240	36.3	29	12.7	701	43.3
6-10	15	11.6	58	9.7	2	0.3	0	0.0	75	4.6
11-15	14	10.9	20	3.3	0	0.0	0	0.0	34	2.1
16-20	9	7.0	10	1.7	0	0.0	0	0.0	19	1.2
21-25	7	5.4	4	0.7	0	0.0	0	0.0	11	0.7
26 OR MORE	44	34.1	3	0.5	0	0.0	0	0.0	47	2.9
TOTAL	129	8.0	600	37.0	662	40.9	229	14.1	1,620	100.0

ranges of 300 to 2,999 and 3,000 to 24,999 (see **Table 8.17**).

Collective Bargaining

An example of a demand on a superintendent's time is in collective bargaining negotiations. In the 1971 and 1982 studies, superintendents said they committed more time to this area than did those surveyed in 1990. The new findings suggest that collective negotiations may have become a more routine management function.

Superintendents in smaller districts more often

negotiate directly with teachers or assist a board member in negotiations (see **Table 8.18**). Of the respondents in the 1992 survey, 29.6 percent indicated they served as chief negotiator for the district in negotiations with teacher unions/associations. This practice is probably true for superintendents in districts not responding to the survey. Most experts in labor-management relations would not recommend such a practice, nor would they encourage lay board members to negotiate, as they do in 19.2 percent of the sampled districts. Again, board members in smaller districts negotiate with teachers much more often than in larg-

TABLE 8.14 NUMBER OF WHITE CENTRAL OFFICE ADMINISTRATORS

No. OF CENTRAL OFFICE ADMINISTRATORS	GROUP A: 25,000 OR MORE PUPILS		GROUP B: 3,000-24,999 PUPILS		GROUP C: 300-2,999 PUPILS		GROUP D: FEWER THAN 300 PUPILS		NATIONAL UNWEIGHTED PROFILE	
	No.	%	No.	%	No.	%	No.	%	No.	%
1- 5	18	15.3	298	53.6	415	97.0	49	100.0	780	67.8
6-10	16	13.6	151	27.2	9	2.1	0	0.0	176	15.3
11-15	9	7.6	58	10.4	2	0.5	0	0.0	69	6.0
16-20	9	7.6	22	4.0	2	0.5	0	0.0	33	2.9
21-25	6	5.1	7	1.3	0	0.0	0	0.0	13	1.1
26 0R MORE	60	50.8	20	3.6	0	0.0	0	0.0	80	7.0
TOTAL	118	10.3	556	48.3	428	37.2	49	4.3	1,151	100.0

TABLE 8.15 NUMBER OF BLACK CENTRAL OFFICE ADMINISTRATORS

No. OF CENTRAL OFFICE ADMINISTRATORS	GROUP A: 25,000 OR MORE PUPILS		GROUP B: 3,000-24,999 PUPILS		GROUP C: 300-2,999 PUPILS		GROUP D: FEWER THAN 300 PUPILS		NATIONAL UNWEIGHTED PROFILE	
	No.	%	No.	%	No.	%	No.	%	No.	%
1- 5	36	41.9	124	89.2	22	100.0	0	0.0	182	73.7
6-10	15	17.4	10	7.2	0	0.0	0	0.0	25	10.1
11-15	6	7.0	1	0.7	0	0.0	0	0.0	7	2.8
16-20	6	7.0	2	1.4	0	0.0	0	0.0	8	3.2
21-25	4	4.7	2	1.4	0	0.0	0	0.0	6	2.4
26 0R MORE	19	22.1	0	0.0	0	0.0	0	0.0	19	7.7
TOTAL	86	34.8	139	56.3	22	8.9	0	0.0	247	100.0

TABLE 8.16 NUMBER OF HISPANIC CENTRAL OFFICE ADMINISTRATORS

No. OF CENTRAL OFFICE ADMINISTRATORS	GROUP A: 25,000 OR MORE PUPILS		GROUP B: 3,000-24,999 PUPILS		GROUP C: 300-2,999 PUPILS		GROUP D: FEWER THAN 300 PUPILS		NATIONAL UNWEIGHTED PROFILE	
	No.	%	No.	%	No.	%	No.	%	No.	%
1- 5	38	74.5	45	84.9	5	83.3	2	100.0	90	80.4
6-10	3	5.9	4	7.5	1	16.7	0	0.0	8	7.1
11-15	4	7.8	0	0.0	0	0.0	0	0.0	4	3.6
16-20	3	5.9	2	3.8	0	0.0	0	0.0	5	4.5
21-25	0	0.0	0	0.0	0	0.0	0	0.0	0	0.0
26 0R MORE	3	5.9	2	3.8	0	0.0	0	0.0	5	4.5
TOTAL	51	45.5	53	47.3	6	5.4	2	1.8	112	100.0

er districts. It is possible that many superintendents, especially in smaller districts, do not have significant funds available to contract for collective bargaining services. Also, the lack of central office staff in small districts precludes the possibility of delegation. Therefore, the superintendent or a board member negotiates with the teachers. This very important task takes a great deal of time and surely creates a time management problem for superintendents.

The younger superintendents were found to be negotiating directly with the teachers more frequently than older groups (See **Table 8.19**). The reason for this situation is unclear. Speculation is that perhaps more members of the younger group are trying to

TABLE 8.17 HOW MANY STAFF MEMBERS REPORT DIRECTLY TO SUPERINTENDENT?

NO> OF STAFF MEMBERS	GROUP A: 25,000 OR MORE PUPILS		GROUP B: 3,000-24,999 PUPILS		GROUP C: 300-2,999 PUPILS		GROUP D: FEWER THAN 300 PUPILS		NATIONAL UNWEIGHTED PROFILE	
	No.	%	No.	%	No.	%	No.	%	No.	%
0	1	0.7	0	0.0	4	0.6	4	1.8	9	0.5
1- 5	37	26.6	241	40.1	221	32.0	42	18.6	541	32.6
6-10	71	51.1	182	30.3	311	45.0	32	14.2	596	36.0
11-15	19	13.7	95	15.8	66	9.6	29	12.8	209	12.6
16-20	6	4.3	40	6.7	20	2.9	40	17.7	106	6.4
21-25	3	2.2	23	3.8	6	0.9	30	13.3	62	3.7
26 0R MORE	2	1.4	20	3.3	63	9.1	49	21.7	134	8.1
TOTAL	139	8.4	601	36.3	691	41.7	226	13.6	1657	100.0

TABLE 8.18 WHO SERVES AS THE CHIEF NEGOTIATOR FOR DISTRICT'S COLLECTIVE BARGAINING AGREEMENT WITH THE TEACHERS?

POSITION	GROUP A: 25,000 OR MORE PUPILS		GROUP B: 3,000-24,999 PUPILS		GROUP C: 300-2,999 PUPILS		GROUP D: FEWER THAN 300 PUPILS		NATIONAL UNWEIGHTED PROFILE	
	No.	%	No.	%	No.	%	No.	%	No.	%
SUPERINTENDENT	17	11.9	136	23.2	257	36.4	87	35.4	497	29.6
PROFESSIONAL NEGOTIATOR FROM OUTSIDE	20	14.0	116	19.8	146	20.7	11	4.5	293	17.4
BOARD MEMBER	2	1.4	35	6.0	167	23.7	119	48.4	323	19.2
PROFESSIONAL NEGOTIATOR FROM INSIDE	68	47.6	149	25.5	29	4.1	3	1.2	249	14.8
BOARD ATTORNEY	5	3.5	84	14.4	77	10.9	7	2.8	173	10.3
NO CONTRACT	31	21.7	78	13.3	50	7.1	26	10.6	185	11.0
TOTAL	143	8.5	598	34.8	726	42.0	253	14.6	1,720	100.0

TABLE 8.19 WHO SERVES AS CHIEF NEGOTIATOR WITH TEACHERS, ANALYZED BY AGE

POSITION	AGE 45-YOUNGER		AGE 46-50		AGE 51-55		AGE 56-60		AGE 61-OLDER	
	No.	%	No.	%	No.	%	No.	%	No.	%
SUPERINTENDENT	172	38.9	134	29.7	103	25.5	67	23.3	23	23.0
PROFFESSIONAL NEGOTIATOR OUTSIDE	59	13.3	82	18.2	79	19.6	52	18.1	19	19.0
BOARD MEMBER	90	20.4	72	16.0	65	16.1	62	21.5	14	14.0
PROFFESSIONAL NEGOTIATOR INSIDE	40	9.0	71	15.7	64	15.8	54	18.8	19	19.0
BOARD ATTORNEY	40	9.0	48	10.6	36	8.9	25	8.7	9	9.0
NO CONTRACT	41	9.3	44	9.8	57	14.1	28	9.7	16	16.0
TOTAL	442	99.9	451	100.0	404	100.0	288	100.1	100	100.0

move their districts away from traditional labor/management bargaining models that are adversarial in nature. Another guess is that many younger superintendents might be in smaller districts where the boards do not wish to expend funds for hiring a professional negotiator.

DISTRICT SCHOOL BOARD CHARACTERISTICS

Superintendents and other administrators express great interest in the characteristics of school boards analyzed in the 10-year studies of the American superintendency. However, the amount of information collected is not extensive, and those with interest in school board demographics should refer to research published by the National School Boards Association and its state affiliates.

Elected or appointed. Nearly all school boards in the nation are elected, with the percentage the same since the 1982 study. Fewer than four percent of board members are appointed, though many very large urban districts have appointed boards.

Size. School boards nationwide generally have five or seven members. The 1982 study found that the average board size was 6.4, also true in 1992.

Tenure. In 1982 the average school board member served 5.4 years. In 1992, school board members are again serving about five years on the average. Three to six years in board tenure was given as a response from 48.6 percent of superintendents. In 20.4 percent of the districts, average terms were less than three years and about one in five districts have board members with an average of between six and nine years of service (see **Table 8.20**).

Turnover. Rapid turnover among board members has made continuity in policymaking and management difficult. The orientation and training of board members is an important task that is made even more difficult by frequent transitions. In addition, superintendents are hired directly by school board members. Superintendents with multi-year contracts might find themselves with a new board after the first or second year in a district, making a good board/administration team especially challenging. The data seem to indicate that only about one in five board members serves a full two terms.

Women and Minorities on School Boards
Given that most boards have five to seven members, the data in **Tables 8.21-8.23** indicate that most board members in 1992, as in 1982, are white males.

About 40 percent of school board members nationally are women (Cameron, 1988). This figure was reported in the 10th annual survey of school board members by the National School Boards Association. The data from the 1992 survey indicate this to be a bit high. The 1992 and 1982 studies indicated that of a seven-member board, typically four or five members were males (Cunningham, p. 85).

Very few minorities are currently found on school boards in the United States (see **Tables 8.24-8.27**). Yet, minorities comprised about 27 percent of U.S. elementary and secondary students in 1990, according to data released by the U.S. Department of Education in 1992. Furthermore, it is projected that minority students will comprise at least a third of public school enrollments by the year 2000. The lack of minority school board members is an important problem for the nation's schools, as is the shortage of minority teachers and administrators.

TABLE 8.20 AVERAGE LENGTH OF SERVICE OF PRESENT BOARD MEMBERS

YEARS OF SERVICE	GROUP A: 25,000 OR MORE PUPILS		GROUP B: 3,000-24,999 PUPILS		GROUP C: 300-2,999 PUPILS		GROUP D: FEWER THAN 300 PUPILS		NATIONAL UNWEIGHTED PROFILE	
	No.	%	No.	%	No.	%	No.	%	No.	%
0 - 3 YEARS	24	16.9	118	19.5	140	19.8	64	25.8	346	20.4
3.1 - 6 YEARS	67	47.2	271	44.9	370	52.4	119	48.0	827	48.6
6.1 - 9 YEARS	33	23.2	132	21.9	136	19.3	40	16.1	341	20.1
9.1 OR MORE YEARS	18	12.7	83	13.7	60	8.5	25	10.1	186	10.9
TOTAL	142	8.4	604	35.5	706	41.5	248	14.6	1,700	100.0

TABLE 8.21 NUMBER OF WHITE BOARD MEMBERS

NO. OF WHITE MEMBERS	GROUP A: 25,000 OR MORE PUPILS		GROUP B: 3,000-24,999 PUPILS		GROUP C: 300-2,999 PUPILS		GROUP D: FEWER THAN 300 PUPILS		NATIONAL UNWEIGHTED PROFILE
	No.	%	No.	%	No.	%	No.	%	No.
1	2	1.4	6	1.0	2	0.3	2	0.8	12
2	3	2.1	8	1.3	6	0.8	0	0.0	17
3	9	6.3	23	3.8	6	0.8	16	6.5	54
4	27	19.0	50	8.3	37	5.2	12	4.8	126
5	38	26.8	197	32.8	230	32.5	114	46.0	579
6	14	9.9	71	11.8	58	8.2	38	15.3	181
7 OR MORE	49	34.5	246	40.9	368	52.1	66	26.6	729
TOTAL	142	8.4	601	35.4	707	41.6	248	14.6	1,698

TABLE 8.22 NUMBER OF MALE BOARD MEMBERS

NO. OF MALE BOARD MEMBERS	GROUP A: 25,000 OR MORE PUPILS		GROUP B: 3,000-24,999 PUPILS		GROUP C: 300-2,999 PUPILS		GROUP D: FEWER THAN 300 PUPILS		NATIONAL UNWEIGHTED PROFILE
	No.	%	No.	%	No.	%	No.	%	No.
0	0	0.0	1	0.2	0	0.0	1	0.4	2
1	3	20.1	8	1.3	9	1.3	10	4.0	30
2	21	14.7	48	7.9	44	6.2	24	9.5	137
3	25	17.5	99	16.3	92	12.9	48	19.0	264
4	37	25.9	174	28.7	188	26.4	69	27.3	468
5	21	14.7	127	20.9	150	21.1	53	20.9	351
6	13	9.1	88	14.5	113	15.9	30	11.9	244
7 OR MORE	23	16.1	62	10.2	115	16.2	18	7.1	218
TOTAL	143	8.3	607	35.4	711	41.5	253	14.8	1,714

TABLE 8.23 NUMBER OF FEMALE BOARD MEMBERS

NO. OF FEMALE BOARD MEMBERS	GROUP A: 25,000 OR MORE PUPILS		GROUP B: 3,000-24,999 PUPILS		GROUP C: 300-2,999 PUPILS		GROUP D: FEWER THAN 300 PUPILS		NATIONAL UNWEIGHTED PROFILE
	No.	%	No.	%	No.	%	No.	%	No.
0	0	0.0	28	4.7	64	9.2	37	15.9	129
1	14	10.0	174	29.5	225	32.4	79	33.9	492
2	36	25.7	171	29.0	171	24.6	62	26.6	440
3	43	30.7	117	19.8	123	17.7	39	16.7	322
4	22	15.7	62	10.5	32	4.6	12	5.2	128
5	14	10.0	21	3.6	25	3.6	2	0.9	62
6	7	5.0	6	1.0	9	1.3	0	0.0	22
7 OR MORE	4	2.9	11	1.9	45	6.5	2	0.9	62
TOTAL	140	8.4	590	35.6	694	41.9	233	14.1	1,657

TABLE 8.24 NUMBER OF BLACK BOARD MEMBERS

NO.R OF BLACK BOARD MEMBERS	GROUP A: 25,000 OR MORE PUPILS		GROUP B: 3,000-24,999 PUPILS		GROUP C: 300-2,999 PUPILS		GROUP D: FEWER THAN 300 PUPILS		NATIONAL UNWEIGHTED PROFILE
	No.	%	No.	%	No.	%	No.	%	No.
1	33	40.7	79	59.0	42	80.8	1	33.3	155
2	23	28.4	27	20.1	7	13.5	1	33.3	58
3	14	17.3	14	10.4	1	1.9	0	0.0	29
4	4	4.9	9	6.7	1	1.9	0	0.0	14
5	4	4.9	2	1.5	1	1.9	1	33.3	8
6	3	3.7	1	0.7	0	0.0	0	0.0	4
7 OR MORE	0	0.0	2	1.5	0	0.0	0	0.0	2
TOTAL	81	30.0	134	49.6	52	19.3	3	1.1	270

TABLE 8.25 NUMBER OF HISPANIC BOARD MEMBERS

NO. OF HISPANIC BOARD MEMBERS	GROUP A: 25,000 OR MORE PUPILS		GROUP B: 3,000-24,999 PUPILS		GROUP C: 300-2,999 PUPILS		GROUP D: FEWERTHAN 300 PUPILS		NATIONAL UNWEIGHTED PROFILE
	No.	%	No.	%	No.	%	No.	%	No.
1	22	66.7	42	75.0	9	47.4	7	63.6	80
2	8	24.2	6	10.7	7	36.8	3	27.3	24
3	1	3.0	4	7.1	1	5.3	0	0.0	6
4	1	3.0	1	1.8	1	5.3	1	9.1	4
5	1	3.0	2	3.6	1	5.3	0	0.0	4
6	0	0.0	1	1.8	0	0.0	0	0.0	1
7 OR MORE	0	0.0	0	0.0	0	0.0	0	0.0	0
TOTAL	33	27.7	56	47.1	19	16.0	11	9.2	119

TABLE 8.26 NUMBER OF ASIAN BOARD MEMBERS

NO. OF ASIAN BOARD MEMBERS	GROUP A: 25,000 OR MORE PUPILS		GROUP B: 3,000-24,999 PUPILS		GROUP C: 300-2,999 PUPILS		GROUP D: FEWER THAN 300 PUPILS		NATIONAL UNWEIGHTED PROFILE
	No.	%	No.	%	No.	%	No.	%	No.
1	8	100	9	100	3	100.0	2	100.0	22
2	0	0.0	0	0.0	0	0.0	0	0.0	0
3	0	0.0	0	0.0	0	0.0	0	0.0	0
4	0	0.0	0	0.0	0	0.0	0	0.0	0
5	0	0.0	0	0.0	0	0.0	0	0.0	0
6	0	0.0	0	0.0	0	0.0	0	0.0	0
7 OR MORE	0	0.0	0	0.0	0	0.0	0	0.0	0
TOTAL	8	36.4	9	40.9	3	13.6	2	9.1	22

TABLE 8.27 NUMBER OF NATIVE AMERICAN BOARD MEMBERS

NO. OF NATIVE AMERICAN BOARD MEMBERS	GROUP A: 25,000 OR MORE PUPILS		GROUP B: 3,000-24,999 PUPILS		GROUP C: 300-2,999 PUPILS		GROUP D: FEWER THAN 300 PUPILS		NATIONAL UNWEIGHTED PROFILE
	No.	%	No.	%	No.	%	No.	%	No.
1	0	0.0	5	55.6	8	72.7	4	57.1	17
2	0	0.0	1	11.1	0	0.0	0	0.0	1
3	0	0.0	0	0.0	1	9.1	0	0.0	1
4	0	0.0	1	11.1	0	0.0	0	0.0	1
5	0	0.0	1	11.1	1	9.1	2	28.6	4
6	0	0.0	0	0.0	0	0.0	1	14.3	1
7 OR MORE	0	0.0	1	11.1	1	9.1	0	0.0	2
TOTAL	0	0.0	9	33.3	11	40.7	7	25.9	27

Conclusion

Public pressure on superintendents and their boards of education for accountability is likely to increase in the 1990s. While most Americans agree that schools need to be reformed and improved, there is no consensus on how this should be accomplished. This poses a problem and opportunity for the nation's school superintendents: Since there is no agreed-upon path or formula for national school reform, solutions may well be developed or chosen at the local level.

EXPERIENCE AND TRAINING

The current corps of superintendents is experienced, with more academic training than ever before and considerable years of experience as superintendents. A greater number of them than in the past have experience in specialized central office positions. as well as at the principalship level. The data indicate they also are sensitive to community input, and place great value on curriculum and instructional program development. Thousands of superintendents are willing and able to provide leadership in education improvement, if they are allowed to do so. However, scarce resources, community pressure, organization size, and an unclear mission are common (but not insurmountable) impediments to change.

Prepare for the Future

The current experienced corps of superintendents may not still be working in 2000. Thus, the training and preparation of superintendents for the 21st century is a critical undertaking. Unfortunately, superintendent preparation is getting very little attention at either the national or state levels. States have made little progress toward establishing certification and training programs that address 21st century leadership concerns. Universities, in which most of the academic preparation is provided, are underfunded and mired in an outdated format of professional preparation based on semester hours of classroom experience.

Superintendents responding to the survey for *The 1992 Study of the American School Superintendency* were very clear in their opinions concerning the necessity of quality preparation for the superintendency. They also indicated they were very interested in mentoring new superintendents or those aspiring to be superintendents. They are concerned about the quality of university programs and think they could be greatly improved.

DEDICATED LEADERS

Perhaps one of the most instructive lessons to learn from the 1992 10-year study is how superintendents prioritize the performance areas of the superintendency. Superintendents (especially in larger districts) are much more interested in executive leadership than outright management. They indicate that the establishment of organizational climate is an important part of their responsibilities, along with providing the very best curriculum and instruction programs. They said that management tasks concerning budget, finance, and facilities were important, but should not be the highest priority.

Superintendents of small districts felt more pressed to perform management tasks on a daily basis. Superintendents in larger districts leaned much more toward executive leadership. The existence of thousands of very small districts may well be a problem in the future, as superintendents are constantly overwhelmed with day-to-day management tasks and do not have time for leadership in strategic planning, curriculum, and instruction. It is quite possible that the leadership of American schools could be greatly improved by the consolidation of thousands of small school districts. This would mean that fewer administrators would need to be prepared for the superintendency and additional resources could be expended by local districts as well as states in preparing and certifying education executives.

UNEQUAL OPPORTUNITIES

The study also shows that women and minorities are underrepresented in the American school superintendency. This is a serious problem, but one with clear antecedents. The existence of role stereotyping in past generations has discouraged or prevented many women from regaining the majority in educational administration they often enjoyed before World War II. Racial discrimination has kept minorities out of the superintendency, except in districts with large numbers of minority students and minority members on boards of education. Policymakers must take decisive action to ensure that qualified women and minorities are encouraged and allowed to take the helm in all types of school districts.

TEAM LEADERS

Finally, the role of an executive leader is to be able to visualize where his or her organization is headed. Superintendents must have a vision for the public school within the context of American society in the 21st century. He or she must be able to lead board members, staff, and the community toward that vision of the future through consensus-building activities. The education of America's most precious asset, its children, must be led by the very best of the educational profession. It is this group's responsibility to lead the effort to regain for children and education the priority of the nation's resources.

American Association of School Administrators. *The American School Superintendency,* Thirtieth Yearbook. Washington, D.C.: AASA, 1952.

American Association of School Administrators. *Goal Setting and Self-Evaluation of School Boards.* Arlington, Va.: AASA, 1982.

American Association of School Administrators. *Guidelines for the Preparation of Administrators.* Arlington, Va.: AASA, 1982.

American Association of School Administrators. *Roles and Relationships: School Boards and Super-intendents.* Arlington, Va.: AASA, 1980.

American Association of School Administrators. *Status and Opinions of AASA Members, 1989-90.* Arlington, Va.: AASA, 1990.

American Association of School Administrators. *Talking About the Superintendent's Employment Contract.* Arlington, Va.: AASA, 1990.

Anderson, Stuart A. *Successful School Board Members.* Springfield, Ill.: Illinois Association of School Boards, 1989.

Angus, David. "The Retirement Plans of Michigan School Administrators." *Bureau of Accreditation and School Improvement Studies.* Ann Arbor, Mich.: University of Michigan, 1986.

Bevan, John K. "Superintendent Turnover in Illinois: A Study of Board Member and Superintendent Expectations." Dissertation, Northern Illinois University, 1988.

Blumberg, Arthur. *The School Superintendent: Living with Conflict.* New York: Teachers College Press, 1985.

Bradley, Ann. "Rapid Turnover in Urban Superintendents: Prompt Calls for Reforms in Governance." *Education Week* 10, 15 (December 12, 1990): 1-2.

Burke, Daniel. "An Analysis of Self-Perceived Operation Authority for Certain School District Decisions by Superintendents and School Boards." Dissertation, Northern Illinois University, 1990.

Burnham, Joan G. "Career Experiences and Career Patterns of Superintendents" Dissertation, University of Texas at Austin, 1988.

Callahan, Raymond E. *The Superintendent of Schools: A Historical Analysis.* Eugene, Oreg.: ERIC, 1966.

Cameron, Beatrice H.; Underwood, Kenneth F.; and Fortune, Jim C. "Politics and Power: How You're Selected and Elected to Lead This Nation's Schools." *American School Board Journal,* January 1988.

Campbell, Ronald E.; Cunningham, Luvern L.; Nystrand, Raphael O.; and Usdan, Michael D. *Organization and Control of American Schools,* 6th ed. Columbus, Ohio: Charles E. Merrill Publishing Co., 1990.

Carlson, Richard O. *School Superintendents: Careers and Performance.* Columbus, Ohio: Charles E. Merrill Publishing Co., 1972.

Chubb, John E. and Moe, Terry M. *Politics, Markets and America's Schools.* Washington, D.C.: The Brookings Institute, 1989.

Cistone, Peter J. *Understanding School Boards.* Lexington, Mass.: Lexington Books, 1975.

Clark, David. *Improving the Preparation of School Administrators: An Agenda for Reform.* Charlottesville, Va.: National Policy Board for Educational Administration, 1989.

Collier, Virginia. "Identification of Skills Perceived by Texas Superintendents as Necessary for Successful Job Performance." Dissertation, University of Texas at Austin, 1987.

Crowson, Robert. "The Local School District Superintendency: A Puzzling Administrative Role." *Educational Administration Quarterly* 23, 3 (1987): 46-69.

Crowson, Robert and Morris, Van Cleve. "The Superintendency and School Leadership." Paper, American Educational Research Association, Boston, April, 1990.

Cuban, Larry. *The Managerial Imperative and the Practice of Leadership in Schools.* Albany, N.Y.: SUNY Press, 1988.

Cuban, Larry. *Urban School Chiefs Under Fire.* Chicago: University of Chicago Press, 1976.

Cuban, Larry. *The Urban School Superintendency: A Century and a Half of Change.* Bloomington, Ind.: The Phi Delta Kappan Educational Foundation, 1989.

Cubberley, Ellwood R. *Public School Administration.* Boston: Houghton Mifflin Co., 1922.

Cunningham, Luvern L. and Hentges, Joseph, eds. *The American School Superintendency 1982: A Full Report.* Arlington, Va.: American Association of School Administrators, 1982.

Davidson, Jack L. *The Superintendency: Leadership for Effective Schools.* Jackson, Miss.: Kelwynn Press, 1987.

Department of Superintendence. *Educational Leadership: Progress and Possibilities.* Washington, D.C.: National Education Association, 1933.

Department of Superintendence. *The Status of the Superintendent.* Washington, D.C.: National Education Association, 1923.

DeYoung, Alan J. "Excellence in Education: The Opportunity for School Superintendents to Become Ambitious?" *Educational Administration Quarterly* 22, 2 (1986): 91-113.

Everett, Ronald and Glass, Thomas. "School Business Administrators in the 1990s: A National Survey of School Business Administrators." *Journal of School Business Management,* 4,1: 15-18

Faber, Charles. *A Manual for School Board Members.* Lexington, Ky.: University of Kentucky, 1976.

Feistritzer, C. Emily. *Profile of School Administrators in the U.S.* Washington, D.C.: National Center for Education Information, 1988.

Feistritzer, C. Emily. *Profile of School Board Presidents in the U.S.* Washington, D.C.: National Center for Education Information, 1989.

Finn, Chester E. and Petersen, Kent D. "Principals, Superintendents and the Administrators Art," *Public Interest* 79 (Spring 1985): 42.

First, Patricia. "How to Effectively Evaluate a Superintendent" *Thrust* 21, 3 (April 1990): 40-44.

Forsyth, Patrick B. "Redesigning the Preparation of School Administrators: Toward Consensus." In *School Leadership: A Blueprint for Change.* Corwin Press, 1992.

Getzels, Jacob; Liphan, James M.; and Campbell, Roald F. *Educational Administration as a Social Process: Theory, Research and Practice.* New York: Harper and Row, 1968.

Getzels, Jacob W. "Educational Administration Twenty Years Later 1954-74" In *Educational Administration — The Developing Decades.* Edited by L. L. Cunningham, W. G. Hack, and R. O. Nystrand. McCutchan Publishing, 1977.

Glass, Thomas E. ed. *An Analysis of Texts on School Administration.* Danville, Ill.: Interstate Press, 1986.

Glass, Thomas E. *The Illinois School Superintendency: A Summary Report of the 1989 Survey of Illinois Superintendents.* Springfield, Ill.: Illinois Association of School Administrators, 1990.

Glass, Thomas E. *The Illinois School Superintendency: A Survey Report.* Springfield, Ill.: Illinois Association of School Administrators, 1991.

Glaub, Gerald. "That Invisible Blob?" *Illinois School Board Journal* 56, 5 (September 1988).

Grady, Marilyn L. and Bryant, Miles. "School Board Turmoil and Superintendent Turnover: What Pushes Them to the Brink?" *School Administrator* 28, 2 (February 1991): 19-25.

Griffiths, Daniel E. *Administrative Theory.* Chicago: University of Chicago Press, 1957.

Griffiths, Danie El. "Administrative Theory." In *Handbook of Educational Research in Educational Administration.* Edited by Norman Boyan. New York: Longman, 1988.

Griffiths, Daniel E. *The School Superintendent.* New York: Center for Applied Research, 1966.

Griffiths, Daniel E.; Stout, Robert L.; and Forsyth, Patrick B. eds. *Leaders for America's Schools.* Berkeley: McCutchan, 1988.

Guthrie, James W. "Effective Educational Executives: An Essay on the Concept of and Preparation for Strategic Leadership." Paper. American Educational Research Association. Boston, April 1990.

Hallinger, Philip and Murphy, Joseph. "The Superintendent's Role in Promoting Instructional Leadership." *Administrators Notebook* 30, 6 (1982), : 1-4.

Havighurst, Robert. *The Public Schools of Chicago.* Chicago: Board of Education, 1964.

Healy, Charles C. and Welchert, Alice. "Mentoring Relations: A Definition to Advance Research and Practice," *Educational Researcher,* 19, 9 (December 1990): 17-21.

Heller, Robert, et al. "Nationwide Survey: Disaster, Controversy" *Executive Educator* 13, 3 (March 1991): 20-25.

Heller, Robert W.; Woodworth, Beth E.; Jacobson, Stephen L.; and Conway, James A. "Disaster, Controversy: Are You Prepared for the Worst?" *Executive Educator* 13, 3 (1991): 20-23.

Hodgkinson, Harold L. *Beyond the Schools: How Schools and Communities Must Collaborate to Solve the Problems Facing America's Youth: AASA Critical Issues Report.* Arlington, Va.: American Association of School Administrators, 1991.

Hodgkinson, Harold. "Facing the Future: Demographics and Statistics to Manage Today's Schools for Tomorrow's Children." *School Administrator.* (September 1988).

Hord, Shirley M., et al. "The Superintendent's Leadership in School Improvement." Paper. American Educational Research Association Boston, 1990.

Hoy, Wayne and Miskel, Cecil. *Educational Administration: Theory, Research, and Practice.* 3rd ed. New York: Random House, 1987.

Hoyle, John R. "Programs in Educational Administration and the AASA Preparation Guidelines." *Educational Administration Quarterly,* 21, 1 : 71-95.

Hoyle, John; English, Fenwick; and Steffy, Betty. *Skills for Successful School Leaders,* 2nd ed. Arlington, Va.: American Association of School Administrators, 1990.

Hunter, Richard C. "The Big City Superintendent: Up Against an Urban Wall." *School Administrator,* 47, 5, : 8.

Institute for Educational Leadership. *School Boards: Strengthening Grass-Roots Leadership.* Washington, D.C.: IEL, 1986.

Konnert, M. William and Augenstein, John J. *The Superintendency in the Nineties: What Superintendents and Board Members Need to Know.* Lancaster, Pa.: Technomic Publishing Co., 1990.

Knezevich, Stephen J. *The American School Superintendent.* Washington, D.C.: American Association of School Administrators, 1971.

REFERENCES

Lantor, Linda. "How Two-Career Couples Juggle Lives to Balance Job Moves." *School Administrator* 47, 9 (October 1990): 9.

Lortie, Dan C. *Schoolteacher: A Sociological Study.* Chicago: University of Chicago Press, 1975.

March, James G. "Almost Random Careers: The Wisconsin School Superintendency." *Administrative Science Quarterly.* 22 (1977): 317-409.

March, James and Simon, H. A. *Handbook of Organization.* Chicago: Rand-McNally, 1965.

McCarthy, Martha, et al. *Under Scrutiny.* Tempe, Ariz.: University Council for Educational Administration, 1988.

Miklos, Erwin. "Administrator Selection, Career Patterns, Succession and Socialization." In *Handbook of Educational Research in Educational Administration.* Edited by Norman Boyan. New York: Longman, 1988.

National Commission on Excellence in Education. *A Nation at Risk: The Imperative for Educational Reform.* Washington, D.C.: United States Department of Education, 1983.

National Commission on Excellence in Educational Administration. *Leaders for America's Schools.* Tempe, Ariz.: University Council of Educational Administration, 1987.

National School Boards Association. *Becoming a Better Board Member.* 3rd ed. Alexandria, Va.: NSBA, 1987.

National School Boards Association. *Education Vital Signs.* Alexandria, Va.: NSBA, 1990.

National School Boards Association. "Twelfth Annual Survey of School Board Members." *American School Board Journal* 190 (1990): 34.

National School Boards Association. *Urban Dynamics: Lessons in Leadership from Urban School Boards and Superintendents.* Alexandria, Va.: NSBA, 1992.

Ornstein, Allan. "Dimensions: Tenure of Superintendents." *Education Week* (November 14, 1990): 3.

Pitner, Nancy J. and Ogawa, Rodney. "Organizational Leadership: The Case of the School Superintendent." *Educational Administration Quarterly* 17, 2 (Spring 1981).

Quality Education for Minorities Project. *Education That Works: An Action Plan for the Education of Minorities.* Cambridge: Massachusetts Institute of Technology, 1990.

Redfern, George B. *Evaluating the Superintendent.* Arlington, Va.: American Association of School Administrators, 1980.

Reeves, Charles. *School Boards.* Westwood, Conn.: Greenwood Press, 1954.

Rhodes, Lewis. "Beyond Your Beliefs: Quantum Leaps Toward Quality Schools." *School Administrator* 47, 11 (December 1990).

Rist, Marilee C. "Race and Politics Rip Into the Urban Superintendency." *Executive Educator* 12, 12 (December 1991): 12-14.

Sass, Michael. "The AASA Performance Goal and Skills Areas: Importance to Effective Superintendency Performance as Viewed by Practicing Superintendents and Professors of Educational Administration." Dissertation, Northern Illinois University, 1989.

Sclafani, Susan. "AASA Guidelines for Preparation of School Administrators: Do They Represent the Important Job Behaviors of Superintendents?" Dissertation, University of Texas, 1987.

Tucker, Harvey J. and Zeigler, Harmon L. *Professionals Versus the Public: Attitudes, Communication, and Response in School Districts.* New York: Longman, 1980.

Tyack, David B. and Hansot, Elisabeth E. *Managers of Virtue: Public School Leadership in America, 1820 to 1980.* New York: Basic Books, 1982.

U.S. Department of Education. National Center for Education Statistics. *Digest of Education Statistics,* 1991

Wissler, Dorothy F. and Ortiz, Flora I. *The Superintendent's Leadership in School Reform.* New York: The Falmer Press, 1988.

Acknowledgments

Dr. Thomas Glass, professor of educational administration at Northern Illinois University, conducted this AASA study and wrote the report.

The 1990 AASA Committee for the Advancement of School Administration helped develop study objectives and select the final survey items.

Along with the researchers across the country who contributed to this report, the author wishes to thank his colleagues Dr. Peter Abrams, who coordinated data processing, and Dr. Raymond Lows, who assisted with sample development.

Special thanks to the 1,724 superintendents who took time out of their busy days to respond to the 1992 survey. Without their efforts, this report would not have been possible.

We also express our gratitude to Luvern L. Cunningham and Joseph Hentges, editors of *The American School Superintendency 1982,* and the directors of all previous AASA superintendent studies.

Gary Marx, AASA senior associate executive director, served as project manager. Natalie Carter Holmes, editor of *Leadership News,* provided editorial guidance, along with Leslie Eckard, associate editor, and Katie Ross, communications assistant. Graphic design was provided by Sans Serif Graphics, Ltd.